LINEAGES OF EMPIRE
The Historical Roots of British Imperial Thought

LINEAGES OF EMPIRE
The Historical Roots of
British Imperial Thought

Edited by
Duncan Kelly

Published *for* THE BRITISH ACADEMY
by OXFORD UNIVERSITY PRESS

Oxford University Press, Great Clarendon Street, Oxford OX2 6DP

Oxford New York
Auckland Cape Town Dar es Salaam Hong Kong Karachi
Kuala Lumpur Madrid Melbourne Mexico City Nairobi
New Delhi Shanghai Taipei Toronto

With offices in
Argentina Austria Brazil Chile Czech Republic France Greece
Guatemala Hungary Italy Japan Poland Portugal Singapore
South Korea Switzerland Thailand Turkey Ukraine Vietnam

Published in the United States
by Oxford Press Inc., New York

© The British Academy 2009

Database right The British Academy (maker)

First published 2009

British Library Cataloguing in Publication Data
Data available

Library of Congress Cataloging in Publication Data
Data available

Typeset by
J&L Composition Ltd, Filey, North Yorkshire
Printed in Great Britain
on acid-free paper by
CPI Antony Rowe,
Chippenham, Wiltshire

ISBN 978–0–19–726439–3
ISSN 0068–1202

Contents

Notes on Contributors

Iain Hampsher-Monk is Professor of Political Theory at the University of Exeter. He is the founder and editor (with Janet Coleman) of the journal *History of Political Thought*, and the author of *A History of Modern Political Thought* (1994). He researches and writes mostly on early-modern political thought, and most recently contributed 'British Radicalism and the Anti-Jacobins' to *The Cambridge History of Eighteenth-century Political Thought* (2006) and edited *The Impact of the French Revolution: Texts from Britain in the 1790s* (2005).

Duncan Kelly is currently University Lecturer in Political Theory in the Department of Politics at Cambridge University, and a Fellow of Jesus College, Cambridge. His work includes *The State of the Political: Conceptions of Politics and the State in the Thought of Max Weber, Carl Schmitt and Franz Neumann* (2003), and he is completing a study provisionally entitled 'The Propriety of Liberty: Persons, Passions and Judgement in Modern Political Thought'. He has written on various aspects of the intellectual history of modern political theory.

Douglas Lorimer is Professor of History at Wilfrid Laurier University, Waterloo, Ontario. He is the author of *Colour, Class and the Victorians* (1978). His recent publications include 'From Victorian Values to White Virtues: Assimilation and Exclusion in British Racial Discourse, *c.* 1870–1914', in *Rediscovering the British World*, edited by P. Buckner and R. D. Francis (2005). He is currently completing a book on racism, the language of race relations, and the sources of resistance to racism in the late Victorian and Edwardian periods, 1870–1914.

Uday Singh Mehta is the Clarence Francis Professor in the Social Sciences at Amherst College. He has taught at several universities including Princeton, Cornell, MIT, University of Chicago, University of Pennsylvania, and Hull, and his publications include *Liberalism and Empire* (2000) and *The Anxiety of Freedom: Imagination and Individuality in the Political Thought of John Locke* (1992).

Jeanne Morefield is an Associate Professor of Politics and Garrett Fellow at Whitman College. She is the author of *Covenants Without Swords: Idealist Liberalism and the Spirit of Empire* (2005). Her recent work includes 'Empire, Tragedy, and the Liberal State in the Writings of Niall Ferguson and Michael Ignatieff', *Theory and Event* (2008) and '"An Education to Greece": The Round Table, Imperial Theory, and the Uses of History', *History of Political Thought* (2007). She is currently working on a book entitled 'Politics in the Passive: Imperial Amnesia and Pluralist Responses in the Long Twentieth Century'.

Karen O'Brien teaches in the English department at the University of Warwick. She is the author of *Women and Enlightenment in Eighteenth-century Britain* (forthcoming), *Narratives of Enlightenment Cosmopolitan History from Voltaire to Gibbon* (1997), and of a number of articles and chapters that form part of her current work on British literature, empire, and political thought in Britain *c.* 1756 to 1820.

Robert Travers is Associate Professor of History at Cornell University, and the author of *Ideology and Empire in Eighteenth-century India: The British in Bengal* (2007). He is currently writing a book about economic thought in relation to the British Empire in India.

James Tully is a Distinguished Professor at the University of Victoria, Canada. He works in the areas of the history of political theory and contemporary political and legal theory. His publications include *Strange Multiplicity: Constitutionalism in the Age of Diversity* (1995), and (as co-editor) *Multinational Democracies* (2001) and *Public Philosophy in a New Key*, 2 volumes (2008).

Phiroze Vasunia is Reader in the Department of Classics at the University of Reading. He is the author of *The Gift of the Nile: Hellenizing Egypt from Aeschylus to Alexander* (2001) and the editor of *Zarathushtra and the Religion of Ancient Iran: The Greek and Latin Sources in Translation* (2007). He is currently completing a monograph on Greece, Rome, and the British Empire. He is the co-editor of the following forthcoming volumes: *The Oxford Handbook of Hellenic Studies* (with George Boys-Stones and Barbara Graziosi), *Classics and National Cultures* (with Susan Stephens), and *Greece, Rome, and Colonial India* (with Edith Hall). His translation of Longus' *Daphnis and Chloe* is forthcoming (in an anthology entitled *Greek Fiction*, edited by Helen Morales).

Richard Whatmore is currently Reader in Intellectual History and Associate Director of the Sussex Centre for Intellectual History at the University of Sussex, UK, at which he has taught since 1993. His research interests centre on eighteenth- and nineteenth-century French, British, and Genevan intellectual history. His publications have mainly been on the political and economic thought of the late eighteenth century, and particularly the period of the French Revolution. His books include *Republicanism and the French Revolution* (2000), and (as co-editor) *Economy, Polity and Society* and *History, Religion and Culture* (both 2000, with Stefan Collini and Brian Young), *Palgrave Advances in Intellectual History* (2006, with Brian Young), and an edition of Emer de Vattel's *Law of Nations* (2008, with Béla Kapossy).

Preface

Recognising the imperial and archipelagic aspects of British history has, in the post-war period, become increasingly central to the enterprise of scholarly writing on the subject.[1] Indeed, this recognition has in turn helped to inspire work in various fields of endeavour, from the history of art, literature, and science, as well as in the rather more obvious fields of political thought and intellectual history. Yet it has not always been so obvious, and indeed scholars have equally well focused on the European dimensions of the early British Empire.[2] Nevertheless, some of the central figures behind the move towards what many in the anglophone world now think of as Atlantic history have been making these sorts of claims for quite a long time.[3] But perhaps the context of our present political climate has helped to cement what now seems completely obvious; that an awareness of the character of imperial enterprise looks to be as central to understanding the British future as much as it has been to its past.

It is in fact something of a commonplace today, in popular as well as in scholarly writing, to reflect upon the nature of empire in the light of recent global politics. Such arguments and concerns, however, are not new and do indeed have a complicated history. The eighteenth and nineteenth centuries were awash with attempts to relate the tasks of the British Empire to the colonial politics and policies of, typically, either the Hellenistic or Roman empires. In the British case, this was often allied to considerations about new settler colonies, where an admixture of historical and contemporary analysis about the state of the world from the Americas to the Antipodes used such historical concerns for novel contemporary purposes. In America itself, ideas of the frontier and of some sort of 'manifest destiny' clearly played an important developmental role in thinking about expansion.[4] Put in these contexts, and in terms

---

[1] J. G. A. Pocock, *The Discovery of Islands* (Cambridge, 2005) collects some of his particularly influential papers on this topic.

[2] Brendan Simms, *Three Victories and a Defeat: The Rise and Fall of the First British Empire, 1714–1783* (London, 2007).

[3] See Bernard Bailyn, *Atlantic History: Concepts and Contours* (Cambridge, MA, 2005).

[4] Frederick Jackson Turner, *The Frontier in American History* (New York, 1920); Anders Stephanson, *Manifest Destiny: American Expansion and the Empire of Right* (New York, 1995).

of the production of this volume as a series of reflections on the historical roots of British imperial thought, it is worth noting how ideas
concerning the possible constitution of a Greater Britain were more or
less coherent amalgamations of these variously competing visions of
empire. Indeed, tracing these overlapping histories and genealogies has
been exceptionally important to contemporary work on the subject.[5]

Such concerns ran alongside still longer-standing debates about
imperial profitability and the position of the East India Company in particular.[6] In a related manner, considerations upon the nature of modern
commercial society as a response to the traditional republican dilemmas
of empire and liberty, of course, also did much to structure the myriad
debates of these two centuries. They continue to shape our own views on
what David Hume called the jealousy of trade.[7] It is still nearly impossible today, even in the light of financial unease in America and Britain, to
read about the lineages of empire without at the same time being told
to reflect upon and compare the character of the Roman Empire with
modern American global power.[8] Whilst modern military adventures
undertaken in the name of freedom and democracy clearly prompt often
rather glib comparisons with a vague idea of Roman military expansionism, these have also provoked discussion about the possible virtues as well
as the obvious scandals of imperial power; some have even seen in
American politics the chance to pursue policies left undone by the British
Empire.[9] The two entities are clearly not the same, though, which makes
the apparent obviousness of the comparison somewhat simplistic.[10] Yet
the imperial turn, if one might call it, has been absolutely central to a
burgeoning field of political theory and intellectual history.[11]

---

[5] Duncan Bell, *The Idea of Greater Britain* (Princeton, NJ, 2007).

[6] Philip J. Stern, '"A Politie of Civil and Military Power": Political Thought and the Late
Seventeenth-century Foundations of the East India Company-State', *Journal of British Studies*,
47 (2008), pp. 253–83.

[7] Istvan Hont, *Jealousy of Trade* (Cambridge, MA, 2006).

[8] See esp. Charles S. Maier, *Among Empires: American Ascendancy and Its Predecessors*
(Cambridge, MA, 2006); Andrew Bacevich, *American Empire: The Realities and Consequences of
US Diplomacy* (Cambridge, MA, 2002).

[9] Niall Ferguson, *Empire: How Britain Made the Modern World* (London, 2004) and *Colossus:
The Rise and Fall of the American Empire* (London, 2005); cf. Nicholas B. Dirks, *Scandals of
Empire* (Cambridge, MA, 2006).

[10] See esp. Bernard Porter, *Empire and Superempire: Britain, America and the World* (New Haven,
CT, 2006).

[11] See David Armitage, *The Ideological Origins of the British Empire* (Cambridge, 2000); Peter N.
Miller, *Defining the Common Good* (Cambridge, 2004); Sankar Muthu, *Enlightenment Against
Empire* (Princeton, NJ, 2003); Jennifer Pitts, *A Turn to Empire* (Princeton, NJ, 2005).

Thus, although ideas of empire and imperialism have been longstanding preoccupations of intellectual history in general, and the history of political thought in particular, it is surely not wrong to sense that our current preoccupation with empire and imperialism is bound up with a desire to trace the genealogy of our current predicament. Indeed, the similarity of concern that connects empire to at least theoretically related concepts such as despotism and tyranny might well account for some of the interest.[12] This is obviously not all that lies behind the continued growth of interest in the topic though, for it is now strongly recognised that a concern with empire has in fact been central to the development of numerous, typically segregated, intellectual disciplines. In other words, histories of art, literature, and science are as infused with debates about the impact, importance, and influence of imperial themes to their development as is political thought. The history of political thought is, in this respect, only the most obvious piece in a much more complicated intellectual jigsaw.

The essays that follow, then, are broadly structured around a very simple but central recognition; that any attempt to understand British imperial thought in the modern world must be historically rooted, and that a relatively expansive notion of what constitutes the history of political thought can illuminate one important aspect of the multiple lineages of empire. However, the symposium at which most of these papers were delivered, and which was held at the British Academy in August 2006, was rather broader than this volume might suggest, and was premised on the recognition that a fully developed theory of the development of British imperial thought would have to encompass developments in those cognate fields of art history and the histories of literature and science as well as political thought. Therefore, participants in the symposium were asked to reflect upon the nature of the relationship between empire and their various fields of expertise, and to try to see if there were any common lessons that might be drawn from their respective endeavours. The fact that this ensuing volume is only one part of this conference, and that it is focused on the history of political thought rather than on the entire range of disciplines discussed at the symposium, serves simply

---

[12] R. Koebner, *Empire* (Cambridge, 1961) is an early reflection on the intellectual history of the idea; see too his article 'Despot and Despotism: Vicissitudes of a Political Term', *Journal of the Warburg and Courtauld Institutes*, 14 (1951), pp. 275–302; cf. Mario Turchetti, ' "Despotism" and "Tyranny": Unmasking a Tenacious Confusion', *European Journal of Political Theory*, 7 (2008), pp. 159–82.

to show that in the attempt to construct a truly interdisciplinary dialogue on the impact of empire upon the development of modern intellectual history, much work remains to be done.

The initial impetus for the symposium and the actual event as a whole therefore permitted a consideration in practice, as well as in theory, of the strengths and weaknesses of interdisciplinary dialogue in the study of imperial thought, history, and imagery. It also proved the rather obvious point that there is certainly much to learn from discrete fields of study in the process of trying to arrive at a more general and synthetic argument about the precise historical character of British imperial thought. The original participants in the symposium were, I am delighted to say, fully committed to constructive engagement and conversation on this front, and I am exceptionally grateful to them, and to the British Academy for providing a wonderfully congenial and appropriate venue within which to discuss such questions. It is clear from the essays in this volume that there is a great deal of material still to be uncovered when thinking about the lineages of empire and the history of political thought, and, rather than summarise other people's arguments, I believe it is much better if the reader begins to read these accounts for themselves; the chapter titles are themselves quite indicative of the scope of the discussion being presented. It only remains for me to undertake the most pleasing aspect of the writing of such introductions, and that is to thank those involved in making it all possible.

Although the original list of speakers and session chairs are available to view in the online archive of events on the British Academy website, because only a fraction of the papers are reproduced here I should especially like to extend my thanks to those who took part and helped to make possible what was an inspiring couple of days. Thus, my very grateful thanks, in alphabetical order, to Mary Beard, Duncan Bell, John Bonehill, Karen O'Brien, Daniel Carey, Natasha Eaton, Jim Endersby, Tim Fulford, Iain Hampsher-Monk, Knud Haakonssen, Graham Harrison, Mark Harrison, Maya Jasanoff, Doug Lorimer, Saree Makdisi, Karuna Mantena, Uday Mehta, Jeannne Morefield, Sankar Muthu, Jennifer Pitts, Geoff Quilley, Sujit Sivasundarum, Miles Taylor, Robert Travers, and Richard Whatmore. For their commissioned essays in this volume I am also deeply grateful for the splendid contributions of Jim Tully and Phiroze Vasunia. I am, nevertheless, acutely aware that this volume has taken some not inconsiderable time to make it to the press after the initial request for support from the British Academy in June 2005 when invitations were sent out. So I should also like to thank all those involved with this volume in particular for their forbearance and patience; I hope at least they can be pleased with the result, which has been further improved with the copy-editing and indexing skills of Penny Rogers and Susan Tricklebank. Finally, but by no means least, I should like to offer my sincere gratitude once more not only to the British Academy in general, but also to Angela Pusey and Jo Blore in particular, for their exceptional administrative and institutional support. Without their help and expertise the event would have run much less smoothly and have been a far less pleasant enterprise than it was. I am very grateful to you all.

Duncan Kelly
Cambridge, December 2008

Part I

GENEALOGIES OF EMPIRE

1

Lineages of Contemporary Imperialism

JAMES TULLY

Introduction

THE AIM OF THIS ESSAY IS TO PRESENT a historical sketch of some major lineages of contemporary western imperialism. It is necessary to make two preliminary qualifications. First, the contemporary mode of western imperialism is the product of the last 500 years of immensely complex interactions between European and Euro-American imperial expansion and non-European responses. It is not possible to present more than a brief and partial sketch of the main lines of descent. Second, contemporary western imperialism is studied under a number of different headings: neo-colonialism, post-colonialism, open door imperialism, free trade imperialism, informal imperialism, liberal or neo-liberal imperialism, world systems imperialism, empire, US imperialism, and so on. Each of these descriptions picks out different aspects of contemporary imperialism as the most salient and seeks to explicate them as the key to the whole. This brief historical sketch is restricted to the limited aspects of contemporary imperialism gathered together under the heading of informal imperialism. The essay begins with a synopsis of defining characteristics of contemporary informal imperialism. The following five sections describe major historical lineages of these characteristics. The final section returns to contemporary imperialism with, I hope, a better understanding of its ancestry.

1. Informal Imperialism

The phrase 'informal imperialism' is now widely used by both defenders and critics of contemporary imperialism. It refers to the mode of global governance that came to predominance during the period of formal

Proceedings of the British Academy **155**, 3–29. © The British Academy 2009.

decolonisation and the Cold War (1940–1989).[1] The adjective 'informal' refers to three features of this new imperial relationship. First, the former great imperial powers, renamed the 'great eight' (G8), and their transnational corporations no longer govern the conduct of the 120 former colonies 'formally' by means of colonies and colonial administration. Rather, they are able to govern the conduct of the former colonies by a host of informal means, from economic aid, trade manipulation, and debt dependency to military dependency, intervention, and restructuring.

Second, the great powers are unable to govern the former colonies 'formatively' in the sense of exercising open and more or less unilateral administrative and military power over them, as in the case of colonial imperialism. Rather, because the former colonies are recognised as formally free and equal sovereign nation states, exercising powers of self-government, although substantively subordinate, dependent, and unequal, the great powers are constrained to govern their development 'informally' in the sense of 'interactively'. They exercise various forms of inducement, constraint, channelling, and response, and employ various means from economic dependency to military intervention, to try to control or govern the way the former colonies or 'developing countries' exercise their powers of self-government. It is thus a more interactive and open-ended imperial game between the hegemonic and subordinate powers than in the case of formal colonial rule.

Finally, this form of governance is informal in yet a third and distinctive sense. The great powers and their multinational corporations neither exercise imperial powers directly themselves, for the most part, nor have they established a world government for this purpose. Rather, they govern informally through coalitions of various kinds and with various members at different times (among the roughly G20) and through institutions of global governance set up at the end of the Second World War.[2] The main institutions are: the concentration of power in the Security Council of the United Nations; the Bretton Woods institutions of the

---

[1] For the specific dates of decolonisation and one of the best histories of western imperialism, see David B. Abernethy, *The Dynamics of Global Dominance: European Overseas Empires, 1415–1980* (New Haven, CT, 2000). The Latin American colonies decolonised in the 1820s and they have experienced informal imperialism by Great Britain and the USA for a correspondingly longer period than the countries that decolonised in the twentieth century.

[2] Even when the USA acts unilaterally rather than multilaterally, it usually garners the tacit or explicit consent of a coalition, and when it appears to act in defiance of some institutions of global governance and international law it usually claims to legitimate its action with reference to others. See, for example, Jutta Brunee and Stephen Toope, 'Slouching Towards New "Just" Wars: The Hegemon after September 11th', *International Relations*, 18, 4 (2004), pp. 405–23.

International Monetary Fund (IMF), the World Bank (WB), General Agreement on Trade and Tariff (GATT), and, in the 1990s, the World Trade Organization (WTO) and its transnational trade regimes; non-governmental organisations (NGOs) and civil society organisations working to westernise non-western societies and citizens; the acceptance of the USA as the leading or hegemonic power; the establishment of dependent economic, political, and military elites in the former colonies; the North Atlantic Treaty Organization (NATO); and the full spectrum global dominance of the US military over land, sea, and space. The former colonies are members of many of these institutions, their elites often have a say in them, and they have some room to manoeuvre within all of them. Nevertheless, the inequalities of power, knowledge, and influence of the hegemonic and subaltern partners are so great that the informal great powers and their corporations are able to prevail in most of the interactions.[3]

Since decolonisation, this complex network of unequal relationships of power between the west and the non-west (or the global north and the global south) has sustained and increased the political and military domination, economic exploitation, environmental degradation, and horrific inequalities in living conditions of the majority of the world's population in the former colonial world that were originally established during the first 500 years of western imperialism prior to decolonisation. The inequalities in this new world order are considerably greater than they were at the high-water mark of ruthless colonial imperialism at the beginning of the twentieth century. An Oxfam snapshot of the growing inequalities between the imperial and imperialised countries puts it in the following way.

840 million people are malnourished. 6 million children under the age of 5 die each year as a consequence of malnutrition. 1.2 billion people live on less than $1 a day and half the world's population live on less than $2 a day. 91 out of every 1,000 children in the developing world die before they are 5 years old. 12 million die annually from lack of water. 1.1 billion people have no access to clean water. 2.4 billion people live without proper sanitation. 40 million live with AIDS. 113 million children have no basic education. One in five people do not survive past 40 years of age. There are 1 billion non-literate adults, two-thirds are women and 98 per cent live in the developing world. In the least developed countries,

---

[3] Gerry Simpson, *Great Powers and Outlaw States: Unequal Sovereigns in the International Legal Order* (Cambridge, 2004).

45 per cent of children do not attend school. In countries with a literacy rate of less than 55 per cent the per capita income is about $600.

In contrast, the wealth of the richest 1 per cent of the world is equal to that of the poorest 57 per cent. The assets of the 200 richest people are worth more than the total income of 41 per cent of the world's people. Three families alone have a combined wealth of $135 billion. This equals the annual income of 600 million people living in the world's poorest countries. The richest 20 per cent of the world's population receive 150 times the wealth of the poorest 20 per cent. In 1960, the share of the global income of the bottom 20 per cent was 2.3 per cent. By 1991, this had fallen to 1.4 per cent. The richest fifth of the world's people consume 45 per cent of the world's meat and fish; the poorest fifth consume 5 per cent. The richest fifth consume 58 per cent of total energy, the poorest fifth less than 4 per cent. The richest fifth have 75 per cent of all telephones, the poorest fifth 1.5 per cent. The richest fifth own 87 per cent of the world's vehicles, the poorest fifth less than 1 per cent.[4]

2. Free Trade Imperialism

What, then, are the major lineages of this latest mode of western imperialism and non-western impoverishment? Among the first scholars to use the phrase 'informal imperialism' were two Cambridge economic historians writing in the immediate post-war period, John Gallagher and Ronald Robinson. In 'The Imperialism of Free Trade' (1953) they argued that this type of informal governance was not new but the descendant of free trade imperialism of the nineteenth and twentieth centuries.[5] In their view the British policy of free trade at the height of British imperialism was not anti-imperial but an alternative form of imperialism to colonialism. The nineteenth-century great powers, with Great Britain in the lead and the USA in relation to Latin America, realised that they could orchestrate the formation of legal and political regimes in non-European countries so they would function to 'open' their resources, labour, and markets to 'free trade' dominated by economic competition among

[4] Jeremy Seabrook, *The No-nonsense Guide to World Poverty* (Toronto, 2003), p. 53. Seabrook explains these inequalities in terms of the history of western imperialism. For the measurement of global inequalities, see Branko Milanovic, *Worlds Apart: Measuring International and Global Inequality* (Princeton, NJ, 2005).

[5] Ronald Robinson and John Gallagher, 'The Imperialism of Free Trade', *Economic History Review*, 6, 1 (1953), pp. 1–15.

European powers, without the need for the expensive and increasingly unpopular old imperial system of formal colonies and monopoly trading companies. In a series of publications in the following decades Robinson, Bernard Semmel, the German imperial historians Wolfgang J. Mommsen and Jürgen Osterhammel, and their followers went on to document the long and complex history of free trade imperialism since the eighteenth century and to argue that decolonisation and the Cold War comprised its triumph over colonial imperialism. Decolonisation and the Cold War, they argued, involved the dismantling of the remaining formal colonies, mandates, and trusteeships; the transfer of limited powers of self-determination to the westernised elites of nominally sovereign, yet dependent local governments in a global network of free trade imperialism; and the transfer of hegemony from Great Britain to the USA. They called this complex transition period 'the imperialism of decolonisation' and 'the end of empire and the continuity of imperialism'.[6] In his classic study of theories of imperialism, Mommsen argued that the theory of informal imperialism was the most important advance in the understanding of imperialism in the twentieth century.[7] At the same time, Harry Magdoff and William Appleman Williams were writing their complementary histories of US 'imperialism without colonies' and 'empire as a way of life'.[8] As we have seen, since the defeat of the Soviet Union and its Third World allies at the end of the Cold War in 1989, other scholars have gone on to document, defend, and criticise the extension of this mode of governance over the planet.[9]

These scholars made three crucial contributions to the study of the lineages of contemporary imperialism. First, they disclosed the historical continuity of contemporary informal imperialism with earlier

[6] Wolfgang Mommsen, 'The End of Empire and the Continuity of Imperialism', in Wolfgang Mommsen and Jürgen Osterhammel (eds), *Imperialism and After: Continuities and Discontinuities* (London, 1986).

[7] Wolfgang Mommsen, *Theories of Imperialism*, trans. P. S. Falla (Chicago, IL, 1980), pp. 86–93.

[8] Harry Magdoff, 'Imperialism without Colonies', in his *Imperialism without Colonies* (New York, 2003), published as a chapter in Magdoff, *Imperialism: From the Colonial Age to the Present* (New York, 1976 [1972]); William A. Williams, *Empire as a Way of Life: An Essay on the Causes and Character of America's Present Predicament, Along with a Few Thoughts about an Alternative* (New York, 1980).

[9] For an introduction to this voluminous literature, see Stephen Howe, *Empire: A Very Short Introduction* (Oxford, 2002); Taraki Barkawi and Mark Laffey, 'Retrieving the Imperial: Empire and International Relations', *Millennium*, 31, 1 (2002), pp. 109–27; and Daniel H. Nexon and Thomas Wright, 'What's at Stake in the American Empire Debate', *American Political Science Review*, 101, 1 (May 2007), pp. 253–71.

experiments with free trade or 'open door' imperialism. Drawing on Kwame Nkrumah's account of 'neo-colonial' (informal) imperialism, Mommsen also highlighted the dual type of corruption characteristic of informal imperialism in the post-decolonisation period. It corrupts the multinational corporations and their support agencies on one side and the local dependent elites and their dependants on the other. Mommsen quoted Nkrumah's famous conclusion that it is the 'worst form of imperialism'[10] because:

> For those who practise it, it means power without responsibility, and for those who suffer from it, it means exploitation without redress. In the days of old-fashioned colonialism, the imperial power had at least to explain and justify at home the actions it was taking abroad. In the colony those who served the ruling imperial power could at least look to its protection against any violent move by their opponents. With neo-colonialism neither is the case.

'In other words', Mommsen concurred, 'the socio-economic structures that had formed during the period of imperialism remained unimpaired after the end of formal colonial rule, and were moreover now exempt from any kind of political supervision, and the same was true of one-sided economic relations designed for the benefit of the former colonial ruler'.[11] Scholars have gone on to study these ever-widening circles of dependency and corruption in the imperial and imperialised countries.[12]

Of equal importance, their research dissolved the ahistorical and misleading distinction between formal (colonial) and informal (post-colonial) imperial periods and types. It showed that these two types of imperialism co-existed in a much broader range of intermediary and overlapping types of imperial governance during the various periods of western imperialism from 1492 to the present, such as protectorates, spheres of influence, indirect rule, private corporation governance, and so on. Scholars have gone on to study and classify this much more complex field and thus to show that there are differences in degree but not in kind between formal and informal types or periods.[13]

---

[10] Kwame Nkrumah, *Neo-colonialism, the Last Stage of Capitalism* (London, 1965), p. xi, cited in Mommsen, *Theories of Imperialism*, pp. 126–7.

[11] Mommsen, *Theories of Imperialism*, pp.126–7.

[12] For the exposure of the corruption of informal imperialism today in the tradition of J. A. Hobson, see Naomi Klein, *The Shock Doctrine: The Rise of Disaster Capitalism* (Toronto, 2007) and Noam Chomsky, *Failed States: The Abuse of Power and the Assault on Democracy* (New York, 2006).

[13] See Abernethy, *Dynamics of Global Dominance*, and Michael Doyle, *Empires* (Ithaca, NY, 1986). It is noteworthy that Hobson argued in 1902 that British imperialism consisted of more

Third, they argued that the field of imperial relationships is so complex precisely because it is *not* a concentrated form of power that is imposed unilaterally over passive and uncivilised non-European peoples and which brings about their linear development towards civilisation or modernisation. Yet, this is how the western legitimating narratives of universal stages of historical development from the Scottish Enlightenment to the latest theories of development, modernisation, globalisation, democratisation, and the spread of good governance and freedom falsely frame the history of imperial expansion. Rather, the actual historical practices of imperialism comprise diffuse and 'interactive' and often 'excentric' (reactive) forms of governance that respond to diverse forms of resistance and collaboration of imperialised peoples in localised, ad-hoc, and unpredictable ways.[14] Their insight created a potential opening within the conservative discipline of imperial history to a movement that was already well underway elsewhere. This broad twentieth-century movement, or counter-movement, consists of the criticism or 'provincialisation' of the western-centric modernisation theories that legitimate western formal and informal imperialism and the writing of contrapuntal histories of western imperialism from the standpoints of the imperialised peoples of Latin America, Africa, the Middle East, India, and Indigenous peoples of the Fourth World, not as passive victims of the gift of civilisation, but as active agents.[15] It is clear from Mommsen's *Theories of Imperialism* that their own work was influenced by authors in this counter-movement, such as Frantz Fanon and Kwame Nkrumah. While scholars on both sides now criticise the legitimating narratives and explore the interactive and corrupting features of informal imperialism, and a few have entered into dialogue across the divide, for the most part these two traditions of historical research on western imperialism remain separate.[16]

---

than thirty different types of relationship over imperialised peoples: J. A. Hobson, *On Imperialism: A Study* (New York, 2005 [1902]).

[14] Mommsen, *Theories of Imperialism*, pp. 86–112. More recently, see Ann Laura Stoler, *Carnal Knowledge and Imperial Power: Race and the Intimate in Colonial Rule* (Berkeley, CA, 2002).

[15] See Dipesh Chakrabarty, *Provincializing Europe: Postcolonial Thought and Historical Difference* (Princeton, NJ, 2000); Walter Mignolo, *Local Histories/Global Designs: Coloniality, Subaltern Knowledges and Border Thinking* (Princeton, NJ, 2000); and Robert J. Young, *Postcolonialism: A Historical Introduction* (Oxford, 2001).

[16] Edward W. Said, *Culture and Imperialism* (New York, 1994) is perhaps the best known attempt to bring the two traditions together. See also Bill Aschcroft, *Post-colonial Transformation* (London, 2001) and Young, *Postcolonialism.*

While these three contributions and the research that has followed in their wake have helped enormously in understanding the lineages of contemporary imperialism, they do not address directly two broader historical questions. How has it come about historically that the great powers and their multinationals now occupy a position within a global field to lord it over the imperialised countries in this informal manner? And, what is the lineage of the languages they use to describe and legitimate their position of 'legal hegemony' *vis-à-vis* the subordinate countries of the world?[17] That is, what is the history of the present institutional and discursive features of the broader field in which free trade and informal imperialism become possible?

3. Colonial and Indirect Imperialism

Since 1415 the European and US imperial powers have employed four broad discourses to describe, explain, and legitimate the imperialisation of non-western countries.[18] The first is the commercial or cosmopolitan right (*ius commercium*) of western states and their companies to enter into 'commercial' relations of two types with non-western societies. The first of these are trade relations dominated by the western companies—the right to trade expanded rapidly to include western access to the resources, labour, and markets of the non-western world. The second type is the right of western religious organisations, scholars, and voluntary associations to enter into 'commerce' with non-westerners in the early-modern sense of studying their customs and ways, and trying to convert them to more 'civilised' ways. The second discourse is the duty of non-western peoples to open themselves to western-style commerce in these two senses, often called the duty of hospitality. If non-western civilisations resist, defend their own economic, legal and cultural ways, close their resources, labour, or markets to trade dominated by the west, or send the companies or missionaries home, then they are said to violate the duty of openness to commerce. Third, a violation of the duty of openness to commerce in either sense, originally formulated as a natural duty under the old law of nature prior to the nineteenth century, triggers a right (of self-defence) of the aggrieved western imperial power to intervene militarily to open the

---

[17] The phrase 'legal hegemony' comes from Simpson, *Great Powers*.

[18] In 1415 a fleet of Portuguese ships left Lisbon to launch an assault on Cueta in North Africa: see Abernethy, *Dynamics of Global Dominance*, p. 3.

closed country to trade and civilisation, and to extract compensation for the company's loss of property and profits. Fourth, the imperial powers have a responsibility or duty to do something more than extract economic profits from the non-western countries. They also have a responsibility or duty to improve the conditions of the imperialised country. This duty to free the lower peoples from their backward ways and guide them up the stages of historical development and progress has been clothed in a number of different names over the last half-millennium: to improve, civilise, develop, modernise, constitutionalise, democratise, and bring good governance and freedom.[19]

Obviously, these four discourses of rights and duties presuppose a set of western institutions that have to be adopted by or imposed on the non-western world for them to be exercised. The right of free trade presupposes the legal and economic institutions of western commerce and capitalism. Accordingly, the non-western legal and economic arrangements of the imperialised society have to be either adapted to western trade, private property, slave and then wage labour, and market organisation, if possible, or, if not, dispossessed and replaced by the imposition of western-style legal and economic organisations. This massive dispossession and restructuring of the non-west is often called the 'second enclosure'.[20] The right of the imperialists to intervene militarily to open societies to trade and protect western companies abroad presupposes a world military, especially a navy, initially called 'gunboat' imperialism. The duty of 'improving' the imperialised peoples of the world presupposes the vast institutions and voluntary organisations of colonial and post-colonial governance whose role is to makeover non-westerners in the image of civilised or modernised westerners.

To simplify a very complex history, these four rights and duties and their corresponding institutional preconditions have been and continue to be spread around the world in three major ways.[21] The first is the implantation of settler colonies in the Americas, New Zealand, and Australia. In

---

[19] I have discussed these imperial rights and duties and their institutional preconditions in detail in 'The Imperialism of Modern Constitutional Democracy', in Martin Loughlin and Neil Walker (eds), *The Paradox of Constitutionalism* (Oxford, 2007), pp. 315–58, and in Emilios Christodoulidis and Stephen Tierney (eds), 'On Law, Democracy and Imperialism', *Public Law and Politics: The Scope and Limits of Constitutionalism* (Aldershot, 2008), pp. 69–102.

[20] John C. Weaver, *The Great Land Rush and the Making of the Modern World, 1650–1900* (Montreal, 2003).

[21] As I mentioned in the previous section, this is a simplification of a much more complex field of types of imperial governance.

these cases of 'replication imperialism' or 'new Europes' the rudimentary colonial structures of western law, commerce, and political forms were imposed over the institutions and traditions of Indigenous peoples, dispossessing them of their territories and usurping their forms of government, by means of 200 years of wars, dishonoured treaties, and the spread of European diseases. Approximately 80 per cent of the 60 million human beings of diverse Indigenous civilisations were exterminated. The remaining population has been forcefully and unsuccessfully assimilated or removed to tiny reserves and ruled despotically by various ministries. When the colonies freed themselves from their respective empires and established western-style states and economies themselves, they retained the European legal, political, and economic institutions and they continue to exercise what the United Nations calls 'internal colonisation' of Indigenous peoples on four continents.[22] The building of the civilising western institutions of free trade and labour discipline in the Americas was carried through by slave labour in Latin America, the opening of Africa to free trade in slaves, the transportation of 12 million to the plantations in Central and North America, and the deaths of millions.

The second major method of imperialisation has been 'indirect' colonial rule. The imperial powers establish a small colonial administration or authorise a private corporation to govern a much larger local population by indirect means. By means of unequal treaties, they recognise the quasi-sovereignty of local rulers, constrain them to adapt their 'customary' laws to trade, private property, contract law, and labour markets, and establish a system of western law at the centre. As Hobson and Leonard Woolf explained, they try to westernise the local elites and make them dependent on their economic bribes and military support, often against their own population, divide and conquer the opposition, train local armies to fight proxy wars to protect the property of foreign companies, and the trading companies often incite local rebellions so they can claim monetary compensation once it is put down.[23] This is the major way the two rights and duties and their institutional preconditions have been exercised in India, Ceylon, Africa, and the Middle East in the twentieth century.

The third major method of imperialisation is free trade or informal imperialism. It has come into practice since the early nineteenth century,

---

[22] See James Tully, 'The Struggles of Indigenous Peoples for and of Freedom', in Duncan Ivison, Paul Patton, and Will Sanders (eds), *The Rights of Indigenous Peoples and Political Theory* (Cambridge, 2000), pp. 36–59.
[23] Hobson, *On Imperialism*; Leonard Woolf, *Empire and Commerce in Africa: A Study in Economic Imperialism* (London, 1920) and his *The Village in the Jungle* (London, 1913).

initially by Britain and the USA in Latin America after decolonisation in the 1820s, after the institutional foundations of western hegemony had been laid by colonial and indirect imperialism. Once the western institutions are in place, an imperial power can withdraw its colonial and indirect apparatus and govern informally or infrastructurally. The paramount power permits local self-rule and educates the population for eventual self-determination, within a protectorate, sphere of influence, or mandate. It exercises paramountcy (now renamed 'hegemony')[24] to induce the local rulers to keep their resources, labour, and markets open to free trade dominated by western corporations and global markets, thereby combining 'empire and liberty'.

The informal means include such things as economic, military, and aid dependency, bribes, sanctions, the education and training of westernised elites in the local military, government, and corporations, and the employment of voluntary organisations to educate the local population to their appropriate place in the global economy. If the local elites fail to act accordingly, then their local laws and constitutions can be overridden by a higher order of law, *lex mercatoria* (merchant's law), the vast body of transnational trade law that has developed in tandem with *ius commercium*.[25] If, in turn, these means fail, then the paramount power threatens to intervene covertly (proxy armies and death squads) or overtly. If the threats fail, military intervention follows to open doors to free trade and to ensure that the sovereign country exercises its powers of self-government properly or be overthrown.[26] As the naval historian Alfred Thayer Mahan argued at the end of the nineteenth century, the ultimate guarantee of free trade and informal imperialism is thus the military capacity of the great powers to intervene. The basis of this—in both British informal imperialism in the nineteenth century and US open door imperialism in the twentieth and twenty-first—is the establishment of small military bases, originally naval coaling stations, in or nearby the countries they govern informally.[27] Taking over from the British in

---

[24] John Agnew, *Hegemony: The New Shape of Global Power* (Philadelphia, PA, 2005).
[25] Clare A. Cutler, *Private Power and Global Authority: Transnational Merchant Law in the Global Political Economy* (Cambridge, 2003).
[26] Hence the common name 'gunboat imperialism' for both British and US informal imperialism. See Michael Lynch, *The British Empire* (Milton Park, 2005); Magdoff, *Imperialism*; Williams, *Empire as a Way of Life.*
[27] Alfred Thayer Mahan, *The Influence of Sea Power upon History, 1660–1783* (Boston, MA, 1932).

the early twentieth century, the USA now has over 750 military bases strategically located around the world, outside its own borders.[28]

In summary, the exercise of these four rights and duties over centuries in these three main ways dispossessed non-Europeans of political and legal control over their own resources and economies, and modified, subordinated, or replaced their forms of organisation with the institutional preconditions of western legal and political domination, economic exploitation, and military control. Adam Smith and Karl Marx called this whole historical invasion and restructuring of the non-European world 'previous' or 'primitive' accumulation and agreed that it constituted the preconditions of free trade imperialism.[29] Hobson, Lenin, Weber, and Luxemburg analysed this history again under the title of 'capitalist imperialism' and 'accumulation by dispossession' in the early twentieth century and the authors mentioned in the previous sections have done the same for post-decolonisation imperialism.[30] All agree that it is the basis of the horrendous inequalities in power and wealth that enable the great powers to lord it informally over the imperialised world.

4. Nineteenth-century Civilisational Imperialism

The four rights and duties that legitimate western imperialism have been formulated in many different ways by the theorists of the different western empires and in response to different historical experiences. Gerrit Gong, Martti Koskenniemi, Edward Keene, and Antony Anghie have shown that they were brought together in their authoritative modern form in the creation of modern international law in the nineteenth century under the 'standard of civilisation'.[31]

The great powers defined their institutions of representative constitutional nation states, private property, openness to free trade, and western 'formal' legal orders as the universal form of a civilised legal, political,

[28] See Andrew Bacevich, *American Empire: The Realities and Consequences of U.S. Diplomacy* (Cambridge, MA, 2002), and sections 6–7 below.
[29] Karl Marx, 'So Called Primitive Accumulation', *Capital* (London, 1990), pp. 873–904. He refers to Adam Smith on the first page (p. 873).
[30] For these authors, see Mommsen, *Theories of Imperialism.*
[31] Gerrit W. Gong, *The Standard of 'Civilization' in International Society* (Oxford, 1984); Martti Koskenniemi, *The Gentle Civilizer of Nations: The Rise and Fall of International Law, 1870–1960* (Cambridge, 2001); Edward Keene, *Beyond the Anarchical Society: Grotius, Colonialism and Order in World Politics* (Cambridge, 2002); Antony Anghie, *Imperialism, Sovereignty and the Making of International Law* (Cambridge, 2005).

and economic organisation and thus the standard by which all other human organisations are judged.[32] The European states (and the USA after 1895) were said to be 'sovereign' and, as such, the sole subjects recognised by international law. Drawing on the four stages theory of world-historical development developed during the Scottish Enlightenment, all other civilisations were classified as uncivilised and ranked according to their level of development relative to the European standard of civilisation. Their legal and political orders, many much older than the European forms, were classified as 'customary' rather than 'formal'. Since they lacked the defining institutions of civilisation, they lacked 'sovereignty' and thus were not subjects recognised under international law. Rather, they were either in a state of nature, if they had not been colonised yet, or subject to the imperial and colonial legal orders of the respective European empires as a result of colonisation and indirect rule summarised in the previous section. The sovereign imperial states were said to have the sacred duty or mission to civilise the inferior peoples under their jurisdiction. The first part of this duty was of course to open their resources and labour to trade dominated by western companies and impose the institutions of western private property law, competitive commerce, and labour discipline, and to modify or undermine traditional cooperative forms of economic organisation and 'customary' law and politics. These institutions, imposed 'despotically' for their own good, would then start the uncivilised and semi-civilised peoples along the stages of development to civilisation and eventual western-style self-government within an international system of law and commerce established and enforced by the western powers. By 1914, 85 per cent of the non-European population were subject to European empires.

Thus, 'civilisation' refers first to a set of European legal, political, economic, and military *institutions* that are said to be a unique and universal standard of civilisation, and, second, to a set of presumptively world-historical civilising *processes* that are said to spread these institutions around the world by means of European imperialism.[33] One of the classic presentations of this imperial vision is given by Immanuel Kant, whose *Perpetual Peace* sets out the European constitutional state form, European international law and a league of European states, and the commercial right of free trade as the universal institutions for every

---

[32] See Gong, *Standard of Civilization*, for the various formulations.
[33] Brett Bowden, 'In the Name of Progress and Peace: The "Standard of Civilization" and the Universalizing Project', *Alternatives*, 29, 1 (2004), pp. 43–68.

people on the planet. And, *Universal History with a Cosmopolitan Intent* asserts that the unremitting wars of imperial expansion will gradually impose these legal, political, and commercial institutions on the non-western world, moving them up from savagery to civilisation to morality. The end result, according to Kant, will be the perpetual peace of a world made over in the identical image of European state and economic forms and under the leadership of a league of advanced European powers. 'Nature' chooses war as the means to spread the civilising institutions of western law and commerce. While Europeans often use unjustifiable force and fraud, non-Europeans (or Europeans) cannot resist, or even inquire into the unjust world order imposed on them, since the coercive imposition of western law and commerce is the precondition of civilisation itself. He carefully explains that the very existence of non-European societies without western-style civil constitutions places them in a lawless state of nature and gives Europeans the pre-emptive right to coercively impose a lawful state over them or drive them off their traditional territories, precisely what they were doing.[34] Since openness to trade and the acceptance of the corresponding domestic and international legal orders are the defining features of civilisation, if a political association asserts its right to govern itself by its own civilisational laws and ways, this proves them to be uncivilised, and their resistance justifies military intervention (in one of the three ways of the previous section).[35]

Western international law was powerless to enforce this sacred duty on the competing imperial states in the nineteenth century. Instead of cooperating in a 'juridical' imperial system based on the new international law, the competing imperial states continued their competitive wars, pillage, slavery, hyper-exploitation, genocide, and destruction, and especially in Africa after the Berlin Conference of 1885, all the while justifying it in the name of civilising the natives. As Wilfred S. Blunt summed up the century in 1900:

> The old century is very nearly out, and this leaves the world in a pretty pass, and the British Empire is playing the devil in it as never an empire before and on so large a scale. We may live to see its fall. All the nations of Europe are making

---

[34] Immanuel Kant, *Political Writings*, ed. H. S. Reiss (Cambridge, 1991), pp. 41–53, 93–130. I have discussed these two texts in more detail in 'The Kantian Idea of Europe', in Anthony Pagden (ed.), *The Idea of Europe* (Cambridge, 2002), pp. 331–58, and 'On Law, Democracy and Imperialism'.

[35] Anghie, *Imperialism, Sovereignty* traces this structure of argument (the four rights and duties) from the sixteenth century to the present; and Koskenniemi, *Gentle Civilizer of Nations* from the nineteenth century to the present.

the same hell upon earth in China, massacring and pillaging and raping in the captured cities as outrageously as in the Middle Ages. The Emperor of Germany gives the word for slaughter and the Pope looks on and approves. In South Africa our troops are burning farms under Kitchener's command, and the Queen and the two houses of Parliament and the bench of Bishops thank God publicly and vote money for the work. The Americans are spending fifty millions a year on slaughtering the Filipinos; the King of the Belgians has invested his whole fortune on the Congo, where he is brutalising the Negroes to fill his pockets. The French and the Italians for the moment are playing a less prominent part in the slaughter, but their inactivity grieves them. The whole white race is revelling openly in violence, as though it never pretended to be Christian. God's equal curse on them all! So ends the famous nineteenth century into which we were proud to have been born.[36]

That is to say, the 'new' imperialism of the late nineteenth century under the duty to civilise was much the same as the 'new' imperialism of the early twenty-first century in Latin America and the Middle East under the duty to bring market freedoms and democracy.[37]

5. Cooperative Mandate Imperialism

The results of unbridled civilisational imperialism culminated in the horrors of the First World War. This 'great war for civilisation' was a global war among the sovereign imperial powers over the control and exploitation of the colonised world.[38] In 1919 it was obvious that the great powers were the barbarians. They were confronted with widespread peace movements at home and with decolonisation and anti-imperial movements in the colonies. They realised that they had to make a transition to a cooperative and informal type of imperialism based on international law. This consisted in two tasks that required a century to complete.[39]

---

[36] Wilfred Scawen Blunt, *My Diaries*, 2 vols (London, 1919–20), vol. 1, p. 464, cited in Louis L. Snyder (ed.), *The Imperial Reader* (New York, 1962), pp. 146–7. Compare Koskenniemi, *Gentle Civilizer of Nations*, pp. 98–178, for similar European views.

[37] For the twenty-first century 'new' imperialism in this light, see Greg Grandin, *Empire's Workshop: Latin America, the United States and the Rise of the New Imperialism* (New York, 2007) and Derek Gregory, *The Colonial Present: Afghanistan, Palestine, and Iraq* (Oxford, 2004).

[38] John H. Morrow Jr, *The Great War: An Imperial History* (London, 2004) and Robert Fisk, *The Great War for Civilization: The Conquest of the Middle East* (London, 2005).

[39] For a history of these two tasks from the perspective of the USA, which is important for the following section, see Neil Smith, *American Empire: Roosevelt's Geographer and the Prelude to Globalization* (Berkeley, CA, 2004).

The first task was to establish a form of international governance that has the capacity to force the imperial powers to end their military competition over the resources, labour, and markets of the colonised world and to embrace some form of military cooperation and continuing economic competition or face the mutual destruction of the contending parties as wars became ever more industrialised and total. The League of Nations was the first attempt. The destructiveness of the Second World War (started by Germany, Italy, and Japan in part because they claimed to be discriminated against by having been stripped of their colonies), made this task all the more necessary. The establishment of the United Nations and the Bretton Woods institutions and the defeat of the Soviet empire during the Cold War brought into being a cooperative military framework of contemporary informal imperialism As both Karl Kautsky and Hobson predicted at the beginning of the century, unless the economic basis of corporate capitalism was transformed in Europe and the USA, this kind of cooperative solution to competitive military imperialism would simply lead to a kind of 'hyper-imperialism' over the colonised world.

The second task was to take the international law duty to civilise out of the jurisdiction of the rapacious individual sovereign empires and place it under international control, which could then guide the uncivilised peoples to free trade and eventual self-government. The first attempt was the Mandate System of the League of Nations. The League classified the imperialised peoples of the world into three stages of development. The first were those in the Middle East who were closest to self-government and whose elites needed only a moderate amount of 'tutelage' in civilisation and modernisation by their respective imperial tutors. The second were those in Africa who were further down the scale of development and required decades of 'guardianship' by their imperial guardians before they could be granted western-style self-government. The third were those who would never be able to be self-governing and would thus always be colonised by their respective superiors. These included South West Africa, the Pacific Islanders, and the Indigenous peoples in the Americas and Australia.[40]

---

[40] For the Mandate System, see Michael D. Callahan, *Mandates and Empire: The League of Nations and Africa, 1914–1931* (Brighton, 1999); Callahan, *A Sacred Trust: The League of Nations and Africa, 1929–1946* (Brighton, 2004); and Anghie, *Imperialism, Sovereignty*, pp. 115–95.

The Mandate System of the League of Nations and the later Trustee System of the United Nations constitute the intermediate step between colonial and indirect rule and the emergence of informal governance after decolonisation. It recognised an international duty to civilise non-Europeans in the form of a mandate on the respective imperial powers. Reciprocally, it recognised most of the colonised peoples, not as free peoples with their own civilisations and modes of development, but as undeveloped peoples who could and should be moulded into western ways of self-government by the developed powers. The great powers were no longer imperialists but mandatories and trustees. Moreover, this new system would, at least in theory, guard and tutor the lower people towards modernisation and self-government through their subordinate participation, as if they were children and pupils.

The defenders could thus contrast the violence, lawlessness, and corruption of unilateral colonial and indirect imperialism in the hands of competing military states with the new, international law-based, multilateral, cooperative, and proto-informal imperialism of the Mandate System. They could thus equate 'imperialism' as a whole with the former, executive mode, and redescribe the new, juridical, and developmental mode as 'non-imperial' and 'anti-imperial', or at least on the path to a post-imperial age. They could thereby employ a language of description of informal imperialism that made it appear to be post-colonial and post-imperial; a language that had been developed already in the nineteenth century by Hobson, Benjamin Kidd, Herbert Spencer, and, earlier, John Stuart Mill and Kant.[41]

This semantic shift gave rise to what are now called the 'two wings' of European and US imperialism. The former is usually unilateral, often in violation of international law, and explicit about the use of military intervention. It is associated with Cecil Rhodes, Theodore Roosevelt, the Bush administrations, and the US National Security Doctrine of 2002. The latter is usually multilateral, in accord with international law, and more reserved and covert about military intervention. It is associated with Woodrow Wilson, the Kennedy and Clinton administrations, and the foreign policy of the European Union. This division between the two

---

[41] The least known of these authors, Benjamin Kidd, a follower of Spencer, presented one of the most influential theories of international law-based, tutelage imperialism and economic exploitation, *The Control of the Tropics* (London, 1898). For John Stuart Mill and imperialism, see Timothy Smith, *Liberalism and Imperial Governance in the Thought of J. S. Mill: The Architecture of a Democratization Theorem* (Berlin, 2008).

wings of western imperialism, with the latter presenting itself as non-imperial even though its objective is to remake the world in accord with the western standard of civilisation, emerged in, and sets the contours of the debate over, the 'new imperialism' of 1880–94 and reappeared in almost identical terms in the 'new imperialism' of 1990–2007.[42] As Gandhi and his many followers observe, the idea that the western powers should not only not intervene, but also withdraw their imperial military and economic institutions from non-western societies and abjure the use of violence and economic sanctions remains beyond the limits of public reason and policy.[43]

With the decline of the League and the dismantling of the Trustee System of the United Nations, the international law duty to civilise could be passed to the new institutions of global governance. In response to the demands of the former colonies at the United Nations, the imperial language of 'civilisation' was removed, yet it was replaced with languages that refer to the same historical processes and institutions: development, modernisation, democratisation, constitutionalisation, freedom, and good governance. The duty to civilise took on the form of transnational trade laws under GATT and the WTO that override the constitutions of the former colonies and open them to exploitation by multinational corporations, neo-liberal structural adjustment and privatisation programmes, the tutelage of civil society and aid organisations, and so on. Informal imperialism could continue apace under a language that removed any reference to imperialism.[44]

Finally, despite its failure at curbing corruption and exploitation, especially in the oil-rich Middle East, the Mandate System also gave the western powers a period to prepare for the eventual transfer of powers of self-determination to the former colonies yet within the continuing field of informal economic and military dependency. This remarkable process

---

[42] For the two wings in the USA, see the debate between Robert Kagan, on the unilateral side, and Robert Tucker and David Hendrickson, on the multilateral side, in the journal *Foreign Affairs* (December 2004 and January 2005), and William K. Tabb, 'The Two Wings of the Eagle', in John Bellamy Foster and Robert W. McChesney (eds), *Pox Americana: Exposing the American Empire* (New York, 2004), pp. 95–103. For the two wings in North American and European political thought, see Tully, 'On Law, Democracy and Imperialism'.

[43] For Gandhi and his influence, see Thomas Weber, *Gandhi as Disciple and Mentor* (Cambridge, 2004). One of the most influential anti-imperial and non-violent Gandhians today is Johann Galtung: see www.transcend.org.

[44] Anghie, *Imperialism, Sovereignty*, pp. 196–244.

of the 'imperialism of decolonisation' is the subject of the next and final sections.[45]

6. US Imperialism

The free trade imperialism of Section 2, the colonial and indirect foundations of Section 3, the civilisational legacy of Section 4, and the two twentieth-century tasks of Section 5 are important lineages of contemporary imperialism. However, to understand how western imperialism was able to survive decolonisation in its current informal mode it is necessary to add the specific roles that the USA played in the two tasks of Section 5. As we have seen, the USA has exercised informal governance over Central and Latin America since the early nineteenth century. The most formative justification of this (in terms similar to the two imperial rights and duties) is the Monroe Doctrine of 1823 and the Corollary to it by President Theodore Roosevelt in 1904, giving the US army and navy 'international police power' over the western hemisphere.[46] At the League of Nations, President Woodrow Wilson went on to claim that the Doctrine is applicable to the whole world. In the Monroe Doctrine and its corollaries the US government gave itself the right and duty to keep the economies of Latin American countries open to US trade and investment and protect its companies from expropriation. The Doctrine is designed to apply against two types of closure: any attempt by the old European colonial powers to exercise a monopoly over Latin American countries and any attempt by Latin American governments to control their own economies and protect them from foreign investment. The USA intervened militarily in the affairs of the sovereign states of Latin America hundreds of times in the nineteenth century alone.[47]

At the end of the nineteenth century, the Monroe Doctrine came to be called the 'open door' foreign policy, associated with the notes of John

---

[45] The phrase 'the imperialism of decolonisation' comes from Ronald Robinson, 'The Imperialism of Decolonization', in James De Le Sueur (ed.), *Decolonization: A Reader* (London, 2003).

[46] *The Monroe Doctrine* (1823), www.ushistory.org/documents/monroe.htm; *The Roosevelt Corollary to the Monroe Doctrine* (1904), http://theodoreroosevelt.org/life/rooseveltcorollary.htm.

[47] For recent surveys, see Robert Kagan, *Dangerous Nation: America's Foreign Policy from the Earliest Days to the Dawn of the Twentieth Century* (New York: Vintage, 2007) and Grandin, *Empire's Workshop*. The classic study from the Latin American side is Eduardo Galeano, *Open Veins of Latin America: Five Centuries of the Pillage of a Continent* (New York, 1997).

Hay concerning opening China to US trade and investment.[48] In 1898, with the transition to 'corporate' capitalism and the need to expand plants and investments aboard, and a remarkably forthright debate about the future of imperialism in the USA and Europe, Charles A. Conant reformulated it in accordance with the duty of civilisation and laid out four possible modes of imperialism to choose from when intervening in Asia:

> Whether the United States shall actually acquire territorial possessions, shall set up captain generalships and garrisons, [or] whether they shall adopt the middle ground of protecting sovereignties nominally independent, or whether they shall content themselves with naval stations and diplomatic representations as the basis for asserting their rights to the free commerce of the East, is a matter of detail . . . The writer is not an advocate of imperialism from sentiment, but does not fear the name if it means only that the United States shall assert their right to free markets in all of the old countries which are being opened up to the surplus resources of capitalistic countries and given the benefits of modern civilization.[49]

The USA continued with the mode of informal imperialism that had served it well in the 'workshop' of Central and Latin America (a mixture of Conant's three non-colonial modes) after the barbaric experiment with colonisation of the Philippines caused a public outcry. The USA initially supported the Philippine independence fighters in their struggle against Spanish imperialism in the Spanish-American War (1898).[50] President McKinley then refused to recognise the independent Philippine Republic, declared his intention to annex the Philippines, and initiated the Philippine-American War against the independence fighters (1898–1902), killing 250,000 Filipinos and 4,200 US troops.[51]

This tradition of informal imperialism through the Monroe Doctrine, open-door gunboat diplomacy, and public opposition to formal colonies (due in part to its own anti-colonial revolution in 1776) is one standard

---

[48] John Hay to Andrew D. White, *First Open Door Note*, www.mtholyoke.edu/acad/intrel/open door.htm; *The Open Door Notes* (1899–1900), www.pinzler.com/ushistory/opendoorsupp.html.
[49] Charles A. Conant, 'The Economic Basis of Imperialism', *North American Review*, 167, 502 (1898), pp. 326–41.
[50] Spain ceded the Philippines, Guam, Puerto Rico, and control of Cuba to the USA under the Treaty of Paris that ended the war. Guantanomo Bay was established in 1901.
[51] The colonisation of the Philippines gave the USA a beachhead into the Pacific and a base to compete with the other great powers to open the Chinese market to trade and investment and put down the Boxer Rebellion. See John Bellamy Foster, Harry Magdoff, and Robert W. McChesney, 'Kipling, the "White Man's Burden", and U.S. Imperialism', in Foster and McChesney, *Pox Americana*, pp. 12–21.

lineage of US imperialism. However, there is another longer and complementary lineage that helps to explain the persistence of and preference for informal imperialism.

At the same time as Conant was explaining the economics of imperialism and the USA was keeping European powers out of Latin American and expanding into the Pacific and Asia, Frederick Jackson Turner presented his famous frontier thesis. He explained that the USA originally moved its civilising frontier westward by means of hundreds of small wars against the savage Indian nations and by establishing armed forts along the frontier of Indian Country. Now that this frontier was closed (having reached the west coast) and private enterprise had to expand beyond the continent, new ways to extend the frontier had to be found. The dispossession of the Native Americans of their traditional territories provided 'free land' for settlers, but now there was no land left and, with the turn to corporate capitalism and wage labour, there was the threat of a socialist revolution. Corporations needed to expand their frontier of open-door commerce abroad to keep the working class employed and satisfied at home.[52] Alfred Thayer Mahan provided the answer to this problem in his account of the role of the British navy and coaling stations in the rise of British imperialism, which he applied to the USA's extension of its civilised frontier into Asia by expanding its navy and overseas stations in his immensely influential lecture tours.[53]

There is thus a continuous lineage of frontier imperial expansion that runs from the wars against the Pequot Indians of the 1630s to Wounded Knee in 1870, through the invasion of Texas and California, military interventions in Central and Latin America, the establishment of Guantanomo Bay (1901), and to the expansion into the Pacific (Hawaii) and Asia at the turn of the century. The militarised frontier was projected further during the Cold War, the overthrow of 'closed' regimes and 'rogue states', and the current war against terrorism. The weaponisation of space is described as the newest frontier by the Pentagon. In each phase, the frontier is invoked to rally public opinion behind the latest step in the

---

[52] George Roger Taylor (ed.), *The Turner Thesis* (Toronto, 1972), Supplement, pp. 30–3.

[53] A. T. Mahan, *Interest of America in Sea Power, Present and Future* (London, 1898), *Lessons of the War with Spain and Other Essays* (London, 1900), and *Armaments and Arbitration, or the Place of Force in the International Relations of States* (New York, 1912). For an introduction to his influence, see Stephen Kinzer, *Overthrow: America's Century of Regime Change from Hawaii to Iraq* (New York, 2006), pp. 33, 37, 83.

'manifest destiny' of US expansion, as historians of US imperialism have shown in detail.[54]

The defining feature of frontier imperialism is, Turner explains, the actual encounter at the frontier: 'the melting point between savagery and civilisation'. As the frontiersman moves west, he loses his European civility and takes on the savage ways of the Indians or else he perishes. He steps from the 'railroad car to the birch canoe' and 'strips off the garments of civilisation and arrays him in the hunting shirt and the moccasin'. Not only does he begin to plant Indian corn and plough with a stick; he engages in savage warfare with the Indians. He 'shouts the war cry and takes the scalp in orthodox Indian fashion'. But this transformation is not the endpoint. Once the frontier is secured, the frontier settler gradually 'transforms the wilderness', not in accord with 'old Europe', but, out of these frontier characteristics, the settlers bring about 'the steady growth of independence on American lines'. This frontier experience of savage wars and transformation of the Wild West into the American way of life is not a single line but a never-ending renewal. It consists in the 'return to primitive conditions on a continually advancing frontier line' and the 'continually beginning over again on the frontier'. It is this unique 'perennial rebirth, this fluidity of American life, this expansion westward' that defines the destiny of the American character. The frontier is important as a 'military training school' that develops the 'qualities of the frontiersman' and produces 'individualism and democracy', 'free land', and 'incessant expansion'. It 'will continually demand a wider field for its exercise'. In the supplements to the original text, Turner turns to the debate over US imperial expansion abroad and projects this frontier thesis on to the political and commercial expansion of the USA into 'lands beyond the seas'.[55]

---

[54] The classic accounts of frontier imperialism are Albert K. Weinberg, *Manifest Destiny: A Study of Nationalist Expansionism in American History* (Baltimore, MD, 1935); Richard Slotkin, *Regeneration through Violence: The Mythology of the American Frontier* (Middleton, WI, 1973); Richard Drinnon, *Facing West: The Metaphysics of Indian-hating and Empire Building* (Norman, OK, 1997 [1980]); Williams, *Empire as a Way of Life*; and V. G. Kiernan, *America, The New Imperialism: from White Settlement to World Hegemony* (London, 2005). For the weaponisation of space as the latest militarised frontier, see Raymond Duvall and Jonathan Havercroft, 'Taking Sovereignty out of this World: Space Weapons and Empire of the Future', *Review of International Studies*, 34, 4 (2008), pp. 755–75. For the overthrow of insubordinate regimes, see Kinzer, *Overthrow*.

[55] Taylor (ed.), *Turner Thesis*, pp. 4–5, 12, 22–3, 31. See Weinberg, *Manifest Destiny*, Slotkin, *Regeneration through Violence*, and Drinnon, *Facing West* for analysis of the Turner thesis in this context.

Turner's influential analysis of US imperialism as a 'perennial rebirth' through the 'return to primitive ways' on the expanding frontier was reinforced by Rudyard Kipling in the famous poem he wrote in support of the colonisation of the Philippines, *White Man's Burden: The United States and Philippine Islands*. Just as Turner argued, Kipling declared that the troops on the frontier had to abandon their civilised ways and engage in 'the savage wars of peace' to defend and extent the frontier of western civilisation. The civilised citizens who protest do not understand why the reversion to savagery is necessary and the uncivilised peoples who resist and hate the imperialists do not understand the gift of civilisation extended to them. The soldier, therefore, must plug his ears to their protestations and stay the course of the civilising mission. This is the thankless 'white man's burden'.[56] When Kipling won the Nobel Prize for Literature in 1907, the Committee praised 'his imperialism' for taking into account 'the sentiments of others'.[57]

In 2003, Max Boot, one of the leading proponents of US informal imperialism today, wrote a celebratory history of the frontier wars that the USA has fought in its rise to world power and an exhortation to continue them. He invoked Kipling's poem in his title, *The Savage Wars of Peace: Small Wars and the Rise of American Power*. In 2006, Robert D. Kaplan, another influential imperialist, interviewed US troops stationed around the world in the frontier bases and savage wars of the 'American Empire' for *Imperial Grunts: On the Ground with the American Military, from Mongolia to the Philippines to Iraq and Beyond*. He begins with a quotation from 1884 which situates the story in the lineage of Indian wars: 'In a campaign against Indians, the front is all around, and the rear is nowhere.' He links this to a quotation from a professor at the Naval War College in Newport, Rhode Island, in 1996: 'Imperialism moved forward . . . mainly because men on the periphery . . . pressed to enlarge the boundaries of empire, often without orders, even against orders.' In the prologue, entitled 'Injun Country', he presents the central thesis: the war against terrorism today is a continuation of the savage frontier wars against the Indians yesterday. This is not an interpretation that he imposed on the interviews. It is how the soldiers themselves understand their situation: '"Welcome to Injun Country" was the refrain I heard from troops from Colombia to the Philippines, including Afghanistan and

---

[56] Rudyard Kipling, *Kipling's Verse: Definitive Edition* (New York, 1940).
[57] Cited in Foster et al., 'Kipling and U.S. Imperialism', p. 17.

Iraq.' The 'war on terrorism', he continues, 'was really about taming the frontier'.[58]

During the early years of decolonisation, one of the first leaders to articulate the compatibility of the granting of self-determination to the former colonies with the continuation and expansion of informal, frontier imperialism was President Woodrow Wilson. He argued that most colonised peoples should be able to exercise the right of self-determination.[59] Yet, at the same time, the USA has the continuing duty to educate the elites, train the military, and intervene from time to time to guide self-determination towards openness to free trade, market economies, and western-style representative democratisation. He saw no contradiction in proclaiming the right of self-determination and intervening militarily in China and Central and Latin America.[60] Major-General Smedley Butler, the famous marine in charge of implementing the Wilsonian doctrine of self-determination and military intervention, called it by its more familiar name in Latin America, 'gangster capitalism':

> I spent 33 years and four months in active service . . . I served in all commissioned ranks from Second Lieutenant to Major-General. And during that time, I spent most of my time being a high-class muscle man for Big Business, for Wall Street and the Bankers. In short, I was a racketeer, a gangster for capitalism . . . I helped make Mexico, especially Tampico, safe for American oil interests in 1914. I helped make Haiti and Cuba a decent place for the National City Bank boys to collect revenues in. I helped in the raping of half a dozen Central American republics for the benefit of Wall Street . . . I helped to purify Nicaragua for the international banking house of Brown Brothers in 1909–1912. I brought light to the Dominican Republic for American sugar interests in 1916. In China I helped to see that Standard Oil went its way unmolested.[61]

Chalmers Johnson, one of the leading historians of US informal imperialism, summarises Wilson's legacy in the following way:

> Wilson . . . provided an idealistic grounding for American imperialism, what in our own time would become a 'global mission' to 'democratise' the world. More than any other figure, he provided the intellectual foundations for an interven-

---

[58] Robert D. Kaplan, *Imperial Grunts: On the Ground with the American Military, from Mongolia to the Philippines to Iraq and Beyond* (New York, 2006), p. 4.

[59] The major exception was the Indigenous peoples of the Americas.

[60] Woodrow Wilson, 'An Address to the Senate', 27 January 1917. See Bacevich, *American Empire*, pp. 114–16. William A. Williams, in *Empire as a Way of Life*, presents Wilson's doctrine as a 'contradiction' a generation ago, but most historians see the two sides of it—self-determination and informal control—as complementary (see note 54 above).

[61] Smedley Butler, 'On Interventionism' [1933], www.fas.org/man/smedley.htm.

tionist foreign policy, expressed in humanitarian and democratic rhetoric. Wilson remains the godfather of those contemporary ideologists who justify American power in terms of exporting democracy.[62]

Following in the traditions of Kant, Mill, and Spencer in the nineteenth century, a wide range of twentieth-century liberal and social democratic political and legal theorists have endorsed this liberal or 'democratisation' wing of US and European imperialism.[63]

7. Contemporary Imperialism

In virtue of these several lineages, the USA and the former imperial powers were thus well prepared to govern informally the transfer of political power to the former colonies during decolonisation; to block alternative, non-aligned forms of self-reliant economic and political development; to overthrow insubordinate regimes; and to control the way the nationalist elites constructed the new nation states so their resources, labour, and markets remain open to a global economy dominated by western multinational corporations, as Gallagher and Robinson explained.[64] They were also able to triumph militarily over Soviet imperialism and its dependencies during the Cold War. Then, as the opening sections foreshadowed, the World Bank, the International Monetary Fund, and official nongovernmental organisations continued the civilising processes, renamed democratisation, that the Mandate System began.[65] New regimes of transnational trade laws that override domestic constitutions and have openness to free trade as their first priority were put in place by GATT and the World Trade Organization. A series of international laws of securitisation after 11 September 2001 through Security Council Resolutions placed further limits on opposition to the neo-liberal order.[66] The burden

---

[62] Chalmers Johnson, *Sorrows of Empire: Militarism, Secrecy, and the End of the Republic* (New York, 2004), p. 51.

[63] For the nineteenth century, see Duncan Bell (ed.), *Victorian Visions of Global Order* (Cambridge, 2007). For the twentieth century, see Jeanne Morefield, *Covenants Without Swords: Idealist Liberalism and the Spirit of Empire* (Princeton, NJ, 2005); Susan Marks, *The Riddle of All Constitutions* (Oxford, 2002); Simpson, *Great Powers*; Koskemienni, *Gentle Civilizer of Nations.*

[64] For more recent scholarship, see Prasenjit Duara (ed.), *Decolonization: Perspectives from Then and Now* (London, 2004).

[65] Alison Ayers, 'Imperial Liberties: Democratisation and Governance in the "New" World Order', *Political Studies*, Online early articles, April 2008, doi:10.1111/j.1467-9248.2008.00723.x.

[66] Kim Scheppele, 'The International State of Emergency: Challenges to Constitutionalism after September 11', unpublished MS (Princeton University, 2007).

of debt, exploitation, environmental damage, and dysfunctional institutions inherited from colonial and indirect imperialism, especially in Africa and the Middle East, deepened the dependency and inequality.[67]

As in earlier phases of western imperialism, the lineage that underlies all the rest is the global military paramountcy of the leading imperial power. For the majority of the world's population would not acquiesce in the present dependency, exploitation, inequality, and 'low intensity democracy' for a minute if it were not backed up by the overwhelming force of arms.[68] No one presents the importance of this lineage more forcefully than one of its leading proponents, Thomas Friedman. He states:

> [T]he hidden hand of the market will never work without a hidden fist—McDonald's cannot flourish without a McDonnell Douglas, the builder of the F-15. And the hidden fist that keeps the world safe for Silicon Valley's technologies is called the United States Army, Air Force, Navy and Marine Corps.[69]

The 750 US military bases around the world provide the local base for the covert and overt exercise of this hidden fist of the old imperial right and duty to keep non-western societies open to free trade dominated by western corporations. The bases in turn are supported by continuous surveillance of the planet by navy, air force, satellites, and the coming weaponisation of space. The Pentagon divides the world into five areas, 'similar', as Kagan observes, 'to the way that the Indian Country of the American West had been divided in the mid-nineteenth century'.[70] These imperial provinces or 'commands' are governed by five US Commanders in Chief (CINC) or 'proconsuls' that report to the Joint Chiefs of Staff. They exercise, as the Pentagon website states, 'full spectrum dominance' over the planet in the name of 'commerce and freedom'.[71]

---

[67] Mahood Mamdani, *Citizen and Subject: Contemporary Africa and the Legacy of Late Colonialism* (Princeton, NJ, 1995). For the continuity of the war in Iraq with earlier indirect imperialism, see Tony Smith, *A Pact with the Devil* (London, 2007) and Fisk, *Great War for Civilization*.

[68] For 'low intensity democracy', see the area studies in Barry Gills, Joel Rocamora, and Richard Wilson (eds), *Low Intensity Democracy: Political Power in the New World Order* (London, 1993).

[69] Thomas Friedman, *New York Times Magazine*, 28 March 1999.

[70] Kagan, *Imperial Grunts*, p. 4.

[71] Joint Chiefs of Staff, *Joint Vision 2010*, www.dtic.mil/jv2010/jvpub.htm. For this global military network, see Bacevich, *American Empire*, Johnson, *Sorrows of Empire* (both authors served in the military), and James Carroll, *The House of War: The Pentagon and the Disastrous Rise of American Power* (New York, 2007).

Conclusion

Fortunately for the future of life on this small planet, this half millennium of tyranny against diverse civilisational forms of self-reliance and association has not gone unopposed. Millions of courageous humans have resisted, modified, and outmanoeuvred its reach (and overreach) and continue to do so today. These counter-traditions in the imperialised and imperial countries are both possible and effective because the informal, interactive, diffuse, and manifestly unjust characteristics of informal imperialism make it impossible for the powers-that-be to exercise effectively full spectrum dominance, let alone hegemony. Moreover, millions have turned away from imperialism as a way of life and kept alive, cultivated, and invented alternative modernities in the interstices of western imperialism. These are alternative forms of political, legal, and economic associations based on self-reliance, fair trade, non-violence, deep ecology, and cooperative networks. This contrapuntal story is for another volume, on the lineages of anti-imperialism and of existing alternatives to imperialism.

Note. I would like to thank the faculty and students of Whitman College, Walla Walla, Washington, for inviting me to give an earlier version of this essay as a public lecture and for offering many helpful suggestions for its improvement. I cannot think of a more stimulating and pleasant intellectual environment in which to discuss these pressing issues.

2

The Social Question and the Problem of History after Empire

UDAY SINGH MEHTA

The only objective that you can set in the modern world is a widespread raising of the people's standard of living.

Jawaharlal Nehru's Speeches 1949–1953 (New Delhi, 1954), p. 20

Our position in the world ultimately depends on the unity and strength of the country, on how far we proceed in the solution of our economic and other problems and on how much we can raise the depressed masses of India.

Jawaharlal Nehru's Speeches 1949–1953 (New Delhi, 1954), p. 7

Introduction

THE DECOLONISATION OF THE EUROPEAN EMPIRES in the twentieth century was spurred, on the part of the colonised, by two broad purposes: first, the desire for independence, and, second, the intention of establishing a sovereign political identity. The most conspicuous feature of the former was, typically, mass anti-imperial movements, organised under the omnibus banner 'they must leave'; and, of the latter, the establishment of constitutional government, which emphasised the identity of the new country in an expressively political and unified form and which featured a central source of power. Notwithstanding their coincidence, there is a complex relationship between the two purposes. Clearly for power to be sovereign it must in some important manner also be independent. It cannot be obligated to the wishes of another power or significantly constrained by the laws of another regime. But, as a matter of fact, the struggle for independence did not typically create the conditions for the exercise of sovereign power. Put differently, the project of the nation state was never complete at the moment of independence. Similarly, the claims and policies of a centralised power in newly independent countries were

Proceedings of the British Academy **155**, 31–49. © The British Academy 2009.

seldom wholly independent, nor did they always reflect the mass movements that had preceded them. And plainly claims of unity were, at best,
prospective.

This essay considers some of the implications of these two broad
purposes, while focusing on the second and drawing mainly on the Indian
experience. What did it mean for newly independent countries to conceive
of their collective identities in primarily political terms? What were the
pressures that informed the claims to political identity and unity? How
did these pressures encourage what might be thought of as a revolutionary mindset in conceptualising constitutional provisions and the ambit of
political power? How does the emphasis on claiming a political identity
relate to the alleged history of the nation as it had been vouched for
during the struggle for independence?

The experience and the consolidation of the state had, of course, been
a salient feature of European modernity from the sixteenth century
onwards. In this respect the emphasis that newly independent countries
placed on political identity and the state was a familiar retreading of
European patterns. But in other respects twentieth-century nationalism
was freighted from the very outset with distinct imperatives. Some of
these imperatives were the unique outcomes of the process of decolonisation and the arguments that had been made in favour of independence.
But they were also intertwined with broader changes that had begun in
the nineteenth century and which continued into the twentieth—changes
in which political power was more and more associated with social issues,
and not merely with settling the general terms of institutional arrangements. Similarly during the nineteenth and twentieth centuries the boundaries and the claims of political unity of European nation states came
under greater pressure to sharpen the demarcation between each other.

In considering the legacies of empire this essay does not distinguish
between those effects that might have been the consequence of broader
changes endemic to the nineteenth and twentieth centuries, and those that
were singularly caused by the process of decolonisation itself. Nevertheless,
what is clear is that in the context of decolonisation the capacious reach
of political power was substantially determined by the pressure of social
questions and the imperative to be able to at least profess political unity.

In her book *On Revolution*, Hannah Arendt claimed 'every attempt to
solve the social question by political means leads to terror'.[1] It is a remark
that casts an important light on the broad context of post-colonial

---

[1] Hannah Arendt, *On Revolution* (London, 1990), p. 112.

politics and the consequences of attempting to address or redress social inequities by political means. By the social question Arendt meant issues of material destitution and inequality. The claim was itself one of the central planks by which she distinguished the American and French revolutions and the constitution settlements that followed them. For her, the singular calamity of the French Revolution, on account of which it led to terror and constitutional instability, was that it attempted to address questions of destitution and social inequality solely within a political framework. In contrast, in the American case, by substantially ignoring the social questions of the day, the constitution was able to limit the ambit of political power, and hence secure the domain of public freedom.[2]

For Arendt, the choices made by the Americans were far-reaching in their consequences and judicious in their implications. They were a fence against the deep, if not inherent, tendency to terror that she identified in modern politics. Given the context and reasons of her own exile from Germany in 1933 it is not surprising that Arendt reflected deeply on the implications of a merciless purposefulness, which she often associated with the grand agendas of modern politics. Yet precisely because she reflected with such moral seriousness about terror and politics, it is important to recognise, as her remark suggests, that she also associated terror with something utterly commonplace, whose reach and provenance extended well beyond the specifics of the Third Reich or even the twentieth century; namely in the political attempt to address social questions. A central feature of Arendt's political vision was that for power to be chastened and public freedom secured, political institutions must be exempt, and must exempt themselves, from shouldering the burden of redressing material and social inequities. Only thus could politics be the realm of ideas and ideals. It was the intermingling of political power with social issues that led the former to become absolute and to exact a heavy price on freedom.[3] In fact, Arendt even saw the reference to 'the pursuit

---

[2] Arendt admitted and was well aware that the question of slavery, the material plight of slaves, and the treatment of Native Americans were also largely ignored at that founding moment. The fact that mass poverty was substantially absent in late eighteenth-century America was just a singular good fortune of the Americans. In contrast, the French faced a more dire situation.

[3] A lot more can be said of this rather pristine conception of politics as an agonistic public domain for the expression of ideas and ideals, substantially relieved of social pressures, including the claim, most often associated with the work of Amartya Sen, in which freedom far from being secured through a disassociation with issues of development is in fact conditional on the success of such a linkage. See in particular Amartya Sen, *Development as Freedom* (New York, 2000).

of happiness' in the Declaration of Independence as an embryonic version of this intermingling, and hence of the potential compromising of an autonomous and circumscribed political domain. Despite this, for Arendt the American constitution served as an ideal in which political power was limited, public freedom secured, and national unity anchored in the structures of political institutions—and all this was possible only because social questions were kept at bay.

But it was the French example that had served as the much more influential model for revolutions in the nineteenth and twentieth centuries. It was one in which political power was constitutionally linked with issues of social uplift and in which, moreover, French national unity was grounded on the shared material destitution of the archetype of the French citizen, namely the French peasant. Citizenship was thus from the very outset a response to a social predicament, and the power of the state was similarly a promissory rejoinder to redress that predicament. The French constitutional legacy has been overwhelmingly influential in the subsequent history of revolutions and in post-imperial constitutionalism. In the founding of new nations and the writing of new constitutions, and thus in the articulation of the powers of the state, the commitment to social uplift and equality has in fact been front and centre of such enterprises. And so it was in India too.

The Context of India's Constitution

In the voluminous writings, debates, and speeches that inform constitutional reflections in India roughly from the mid-1940s onwards, three issues have an unmistakable salience. First is an overriding concern with national unity; second, a deep and anxious preoccupation with social issues such as a poverty, illiteracy, and economic development; and, third, there is a palpable focus on India's standing in the world and with foreign affairs more generally. These three broad issues constitute the template for much of the subsequent politics of the country; in fact it seems fair to say that they characterise with an enduring intensity the general contours of the politics of many newly independent countries in the second half of the twentieth century.

In the Indian case each of these three concerns had obvious exigent reasons that explain their prominence in expert and popular attention. It is plain that a country on the verge of independence, marked by dizzying, often fractious, and potentially centrifugal diversity—not to mention a diversity that had long been used to justify imperial subjection and one in which the prospect and then the reality of partition had loomed for many years—would be vigilant, indeed, obsessed with national unity. Similarly, under the depressing extant conditions of near ubiquitous social despair, illiteracy, and many forms of destitution, the concern with such matters could hardly have been anything other than anxious and urgent. And, finally, given the long history during which national identity had been denied, distorted, and disparaged, and the struggle for independence during which it had been asserted as having a historical and objective warrant, it is only to be expected that a pressing and guiding feature of national idealism would have it alloyed with the question of recognition and standing in the international arena. If, as was the case, the claims of western empires had been underwritten by a normative universality, which since the time of Locke, if not Alexander, vouched for themselves in terms of some amplified normative Reason, nationalism in its opposition to empire had to assert an alternative universality of which the nation was an agential exemplar. No doubt nationalism had its particularistic and culturally specific leanings, but at least among its more thoughtful advocates—figures such as Gandhi, Nehru, and Fanon—nationalism was also always tethered to an ideology whose transformative political and spiritual energies were thoroughly universal. Aurodindo's claim that 'the attainment of independence for me is the search for truth' had political and spiritual analogies with the thought of Gandhi, Nehru, and Tagore. Hence the claim of independence, not unlike that of imperial authority and imperial subjection, had to be, at least partially, vindicated by a referent beyond itself.

The three issues thus drew on urgencies and imperatives that were both historical and contemporaneous. They had a logic that was both conceptual and material. Moreover, in their centrality, they explicitly signalled to a tradition of political thinking that extended back to the American war of independence and the constitutionalism that followed it, along with the French and Russian revolutions. The three issues also anticipated much of the constitutional reflections that were to follow in the second half of the twentieth century. A conspicuous feature of constitutionalism in the twentieth century was the emphasis it placed on national unity and identity, on social uplift and equality, and on international standing.

Temporising on Freedom

Notwithstanding these informing urgencies, there is a revealing irony in the emphasis that these issues assume. Much of democratic constitutionalism, and more generally anti-colonial nationalism, conceived of their provenance as a response to tyranny, and to the umbrage to collective freedom provoked by imperial subjection. In political terms, the response to tyranny and subjection could only have been an insistence on freedom. In the Indian and other colonial contexts this meant freedom *from* the tyranny of imperial subjection. Yet issues of national unity, social uplift, and recognition—and this is the irony—make that freedom conditional on an uncertain period of gestation, through which unity alone can be secured; on resources and extended effort, which are the prerequisites for social transformation; and on the vagaries of an international context, in which the assertions and recognition of sovereignty are at best conditionally secure. As a response to the temporising and the various conditionalities with which empires typically opposed the demand for national freedom, it is ironic that newly independent nations, such as India, should themselves have made the assertion of freedom conditional on achievements which could at best be only prospective.[4]

The irony goes beyond the familiar claim in which it is often remarked that new states tended to imitate the constitutional forms of their former imperial masters. What is far more significant is that the terms in which new states conceived of freedom, once independence was secured, made its affirmation a most capacious and promissory *project* that was issued not just to all members of the nation itself, but to the world at large. It professed an agenda in which one could not, at any given point and certainly not at the moment of independence, securely anchor the sentiment and singularity of national being on which the nationalist struggle had wagered so much. The nation and its freedom, following independence, was thus a project for the future. Independence, one might say, illuminated—revealingly, in the Indian case, at the 'midnight' hour—a condition of inadequacy. The irony is that the successful culmination to free oneself from imperial subjection led almost immediately to freedom itself becoming a subsidiary concern; that is, subsidiary to national unity, social uplift, and a concern with recognition. To paraphrase and extend Homi Bhabha's insight regarding agency under condition of imperial subjec-

---

[4] Uday S. Mehta, *Liberalism and Empire* (Chicago, IL, 1999), see esp. ch. 3.

tion, one might say that independence turned on a sly continuance of the ideology and practice of the empire.[5]

Where freedom was only a prospective condition of the nation it became, in effect, an ambivalent and incalculable measure of the public or national interest. It could not stand alone as something secured through independence itself or through the articulation of individual rights or even constitutional government. Instead it indicated a collective journey to a still distant 'tryst with destiny'. In such a view, freedom is never in the moment, never singular or purely expressive because it cannot be tangential to the larger national and collective purposes with which it is constitutionally braided. Nor could it be asserted by reference to the everyday social materiality of life because that was deemed to simply expose deficient conditions, for which constitutional idealism offers a compensatory, even if, distant promise. The social conditions—matters defined by religion, caste, extant economic conditions, and historically prescribed identities—all get imbued with the presumption of being antithetical to freedom.

Independence and the decades that follow are thus marked by an unremitting solemnity and the prospect of an arduous collective intensity. Even individual freedom is vouched for, not by reference to the everyday conditions of life, but primarily to the extent that the individual now bears the imprimatur of being a citizen, and hence can be conceived of as a part of a unitary national whole. Indeed the enfranchisement of the individual, as citizen, becomes necessary not because he or she is 'ready' or 'educated' or 'free' from sedimented parochial social identities—as classical liberal theory would have required—but because citizenship is the only category through which the nation can ratify its own purposefulness as an entity that will deliver on the promise of freedom.[6] Freedom, as the tenor of Arendt's views prophesied, is muffled by the gravity of national purposefulness.

Constitutionalism: A Revolutionary Agenda

If, as I am suggesting, the idea of being free does not adequately capture that post-imperial moment which, in the Indian case, extends roughly

[5] Homi Bhabha, *The Location of Culture* (London, 1994), pp. 86 ff.
[6] John Stuart Mill, *On Liberty*, esp. ch. 1, and *Consideration on Representative Government*, esp. ch. 18, in Mill, *Three Essays* (Oxford and New York, 1975).

from the mid-1940s through to at least the late 1960s, it is because freedom itself is just an appealing and weighty lure of a future condition.
One is therefore led to ask how should one conceive of that specific and
very distinctive energy that marks constitutional reflection and political
practice in India—and as it turns out elsewhere in the second half of
the twentieth century? Specifically one needs to ask what it is about
national unity, social uplift, and international standing that gather in
their fold the vision—of which the constitution is one concrete expression, but which may also be the omnibus matrix—of Indian political
culture.

The constitutional moment in India was underwritten by an ethos,
which combined the patience that was required for the lofty ambitions
to be fulfilled with an all-encompassing urgency, which they also
required. The Constituent Assembly Debates (1946–9) are full of the
sentiment that the nation had to be strong; it required enormous forbearance, fortitude, and dedication, and, above all else, it had to be a
purposeful unified entity oriented to a broad though singular vision.[7]
When such sentiments are repeated, in debate after debate, by one
national stalwart followed by another, one begins to realise that these
are not just the grand pieties that momentous and grave occasions
necessarily bring forth.

What then is it about the language of unity and social uplift that
allows it to serve as a caption for this broader national endeavour, in a
way in which the securing of public freedom had served as the caption for
American constitutionalism in the eighteenth century?[8] It is in this
language, for which, I have suggested, there are of course obvious and
exigent reasons and explanations, that something else resides, and in
virtue of which the constitution can be seen as doing something quite
radical; indeed as connecting Indian constitutionalism with that other
constitutional moment of the eighteenth century, namely the French revolutionary tradition. Unity and social uplift are the terms through which
a purely political and instrumental national vision is articulated and other

---

[7] 'I hope and trust that this Constituent Assembly will in course of time be able to develop the
strength as all such assemblies have done. When, an Organisation like this sets on its work it
gathers momentum, and as it goes along it is able to gather strength which can conquer all difficulties and which can subdue the most formidable obstacles in its path. Let me pray and hope
that our Assembly too will gather more and more strength as it goes along': Dr Rajendra Prasad
(Chairman) *CAD* (New Delhi, 1972), vol. 1, p. 52.
[8] See Judith N. Shklar, *Redeeming American Political Thought* (Chicago, IL, 1998), esp. ch. 11.

forms of power and authority eclipsed or, at least, rendered secondary. Politics and the power of the state become the grounds for national unity and the redressing of social issues the central venue through which this ground and unity are constantly reaffirmed.

In the English tradition of political thinking Thomas Hobbes was the crucial theorist who tightly linked the securing of life and living well (in his terms self-preservation and felicity) with political power. But what is at least as crucial in his broader argument (a point which Richard Tuck has emphasised in his interpretation of Hobbes) is the claim that political power itself can be secured only through a prior, or rather constitutional, establishing of unity. It is the making of 'a people' that constitutes the ground for the exercise of that distinct form of power which Hobbes calls political power. With Hobbes this unitary politics becomes the decisive condition for order and progress and where all other forms of unity and distinction exist at the mercy of political power. The fact that he endorses a form of political absolutism, one which democratic constitutions like the Indian constitution expressly eschew, does not by itself settle the question of whether such constitutions can in fact secure a principled and practical distinction with the form of power Hobbes advocates. The Indian constitution bespeaks a conception of power, which by emphasising national unity articulates a vision that is in fact revolutionary in precisely the sense that Hobbes viewed politics as a revolutionary and distinctive modern form of order.

Such a claim requires justification because it appears to fly in the face of the obvious facts about the constitution, the debates that led to its adumbration, and to the relevant aspects of independence itself. It is a familiar and often repeated fact that Indian independence, the event that occurred on 15 August 1947, was marked not so much by metaphors of novelty and revolutionary rupture, but, rather, by those of transference and continuity. This is of course not merely a metaphorical claim. It was literally, that is to say politically and juridically, the case. An extant 'interim' government, of which Nehru had been the executive head, became the Government of India, and of which, following independence, he remained the head. Technically, King George VI, who had been titular sovereign prior to August 1947, remained sovereign until 1949. In terms of governmental and administrative machinery, the 'transfer of power', as it was called, was just that. It represented the simple succession of 'personnel'. Similarly the Constituent Assembly and the constitution that it produced were anchored in strict legislative precedent because they were husbanded by the 1935 Government of India Act along with the additional guidance of the Viceroy and Cabinet Mission's Statement of May 1946.[9]

All these facts and circumstances suggest that the constitutional moment was anything but revolutionary, because it was braced by clear judicial precedent, legislative authorisation, and deference to political convention. Moreover, unlike the French Revolution, and instead more akin to the American Revolution, in the Indian case the constitutional moment was not burdened by an inheritance of absolutism. Whatever one might say about British imperial governance, at least by the mid-1940s, it bore no resemblance to Bourbon absolutism of the late eighteenth century. To the important extent that revolutions are predetermined by the regimes they overthrow, the inheritance of responsible and limited government might further vitiate the idea that Indian constitutionalism represented something revolutionary. Finally, one might add, again as in the American case, Indian constitutionalism plainly occurred in a context similar to that which Burke had celebrated in the Hastings trial, where there existed a complex social skein of power and authority, and where therefore neither anarchy, nor the void of power, was present to escalate revolutionary demands.

But along with these familiar facts there is another set of facts pertaining to the Indian constitution. Here was a document which granted universal adult franchise in a country that was overwhelmingly illiterate; where, moreover, the conditionality of acquiring citizenship made no reference to race, caste, religion, or creed and in which, it is worth mentioning, there were no additional or more stringent conditions for the former British rulers to become citizens. It committed the state to being secular in a land that was by any reckoning deeply religious, and evacuated as a matter of law every form of social hierarchy under extant conditions that were marked by a dense plethora of entrenched hierarchies. Moreover, it granted a raft of fundamental individual rights in the face of virtual total absence of such rights. Here was a constitution which in its preamble committed the state to the most capacious conception of justice, including thereby 'social, economic and political' justice, 'liberty of thought, expression, belief, faith, and worship', equality understood to include that of 'status and opportunity', and in which under the heading of 'fraternity' it professed to ensure 'the dignity of the individual and the unity

---

[9] See Granville Austin, *The Indian Constitution: Cornerstone of a Nation* (Oxford, 1966); Sir B. N. Rao, *India's Constitution in the Making* (New Delhi, 1966), and H. M. Seervai, *Constitutional Law of India* (New Delhi, 1999), vol. 1, chs 1 and 1A.

and integrity of the Nation'. Most importantly, the constitution created a federal democracy with all the juridical and political instruments of individual, federal, local, and provincial self-governance where the nearest experience had been of imperial and princely authority. Similarly, when one considers, for example, the Directive Principles of the Constitution, or the 'strivings' of the state, they include an avid engagement with matters of health, education, individual and communal safety, equality, and prosperity.

A lot can be said about this document, which has aptly been called the 'cornerstone of a nation'. For one thing, it points to a truly remarkable self-confidence on the part of the framers and the Indian elite as they envisioned the future of this nation. One cannot but be awed by the extent and reach of such a political and social agenda. This constitutionally enshrined vision of the future is what has often been seen as implying an activist and capacious state that was responsible for the eradication of poverty, undoing the stigmas of casteism, improving public health and education, building large industry, facilitating communication, fostering national unity, and, most broadly, creating conditions for the exercising of freedom.

It is this second set of facts about the constitution, which I wish to suggest constitute the grounds of national unity in a rather interesting and distinct way. And again it is these facts that I want to argue articulate a revolutionary agenda including in the familiar sense that implies an attempt at a radical disjunction and rupture with the past and the present. There are obvious similarities here with the American constitutional founding. Despite the frequency with which ancient authors and examples are invoked and Montesquieu in particular praised, the consensus of opinion among the Federalists suggests a decisive distancing from any exemplary past. The first three words of the American constitution, 'We the People', alone suggest that break. They refer, as Judith Shklar pointed out, neither to the plebs of Rome nor to the 'commons' of England, but rather to everyone.[10] They summarise what Benjamin Franklin had said at the Convention: 'We have gone to back to ancient history for models of Government, and examined the different forms of those Republics . . . we have viewed Modern States all around Europe, but find none of their Constitutions suitable to our circumstances.'[11]

---

[10] Shklar, *Redeeming American Political Thought*, p. 160.
[11] Quoted in Max Farrand (ed.), *The Records of the Federal Convention of 1787* (New Haven, CT, 1966), vol. 1, p. 397.

What is crucial both in the Indian and the American case is that the forswearing of a past was part of a piece with the denial of extant social conditions as being the basis of democratic citizenship. The constitution in fact breaks with the everyday materiality or experience of life. In both the American and Indian cases the vote and the terms of franchise were the crucial grounds for authorising a new kind of power and conceiving a new kind of specifically political unity. In the Indian case there was a clearly conceived sense that the vote and citizenship would create a new network of linkages that were specifically political and, as such, relatively free from long-entrenched and crowded social identities.[12] Voting did not stem from a historical entitlement, but rather a natural right in which poverty, caste, gender, educational disadvantage, and the absence of property were not disqualifications. In the American case of course the specific European fear of the propertyless armed with the vote was absent largely because mass poverty itself was absent and the plight of slaves and Native Americans ignored. But, in the Indian case where one might have expected the elites to have such a fear, that worry is clearly compensated for by the consolation that universal franchise would work to the advantage of a new kind of state power.

The same argument in favour of political power as the ground of a new national purposefulness also addressed a familiar and longstanding colonial objection to independence. That argument had been a claim that countries such as India had not articulated themselves into that specific form of society that could represent itself politically. Whatever forms of collective action they were capable of they were not capable of political self-representation. They were caught between anarchy, despotism, or, as J. S. Mill emphasised regarding India and the East, a surfeit of social norms and customary mores. They lacked and were as yet incapable of a political will of which a state was the only evidence. They had no state, which in effect could claim to be authorised by 'We the People'.

There were only two ways to disable this argument. There was the Gandhian alternative in which political agency, to the extent that it required a monopoly on the means of violence and clear territorial demarcations, was not in any case to be celebrated, and where, for precisely those reasons, agency did not turn on the authorisation of a central and unified state. Rather, agency rested on an adherence to universal ethical principles that were free from the instrumental logic of modern

---

[12] See *Report of the Indian Franchise Committee* (Calcutta, 1932).

politics and were largely nested in extant social relationships. For Gandhi, the strands from which freedom, both individual and collective, was to be crafted existed in the integuments of extant social life. They did not therefore require a specifically political cast. Gandhi was challenging the very conception of politics and agency that underwrote the colonial claim, including the argument that required transcending of the social and the diversity that was implied by it. The issue of the requisite unity of politics and representation was thus challenged by affirming the universality of ethics and the inherent diversity of the social. Gandhi, in effect, disabled the colonial argument by disputing its underlying premise, which made political unity and the state the condition for collective agency.

The second alternative was the constitutional and democratic alternative in which the answer to the colonial question 'Is there a political order and whom does it represent?' could only be, 'First that we have an order which is vouched for by a corresponding unity and it is one in which everyone is represented.'[13] The answer of course was itself largely wishful, especially under conditions where social identities were deeply entrenched and where in particular the very issue of the representation of minorities hardly felicitous. Yet it was an answer which if nothing else indicated a clear constitutional orientation in which politics was to be the ground of a prospective unity.[14]

This is not the appropriate context in which to discuss why constitution making has not been recognised as a truly revolutionary political moment. I hope it suffices to say that in the modern western tradition of political theory revolutions have been associated with that dramatic and tumultuous moment when individuals, in for example John Locke's understanding, contracted with each other to leave the state of nature and form a new 'body politic'. In contrast, constitutions have been associated with that orderly act where the body politic 'entrusted' its power in a particular form of government. As Thomas Paine put it when writing of the American experience, 'A constitution is not the act of a government, but of a people constituting a government.'[15]

---

[13] 'We cannot say that the republican tradition is foreign to the genius of this country. We have had it from the beginning of our history . . . Panini, Megasthenes and Kautilya refer to the Republics of Ancient India. The Great Buddha belonged to the Republic of Kapilavastu': Sarvepalli Radhakrishnan, speech to the Constituent Assembly on 20 January 1947, *CAD*, vol. 1, p. 272. Also see Dipesh Chakrabarty, *Provincializing Europe* (Princeton, NJ, 2000), pp. 9–11.

[14] I am indebted to Pratap Banu Mehta for some of the formulations in this and the previous paragraph.

[15] Thomas Paine, *The Rights of Man*, ed. I. Kramnick (London, 1990), part 2.

The Question of History

In the Indian case, I am suggesting, it is quite the reverse of what one has come to understand through this generic Lockean narrative, and of which the American example is taken as paradigmatic. In India instead it is the constitutional moment that is revolutionary and rupturing. But this claim obviously provokes questions: revolutionary with respect to what and rupturing of what? What does the Indian constitution rupture? Or, more generally, what did it mean to be post-imperial? I think the answer is that the constitution ruptures a particular relationship with time and with historically sanctioned social practices as an expression of that relationship. It is from this rupture or distancing of history that sovereignty, and the political, as an expression of a capacious public will, comes to be formed.

To put the point somewhat polemically, the Indian constitution, along with the conception of the political that it puts in place, does not so much emerge from history as it emerges in opposition to history and with a firm view of the future. If political absolutism in Europe had defined itself following Bodin and Hobbes as *potestas legibus soluta*, i.e. power absolved from laws, one might say that in India, following the constitution, the political became power absolved from history.

The relationship of power to history is fraught with imperial associations. In the nineteenth century every major expression of European political thought had made history the evidentiary ground of political and even moral development. In Hegel, Marx, and J. S. Mill, notwithstanding their differing accounts of historical development, history was the register through which alone a society's political condition and political future could be assessed. Hegel's articulation of the state as the embodiment of a concrete ethical rationality represented the realisation of a journey of Reason that originated in the distant recesses of the East. Marx's vision of a proletarian future had its explanatory and political credence in overcoming the contrarian forces that fetter and spur historical movement. J. S. Mill's ideal of a liberalism that secured the conditions for the flourishing of individuality again explicitly rests on having reached a point of civilisational progress 'when mankind have become capable of being improved by free and equal discussion'.[16]

These arguments had a specifically imperial inflection. In J. S. Mill, who was by far the most influential liberal advocate of the empire, the

---

[16] Mill, *On Liberty*, p. 16.

argument went broadly along the following lines. Political institutions such as a representative democracy are dependent on societies having reached a historical maturation, or, in the language of the times, a particular level of civilisation. But such civilisational maturation was differentially achieved. That is, progress in history itself occurs differentially. Hence, those societies in which the higher accomplishments of civilisation had not occurred plainly did not satisfy the conditions for a representative government. Under such conditions, liberalism, in the form of the empire, serviced the deficiencies of the past for societies that had been stunted through history. This, in brief, was the liberal justification of the empire. Its normative force rested squarely on a claim about history. It is what Dipesh Chakrabarty has called the 'waiting room' version of history;[17] the idea being that societies, such as India, had to wait until they were present in contemporary time or what amounts to the same timing in contemporary history. They had to wait because their history made it clear that they were not 'as yet' ready for political self-governance. The denial of an autonomous political realm was the debt paid by the present on behalf of a deficient and recalcitrant past.

The nationalist response to this historically anchored waiting-room model was to agree with the idea and the logic of argument but to disagree with particulars of its application. Here, as elsewhere, Gandhi is the exception because his conception of civilisation and its cognate progress was never historically driven. When Gandhi speaks of civilisation, it is invariably as an ethical relationship that an individual or community has with itself, with others, and with its deities.[18] Whatever else this does, it cuts through any reliance on history as the register from which alone progress can be read, evaluated, and directed. But the more typical nationalist response, including among the social reformers of the nineteenth century, was to concur with the claim that progress was historical but to demur on the point that India was not 'as yet' ready. The nationalist claim instead was that India was in fact ready, that it had paid its debt on behalf of a 'backward' past through two centuries of tutelage. Its claim to political autonomy was simply the other side of the claim that it was present in contemporary time and thus freed from the residual vestiges of historical time. As an aside it is worth pointing to a curious resonance that this Indian political vision has with the nation where one

---

[17] Chakrabarty, *Provincializing Europe*, p. 8.

[18] For Gandhi's views on civilisation and history, see M. K. Gandhi, *Hind Swaraj and Other Writings* (Cambridge, 1997).

might have expected a preponderant reliance on history as a ground of unity, namely Israel. The following quotations from Theodor Herzl's *The Jewish State* are startlingly illustrative in this respect:

> I think the Jewish question is no more a social than a religious one, notwithstanding that it sometimes takes these and other forms. It is a national question, which can only be solved by making it a political world-question to be discussed and settled by the civilised nations of the world in council.[19]

> No human being is wealthy or powerful enough to transplant a nation from one habitation to another. An idea alone can compass that; and this idea of a State may have the requisite power to do so.[20]

> It is true that the Jewish State is conceived as a peculiarly modern structure on unspecified territory. But a state is formed, not by pieces of land, but rather by a number of men united under sovereign rule.[21]

The Absolute Reach of Political Power

What did it concretely mean to be freed from history? And to be present in what I am calling contemporary time? It did not mean that India was not affected or influenced by its past, or that the problems of poverty, caste, and numerous other social and economic woes were without a historical dimension. That would have been rank stupidity, but the framers of the constitution and the members of the Constituent Assembly were not fools.

Instead I think the historical aspect of these problems is taken as part of their social scientific and political nature, but not as an inheritance that limited the potential of political power. All social issues in which there was plainly a historical dimension, including, crucially, issues of economic destitution and caste inequality, were automatically and immediately translated into the language of social science. Through this translation they lost any temporal dimension that linked them with the past. To put the point perhaps overly starkly, the challenge of caste injustice became analogous to that of building industry or large dams. Both became issues for which politics was deemed to be the only form of redress. They represented challenges in which the state drew on and leaned on the guiding primacy of science and social science. History

---

[19] Theodor Herzl, *The Jewish State* (New York, 1989), p. 15.
[20] Ibid., pp. 19–20.
[21] Ibid., pp. 63 ff.

became a social and contemporary fact on which politics did its work. History was translated into a medium where it became available for political modification. It did not in this form constitute a limit on political power. In this translation of history from being a domain of experience into one of political modification social science and science play a crucial role. This conception of the political is nothing if not presentist; it loses an element of temporality that one associates with notions such as inheritance. It is anchored in the amplitude of choice; everything becomes an issue of choosing because the conception of politics that it belongs to is supremely about choosing.

It is in this context that the concern with social issues, which is such a conspicuous feature of the Constituent Assembly debates and the constitution, becomes relevant and urgent. Issues such mass poverty, mass illiteracy, and near ubiquitous destitution belong to the realm of necessity because they put human beings under the pressing dictates of their bodies. To the extent that political power concerns itself with, and under modern conditions it has to, this dimension of human life, it too becomes subject to a necessity. It can represent freedom only as something prospective. Its immediate ambit is dictated by the intensity of 'mere life'. And this ambit can have no limiting bounds. This simple logic transforms power from a traditional concern with freedom to a concern with life and its necessities.

Conclusion

Hannah Arendt may have been wrong to identify politics that concerns itself with social questions as leading to terror. But her exaggeration offers an insight into a related feature of when politics is placed under such necessity, which is its absolutism. Here absolutism refers not to the capriciousness of the Prince or the Leviathan who can take his will as a synonym for right and power. That aspect of absolutism is clearly checked by democratic constitutionalism. But absolutism understood as something in which there are no substantive limits on the domain of the political is a feature of power that is committed to alleviate the pressing exigencies of life. It is also the very pressing concerns of life that become a central mechanism for conceiving of and emphasising the unity of the nation. Not unlike the Jacobin projection of *le peuple, toujours malheureux*, which served as a ground of French unity, poverty, illiteracy, and destitution served as a constitutional warrant for Indian unity.

It is tempting to think of the perspective that proffers the generality of the *suffering people* as stemming from compassion. Much of the language of the Constituent Assembly's deliberations in fact suggests this sentiment as a motive for what the members did and thought. No doubt for many of the members of the Assembly the concern for the suffering of their fellow citizens was deeply felt and the subjective response it provoked was indeed a form of compassion. Despite this and what may have been a genuine sentiment, I believe it would be a mistake to understand the collective project of which it was a part as a form of compassion. Compassion, in the face of suffering, has as its operative modality a commitment to co-suffering, to put oneself in the position of the sufferer or minimally to share in the suffering. It is tethered to a logic of singularity and exemplarity, i.e. of taking the place of the sufferer. On both counts, it repudiates the distance or the vantage that is required to produce a conception of a whole people, let alone a way of redressing the plight of a whole people. The perspective of compassion cannot produce the idea of a nation, or rather of a unitary entity that is a nation because the object of compassion is always singular. Moreover, compassion, as Martha Nussbaum and Roberto Unger have insightfully pointed out, is deeply, even if not essentially, wedded to an epistemic and ontological uncertainty, i.e. to the question of whether the suffering was adequately appraised and fully shared.[22] For these reasons compassion for the most part has been politically mute. It is, one might say, an ethical but not a political virtue. Of course in rare instances, such as with Gandhi, the idea of compassion has profoundly affected the political realm—but even then it typically manifests a philosophical and temperamental reluctance towards the ordinary rationale of national politics.

In contrast, the perspective of pity faces no such obstacles. Because pity maintains a distance from its object, it can conceive of the object as embodying an abstraction, or representing a type, such as the poverty stricken or the disadvantaged castes of the people of India. And because it is not limited by the injunction to share in the plight of those it perceives it can imagine a redress to their condition that corresponds to the generality of its perspective. Pity maintains a distance from its object, and through that distance it can and does offer up a general remedy to their condition. Moreover, the perspective of pity is replete with the potential for solidarity and hence unity, because it conceives of some-

---

[22] Martha Nussbaum, *Upheavals of Thought* (Cambridge, 2000), esp. chs 7 and 8; Roberto Unger, *Passion: An Essay on Personality* (New York, 1984).

thing as embodying or, more precisely, representing something general, such as poverty. Pity, in this sense, has the potential of immense political instrumentality. There is an important and still grossly under-explored relationship that links pity with the politics of modern nationalism.

The main point of this essay can be made by way of a contrast. American constitutionalism in the eighteenth century, whatever else it was, stemmed from a deep distrust of power—of which a distrust of the absolutist prince was just a single instance. The first impulse of this constitutionalism was thus to limit political power, to be suspicious of it, and to constrain its reach. This was one of the things that most struck Tocqueville as he reflected on democracy in America—namely, that the central government was virtually absent and, at best, severely limited in the power at its disposal. In this view, the happiness and the freedom of the individual could never be assigned to a distant prospective hope. It already existed in the materiality of everyday life. Perhaps because the American Founding Fathers did not have to contend with the problem of mass poverty and had little concern with the issue of slavery, or perhaps, because they were the last adherents to the idea that politics was about freedom and not the pressing necessities of life and the body, they could still articulate a constitutional vision in which political power was not absolute. When John Adams announced in the manner of Montesquieu, 'Power had to be opposed by power', he meant by this that power, specifically political power, had to be limited. A central part of that limitation was that it would not redress the sufferings of the body and would not allow its vision to be guided by that goal. Of course, in our own times, it has become clear that there is indeed an inhumanity to that limitation on power and the conception of the public interest that it can fashion. Ironically, despite the inspiration that American anti-colonial nationalism and constitutionalism gave, and continues to give, to subsequent nationalisms, its essential impulse is profoundly different to its enduring rhetorical effect. This, no doubt, is one reason why the USA is typically confounded by other people's nationalism.

Such a chastened conception of power and politics is plainly not the case with constitutionalism in much of the twentieth century and in India in particular. This constitutionalism must and does constitute power and increase and celebrate its ambit. It is only through politics that the nation can be imagined, let alone administered. In the Indian case, once partition wrecked the geographical grounds of nationhood, politics became even more central to stitching the nation and giving expression to the existential needs of the unitary whole.

Part II

HISTORICAL DEBATES

3

'Neither Masters nor Slaves': Small States and Empire in the Long Eighteenth Century

RICHARD WHATMORE

I

EVERYONE KNOWS THAT A VIEW OF the British Empire as a moral phenomenon—a force for education, civilisation, and progress—became commonplace in the nineteenth and early twentieth centuries.[1] British rule was often described as benevolent, supportive of self-government, and respectful of the customs and laws of the dependent states of the empire.[2] Britain's purportedly liberal approach to empire was variously ascribed to the moral and moderate element in its national character exemplified by Wilberforce's attack on the slave trade, to the fact that Britain had itself always been a composite state with a successful history of dealing with provinces, to the emphasis on commerce rather than conquest as the purpose of the empire.[3] The distinctiveness of Britain's imperial role was, in

---

[1] Thomas Erskine May, *The Constitutional History of England since the Accession of George the Third, 1760–1860: With a New Supplementary Chapter, 1861–1871*, 4th edn, 3 vols (London, 1873), vol. 3, p. 384: 'Beyond these narrow isles, England has won, indeed, a vast and glorious empire. In the history of the world, no other state has known how to govern territories so extended and so remote, and races of men so diverse, giving to her own kindred colonies the widest liberty . . . To the Englishman may it not be said . . . "having won freedom for thyself, and used it wisely, thou hast given it to thy children, who have peopled the earth; and thou hast exercised dominion with justice and humanity".' For a later, similar, example, see Ramsay Muir, *The Character of the British Empire* (London, 1917).
[2] For illustrations, see Arthur Mills, *Colonial Constitutions: An Outline Constitutional History and Existing Government of the British Dependencies* (London, 1856) and Leone Levi, *International Commercial Law: Being the Principles of Mercantile Law of the Following and other Countries, viz.: England, Scotland, Ireland*, 2nd edn, 2 vols (London, 1863), vol. 1, pp. 3–5.
[3] John Macgregor, *Sketches of the Progress of Civilization and Public Liberty: With a View of the Political Condition of Europe and America in 1848* (London, 1848), pp. 61–3, and Homersham

---

Proceedings of the British Academy **155**, 53–81. © The British Academy 2009.

the nineteenth century, deemed by many to parallel its role in European politics, in maintaining a balance of power supportive of trade but opposed to the rise of land-based empires in Europe, historically associated with Spanish and French aspirations, and latterly with Russian ambition.[4] In the twentieth century, Britain became involved in world wars initially on the grounds of defending the independence of Europe's small states. British policy was never inflexible, and was often contested, but a commitment developed to the independence of the small states of Europe which emerged intact from the Napoleonic Wars, such as Portugal, or which subsequently sought to become independent, with the first example being Greece in the 1820s.[5] The rationale for Britain's commitment was partly commercial, to develop trade in peaceful times, but was also linked to the desire to maintain Britain's reputation as a defender of liberty abroad, because of its self-perception as the archetypal free state.

Britain had always been seen to be related, with respect to general culture and manners, to the small republics of Europe.[6] Partly this was due to England's own republican past, but it had more to do with a perception among the small states that Britain's constitution, although mixed and monarchical, was far closer to those of the small republics than it was to Europe's absolute monarchies.[7] By the 1790s, British protection was seen for many to be the surest means of maintaining Europe's small

---

Cox, *The British Commonwealth, or, A Commentary on the Institutions and Principles of British Government* (London, 1854), pp. 516–67.

[4] John Finlay, *Miscellanies: The Foreign Relations of the British Empire* (Dublin, 1835), pp. 1–22.

[5] For a summary view of attitudes during the French Revolutionary Wars, see William Pitt's speech of 3 June 1803 in *The Speeches of . . . William Pitt, in the House Of Commons*, 2nd edn, 3 vols (London, 1808), vol. 3, pp. 273–87. For the defence of small states as key to a 'liberal empire', see George Canning, 'On Granting Aid to Portugal', House of Commons, December 1826 in W. J. Bryan (ed.), *The World's Famous Orations: Great Britain II*, 10 vols (New York, 1906), vol. 4. See also Arnold-Hermann-Ludwig Heeren, *A Manual of the History of the Political System of Europe and Its Colonies, From Its Formation at the Close of the Fifteenth Century to Its Re-establishment upon the Fall of Napoleon* (London, 1846), pp. 503–5, and Frederick Strong, *Greece as a Kingdom, or, A Statistical Description of that Country from the Arrival of King Otto, in 1833* (London, 1842), pp. 52–70.

[6] Jean-Charles-Léonard Simonde de Sismondi, 'On Constitutional Monarchy', *Political Economy and the Philosophy of Government* (London, 1847), pp. 417–47, and William Cargill, *An Examination of the Origin, Progress, and Tendency of the Commercial and Political Confederation against England and France* (Newcastle, 1840), pp. 30–40.

[7] For the classic evaluation of Britain's constitutional relationship to republics and absolute monarchies, see Jean-Louis Delolme, *Constitution d'Angleterre* (Amsterdam, 1771). On the legacy of English republicanism, see B. Worden, *Roundhead Reputations: The English Civil War and the Passions of Posterity* (London, 2001).

republics. The Parisian dramatist Jean-Louis Mercier spoke for many, in linking the survival of the small republics to a balance of international power regulated by Britain, rather than a union of European states or a concert of the major powers:

> England has figured on the globe as a power protecting the general liberty of Europe; and in this point of view may be considered as the patroness of the human race. Had it not been for England, France, or perhaps Spain, would have acquired an ascendancy over Europe a century ago; and religious liberty at least would have been destroyed.
>
> However chimerical the equilibrium of Europe may be, it supplies to each state a persuasion of its personal security. The little republics subsist almost entirely under the shelter of this theory; while it is extremely probable, that a general confederacy of all the powers of Europe would be far more injurious to the personal liberties of the human race, than those oppositions of state to state, which prevent the flux and reflux of nations, and establish the privileges of each principality on the basis of an equal resistance. Hence has the league of certain kings demonstrated all the mischief which may result from that union which invariably bears hardest on the freer nations of Europe . . . That Europe may be made to form but one and the same society is an admirable speculation. But when a supernatural being shall descend from heaven, and take his seat on a throne, and not till then, I shall admit the necessity of destroying the system of that balance, which, not withstanding the wars that result from it, allows a useful division to subsist.[8]

The history of Britain's role as the protector of small states is far from straightforward, because in turbulent times Britain was often accused of failing such states, and building an empire that entailed their loss of independence.[9] Furthermore, politicians in powerful empires have always claimed to be exercising the moral duty to protect weaker states in their various enterprises, whether this was substantially true or merely rhetorical. The purpose of this essay is not to provide such a history. It is rather to examine the origins of the perception of Britain as a defender of small states, and more particularly of Europe's small republics, by the republicans who viewed Britain as foreigners. The story is important, because it illuminates a perceived change in the nature of Britain's empire between the eighteenth and nineteenth centuries, one which fostered notions of liberal empire, and an imperial identity that necessitated more direct involvement in Europe.

---

[8] Louis Sébastien Mercier, *Fragments of Politics and History*, 2 vols (London, 1795), vol. 1, pp. 371–3: reference to the 'mischief' of 'the league of kings' is to the dismemberment of Poland.
[9] George Browning, *The Domestic and Financial Condition of Great Britain: Preceded by a Brief Sketch of Her Foreign Policy* (London, 1834), p. 19.

Study of Europe's small republics and their ultimate reliance upon Britain requires a reconstruction of the strategies for independence of the small republics and their attitude to empire. The argument of the essay is that the rise of commercial empires like Britain and France, which were locked into competition for trade and influence that resulted in a series of global wars, altered the survival strategies of Europe's small republics in the eighteenth century. Many of their citizens turned to Britain as the only state capable of sustaining a commercial empire whose prosperity was dependent upon international peace, or at least upon peace in Europe. In describing such an empire, they were forced to speculate on the likely future of Britain, and more especially upon the effects of Britain's 'mercantile system'. Britain's mercantile system was often portrayed as the fundamental impediment to Britain's pacific role in international affairs; the system was a source of reason of state politics, of war, and a likely cause of the collapse of Britain's empire. The essay begins with an examination of eighteenth-century perspectives upon empire, and goes on to examine the survival strategies of Europe's small republics, and the bankruptcy of traditional policies for maintaining national independence by the mid-eighteenth century. The essay closes with the perspective on Britain as the saviour of the small republics fully articulated, if frequently challenged, by the time of the Vienna Settlement.

II

What was distinctive about empire in the eighteenth century and what was its likely future? In 1712 these questions were addressed by Pierre-Daniel Huet (1630–1721), formerly bishop of Soissons and of Avranches, in his *Le grand tresor historique et politique du florissant commerce des hollondois, dans tous les etats et empires du monde*. The subject was surprising for an aged Jesuit and Academician, having hitherto authored editions of Latin classics, commentaries on Descartes, and biblical exegesis, and who had come to prominence for taking the side of the ancients in the famous *querrel*. Yet *Le grand tresor* proved a publishing success, seeing English and Spanish translations within five years, and being republished many times in the following two decades.[10]

---

[10] Pierre-Daniel Huet, *Le grand tresor historique et politique du florissant commerce des hollondois, dans tous les etats et empires du monde* (Rouen, 1712).

Huet was convinced that the nature of empire had changed for moderns because of the direct relationship between success in commerce and success in war. Trade had become so closely tied to self-defence that the development of commerce had become the most important arm of statecraft, and the area in which international competition was greatest. In 1742, David Hume followed Huet in speculating upon 'the alterations which time has produced, or may produce in politics', and agreed that 'trade was never esteemed an affair of state till the last century'.[11] A further step was taken by Hume in aligning national interest in trade with the fact that in recent times 'monarchical government seems to have made the greatest advances towards perfection'. Civilised monarchies, he affirmed, could now be described as governments of laws rather than of men, which in the past was only legitimately said 'in praise of republics'.[12]

Such monarchies had not only become stable polities, but ones in which property was secure, and where industry and the arts could flourish. Hume did not go so far as to reject the established maxim that free states were more capable of advancing trade than absolute monarchies, but he did want to question it, by noting that the only limit upon trade in such monarchies arose from the lack of honour associated with commerce.[13] Both Huet and Hume considered France to be the most advanced civilised monarchy. Hume, like so many contemporaries, was fascinated by the consequences of a rapaciously commercial France for Europe, and more particularly for Britain. He also shared a concern that commercial empires like Britain and France, despite being civilised monarchies, might destroy themselves because of their ongoing war for international supremacy in politics and in trade which lasted through the long eighteenth century (1689–1815).[14]

[11] David Hume, 'Of Civil Liberty', in *Political Essays*, ed. K. Haakonssen (Cambridge, 1994), p. 55. See further John Payne, *An Epitome of History; or, A Concise View of the Most Important Revolutions and Events*, 2nd edn, 2 vols (London, 1795), vol. 1, p. 85.

[12] Hume, 'Of Civil Liberty', pp. 52, 55, 56; see also 'Of the Rise and Progress of the Arts and Science', in *Essays and Treatises on Several Subjects* (London, 1758), pp. 78–9, and *The History of England, under the House of Tudor*, 2 vols (London, 1759), vol. 1, p. 18.

[13] Hume, 'Of Civil Liberty', p. 55. For a classic statement of the positive link between liberty and commerce, see Voltaire, 'Letter X, Of Trade', *Letters Concerning the English Nation* ([Dublin], 1733), pp. 59–60.

[14] Arthur Maynwaring, *Advice to the Electors of Great Britain; Occasioned by the Intended Invasion from France* (Edinburgh, 1708) and *Remarks upon the Present Negotiations of Peace Begun between Britain and France* (London, 1711); Anon., *The Present State of the Revenues and Forces, by Sea and Land, of France and Spain: Compar'd with those of Great Britain* (London, 1740), pp. 5–10; Anon., *Considerations on the Politics of France, with Regard to the Present Critical Situation of Affairs: Wherein the following proposition, viz. that the true interest of Great*

Istvan Hont has recently provided the most in-depth intellectual history to date of the clash between Europe's empires in the long eighteenth century.[15] Hont argues that 'modern' politics were born when Machiavellian ideas about maintaining states were applied to the commercial realm, making the issue of the corrupting effects of trade an urgent political issue, encapsulated in the term 'jealousy of trade'.[16] A key turning point in European history occurred in the sixteenth and seventeenth centuries when the politics of necessity in city republics was applied to the external relations of large territorial monarchies, in order to ensure the latter's national security, overruling in the process justice, morality, and law, and becoming known as 'reason of state'.[17] Hont's new insight is that Renaissance republicanism and commercial modernity also developed important political linkages 'chiefly between the republican doctrine of national grandeur and the modern politics of global markets'.[18] When reason of state was applied to international commerce in the form of jealousy of trade and when the sense of self-defence that it entailed was coupled with republican patriotism, it justified imperialist designs towards extra-European nations and resulted in external economic aggrandisement. When reason of state and republican patriotism was applied to the trade of states within Europe, which occurred from the end of the seventeenth century, very different forms of national politics emerged. War against 'monopolists' began to be justified by statesmen and commentators. Economic practices became commonplace which entailed the destruction of the trade of neighbouring states; the classic case here was the control and limitation of Ireland's trade by greater

---

Britain must always consist in opposing the designs, . . . of that ambitious power, is . . . demonstrated (London, 1744). For a summary and critique of such arguments, see Robert Wallace, *Characteristics of the Present Political State of Great Britain* (London, 1758), pp. 200–35. See also Anthony Pagden, *Lords of All the World: Ideologies of Empire in Spain and France c. 1500–c. 1800* (New Haven, CT, 1995) and John Huxtable Elliott, *Empires of the Atlantic World: Britain and Spain in America 1492–1830* (New Haven, CT, 2006), pp. 292–324.

[15] Istvan Hont, *Jealousy of Trade: International Competition and the Nation State in Historical Perspective* (Cambridge, MA, 2006), 'Jealousy of Trade: An Introduction', pp. 1–156.

[16] Ibid., pp. 1–30, and 'Free Trade and the Economic Limits to National Politics: Neo-Machiavellian Political Economy Reconsidered', pp. 185–266.

[17] Richard Tuck, *Philosophy and Government, 1572–1651* (Cambridge, 1996), pp. 31–64, and *The Rights of War and Peace: Political Thought and the International Order from Grotius to Kant* (Oxford, 2000), pp. 1–15; Jonathan Haslam, *No Virtue Like Necessity: Realist Thought in International Relations since Machiavelli* (New Haven, CT, 2002); H. Driezel, 'Reason of State and the Crisis of Political Aristotelianism: An Essay on the Development of Seventeenth-century Political Philosophy', *History of European Ideas*, 28 (2002), pp. 163–84.

[18] Hont, *Jealousy of Trade*, pp. 10–11.

Britain.[19] A far less secure world emerged with the clash of commercial monarchies seeking empire through economic and political dominion. Hume called such monarchies 'civilised', but this was far from the case in practice, as they acted like republics when invoking patriotic war with an economic rationale, and behaved ruthlessly towards fellow states. One area that has been neglected by recent scholars is the consequence of the rise of these militarily and economically awesome but insecure empires for the small states of Europe.

The variety of small state forms across the continent was remarkable, with hundreds of sovereignties in Germany and Italy alone, ruled by archbishops, bishops, princes, landgraves, dukes, marquises, and counts.[20] Complicated series of relationships had developed with larger neighbours, which frequently altered with the traditional crises within Europe's dynastic families.[21] With the fall of the republics of Novgorod (1478), Siena (1167), Florence (1537), and Pisa (1509), Europe's surviving republics included Venice, Genoa, Lucca, the Grisons, St Marino, Switzerland, Geneva, and Ragusa. The United Provinces is a special case, in establishing itself as a republic and then maintaining its commercial empire, despite decline in terms of trade and political influence in the eighteenth century relative to Europe's commercial monarchies.[22] Venice is also distinctive, in becoming the archetypal dying republic, despite maintaining elements of its former empire, in the midst of Italian states ever more dependent upon larger monarchies.[23] The attempts of the

---

[19] For an overview, see David Armitage, *The Ideological Origins of the British Empire* (Cambridge, 2000), pp. 146–69.

[20] Tobias George Smollett, *The Present State of All Nations: Containing a Geographical, Natural, Commercial, and Political History of All the Countries in the Known World*, 8 vols (London, 1768–69), vol. 5, gives a list of the German states; John Payne, *Universal Geography formed into a New and Entire System; Describing Asia, Africa, Europe, and America*, 2 vols (London, 1791), vol. 2, p. 5.

[21] See Anon., *The Present State of Europe: or, A Genealogical and Political Description of All the Kingdoms, States and Principalities Thereof* (London, 1705), pp. 364–460, and 'An Alphabetical INDEX of the Principal FAMILIES'.

[22] On the distinctive Dutch case, see Hans Blom, 'The Republican Mirror: The Dutch Idea of Europe', in Anthony Pagden (ed.), *The Idea of Europe from Antiquity to the European Union* (Cambridge, 2002), pp. 91–115. On Dutch decline and Louis XIV's antagonism towards this state, see Voltaire, *Le siecle de Louis XIV* (London, 1752), pp. 79, 236.

[23] Venice lost Cyprus (1571), Crete (1669), and the Peloponnese (1715) but maintained lands in Dalmatia and certain islands in the Ionian and Adriatic seas. On the decline of Venice, see John Andrews, *An Inquiry into the Manners, Taste, and Amusements, of the Two Last Centuries, in England* (London, 1782), p. 81; Claude-Etienne Savary, *Letters on Egypt*, 2 vols (London, [1787]), vol. 2, p. 294; Johann Wilhelm von Archenholz, *A Picture of Italy*, 2 vols (London, 1791), vol. 1, pp. 27–8; Richard Rapp, *Industry and Economic Decline in Seventeenth-century Venice* (Cambridge, MA, 1976).

republics to survive in a world dominated by imperial monarchies—republics such as the Swiss states or Geneva which had never developed an empire—became staples of political conversation.

Whether republics could remain independent in the modern world and how they might do so formed major themes of such works as Montesquieu's *De l'esprit des lois* (1748) and Rousseau's *Contrat social* (1762).[24] Old tropes were reiterated that small republics would maintain themselves as they had always done; against corruption and luxury by firm and decent manners rigorously enforced by law, and against the commercial empires by the presumed interest that large monarchies had in keeping them independent for the sake of their trade.[25] With less and less frequency, and mainly through the republication of historic authors, the Machiavellian view was expressed that small republics could defend themselves in war because of their civic valour, which was a product of their liberty.[26] An equally long-held view became commonplace, predicting the inevitable decline of such states, because ancient history showed that the rise of a new Carthage or Rome (Britain and France) always led the number of the states in Europe to fall. One of the most neglected subjects in recent intellectual history has been the debate about the number of European states compatible with peace, global markets, and empire.[27] Small republics could not, it was argued, cope with luxury, could not defend themselves against larger states, and had been in terminal decline for two centuries through their 'intestine perfidy, corruption

[24] For a summary view, see Gabriel Bonnot de Mably, *Entretiens de Phocion, sur le rapport de la morale avec la politique; traduits du grec de Nicoclès, avec des remarques* (Amsterdam, 1763), pp. 151–231.

[25] Charles Irénée Castel de Saint-Pierre, *Annales politiques de feu Monsieur Charles Irenée Castel* (London, 1757), vol. 2, pp. 18–19; Jacob Green, *Observations on the Reconciliation of Great-Britain and the Colonies: By a Friend of American Liberty* (New York, 1776), p. 9; Ligier, *What Has Been at All Times the Influence of Commerce upon the Genius and Manners of the People? A Discourse which Obtained the Premium in the Academy of Marseilles. In the year M.DCC.LXXVII* (London, 1779), pp. 4–5.

[26] Algernon Sidney, *Discourses concerning Government. To Which are Added, Memoirs of His Life, and an Apology for Himself* (London, 1751), p. 104, and John Thelwall, *Strike; But Hear!!! A Dedication to His Majesty's Ministers, the Crown Lawyers, and the Majority of Both Houses of Parliament. With a Farewell* (London, 1796), p. 8.

[27] George St Amand, *An Historical Essay on the Legislative Power of England: Wherein the Origin of both Houses of Parliament, Their Antient Constitution* (London, 1725), pp. 1–3. As Henry Lloyd put it, 'we may venture to foretell, that in less than a century there will not be above seven or eight sovereignties in all Europe where formerly there were above a thousand' (*An Essay on the Theory of Money* (London, 1771), pp. 60–1).

and fermentation'.[28] The marquis de Chastellux clearly had contemporary experience in mind when he wrote:

> ... nothing can be more deplorable, and at the same time more contemptible than republics in their decline. Their ancient customs seem to be new sources of vice and ignominy. Their public councils become, henceforward, no better than the vulgar bawlings of the market, or the abusive clamors, which prevail amongst the meetings of the mob. The love of glory is extinguished, and in its place, appear an empty ostentation, and a mean presumption, which render these vices, thus odious in themselves, so particularly ridiculous.[29]

All authors agreed that the small republics could no longer stand alone militarily against commercial empires. Accordingly they would have to adapt themselves to the modern lust for trade and empire, and work out means of avoiding collapse in circumstances where Britain or France might seek to conquer them, or see competitors in the east of Europe do likewise, in the manner of the dismemberment of Poland.[30] The situation was neatly summarised by Adam Ferguson in *An Essay on the History of Civil Society*, in explaining that the small republics were no longer masters of their own destiny, while refusing to give up their precarious liberty:

> The small republics of Greece, indeed, by their subdivisions, and the balance of their power, found almost in every village the object of nations. Every little district was a nursery of excellent men, and what is now the wretched corner of a great empire, was the field on which mankind have reaped their principal honours. But in modern Europe, republics of a similar extent, are like shrubs, under the shade of a taller wood, choked by the neighbourhood of more powerful states. In their case, a certain disproportion of force frustrates, in a great measure, the advantage of separation. They are like the trader in Poland, who is the more despicable, and the less secure, that he is neither master nor slave.
>
> Independent communities, in the mean time, however weak, are averse to a coalition, not only where it comes with an air of imposition, or unequal treaty, but even where it implies no more than the admission of new members to an equal share of the consideration with the old. The citizen has no interest in the annexation of kingdoms; he must find his importance diminished, as the state is enlarged: but ambitious men, under the enlargement of territory, find a more plentiful harvest of power, and of wealth, while government itself is an easier

---

[28] François-Ignace Espiard de la Borde, *The Spirit of Nations* (London, 1753), pp. 129, 132.

[29] François Jean, marquis de Chastellux, *De la félicité publique, ou, Considérations sur le sort des hommes dans les différentes epoques de l'histoire* (Amsterdam, 1772), p. 115 (translation from *An Essay on Public Happiness*, 2 vols (London, 1774), vol. 2, pp. 217–18).

[30] William Augustus Miles, *Authentic Correspondence with M. Le Brun, the French Minister, and Others, to February 1793, Inclusive* (London, 1796), p. 125.

task. Hence the ruinous progress of empire; and hence free nations, under the shew of acquiring dominion, suffer themselves, in the end, to be yoked with the slaves they had conquered.[31]

The following two sections deal with some of the old and new fears about the decline of commercial states that accompanied the clash of the British and French empires. The essay subsequently deals with the strategies developed by certain Swiss and Genevan writers to retain their national independence, and their turn to Britain as the only state with an interest in an economic balance of power premised upon their survival. The Swiss cantons are significant because of their ancient association with republican patriotism, and the historic success of their traditional strategies for maintaining themselves, neutrality and confederacy. Geneva is important as the most commercial of republics, as a direct neighbour to France with strong religious and trading links to Britain, and as a centre of international Calvinism.

III

In *Le grand tresor*, Huet focused upon the Dutch empire as the most remarkable of recent times, and sought to work out 'by what means [the Dutch] have made themselves masters of all the trade of Europe'.[32] He came to the conclusion that it was a universal truth that 'states flourish in proportion to commerce'. All states had in consequence to 'regulate their principal interest always with an eye to their commerce', and consider 'agriculture and commerce [as] the breasts which suckle and nourish the state'. This fact could be gathered 'from what the Holy Scriptures teach us, in relation to the Tyrians and Sidonians', or from the evidence of recent history, exemplified by the statement of 'the great [Gustavus] Adolphus' that 'to put his soldiers' valour to the proof, he was often obliged to have recourse to his merchants'.[33]

At the same time, however, Huet accepted that ancient history, sacred history, and even the experience of recent generations, could not fully explain the nature of the eighteenth-century world as he saw it, which had irredeemably altered in significant respects. First, the greatness of the

---

[31] Adam Ferguson, *An Essay on the History of Civil Society* (Edinburgh, 1767), p. 91.
[32] Translations are from Huet, *Memoirs of the Dutch Trade in All the States, Kingdoms, and Empires in the World* (London, n.d. [1717]).
[33] Ibid., pp. ii–iii.

commerce of a state or empire no longer appeared to be proportionate to its geographical extent, population size, or natural resources:

> But nothing can come up to what the Dutch have done by commerce; and it will ever be a subject of astonishment and wonder that a handful of merchants, that fled into a little country which produced scarce enough to subsist its new inhabitants, should beat down the exorbitant power of the Spanish monarchy, and make that King sue for peace.[34]

Second, relations between states internationally had altered in the light of the capacity of smaller states to use commerce to develop beyond their manifest 'natural' limits. Proof lay in the fact that 'so mighty a republick' as Holland was for the first time in history 'at present in some manner [holding] the balance between all the other powers of Europe'.

Each of these points would have struck readers of the day as somewhat peculiar. Huet was one of a very small number of authors for whom the size of the state did not matter. Furthermore, most observers were convinced well before the first decade of the eighteenth century that Holland had declined both in commercial and in military terms, since the time of the Anglo-Dutch wars.[35] These wars, 'occassioned by the jealousy of trade', were intended to pave the way for English merchants to humble the maritime power of the Dutch, in order to prevent them from acquiring 'all the commerce of Europe, as they had already done that of the Indies'.[36] It became increasingly clear that the Dutch were not only failing to dominate European commerce, but were experiencing relative decline because of their small size and relative poverty with respect to natural resources.[37] All the small states of Europe were faced with the

---

[34] Ibid., p. v.

[35] The best known comment was Sir William Temple's in *Observations upon the United Provinces of the Netherlands* (London, 1673): 'It must be avowed, that this state in the course and progress of its greatness for so many years past, has shined like a comet, so in the revolutions of this last summer [1672], it seem'd to fall like a meteor, and has equally amazed the world by the one and the other.'

[36] Paul Rapin de Thoyras, *The History of England. Written Originally in French by M. Rapin de Thoyras. Translated into English by John Kelly*, 3 vols (London, 1732–7), vol. 3, p. 91.

[37] Malachy Postlethwayt, *Britain's Commercial Interest Explained and Improved; In a Series of Dissertations on Several Important Branches of Her Trade and Police*, 2 vols (London, 1757), vol. 2, p. 300; Anon., *The Politician's Dictionary; or, A Summary of Political Knowledge Containing Remarks on the Interests, Connections, Forces, Revenues, Wealth, Credit, Debts, Taxes, Commerce, and Manufactures of the Different States of Europe*, 2 vols (London, 1775), vol. 2, pp. 350–1; Rowland Hunt, *The Prosperity of Great Britain, Compared with the State of France, Her Conquests and Allies. Addressed Principally to the Freeholders, Farmers, . . .* (Shrewsbury, 1796), pp. 16–19.

commercial supremacy of Britain and France, the polities which had managed to couple flourishing trade with being monarchical Leviathans.

Huet was convinced that the third new development 'ought most to surprise us', being that in the case of the Dutch, 'wars never interrupted their Trade, and that it was in the very heat of war that they laid the foundations of that [commerce] of the East Indies and the Coasts of Africa'. Whereas historically war and trade had been forces at odds with one another, and never compatible, the contemporary world was characterised by their concordance, which in part explained the number of conflicts between states that had occurred from the first decades of the seventeenth century onwards. The latter perception was linked to the heavily underlined intention behind Huet's work, which was signalled in the final part of the title of the French original of his book, but which was omitted from the English translation: *Le grand tresor* sought to reveal the means to 'rétablir le commerce de France'. Commerce, Huet contended, continued to be 'so little understood in France'. Yet he was certain that if this state continued the policy of Colbert, French merchants would 'make our nation the most flourishing in the world'.[38] Huet reminded his readers of a comment ascribed to Lord Bellasis:

> That if God should one day make the Turks know what they could do at Sea, and the French how far they might extend their commerce, all Europe would soon fall a conquest to those powers.[39]

Commerce was the key to the reassertion of French power and the establishment of a global French empire. Commerce and war together, the branches of statecraft in which the French were potentially most gifted, would allow this state to grow beyond its geographical limit, and enable it to expand massively its access to natural resources for wealth and for defence.

In emphasising the importance of commerce to empire and in stating that France was best equipped to become the foremost European power, Huet was following better known authors, such as the great natural jurist Samuel Pufendorf, for whom, writing a generation earlier, France had become 'the most Potent Kingdom in Christendom', with the consequence that 'those lesser States bordering upon France are in great danger

---

[38] Huet's continued support for Louis XIV's minister Colbert is clear from the dedication 'A Monsieur Colbert, Ministre et Secretaire d'Estat' in *Histoire du commerce, et de la navigation des anciens* (Paris, 1716), pp. 1–3.

[39] Huet, *Le grand tresor*, p. vii. Thomas Bellasis, first Earl Fauconberg (1627/8–1700), was sometime ambassador-extraordinary to France.

to be devour'd by so flourishing a Kingdom'.[40] France was widely held to have aspired to universal monarchy under Louis XIV.[41] Many eighteenth-century commentators expected France to renew this attempt, and to be bolstered with respect to the practicality of its aspirations once Colbertist policies to make France a commercial empire were reasserted.[42] Huet's point was that the synergy between commerce and war could make France into a new kind of empire.

IV

Difficulties with Huet's vision of a France made supreme in trade and war arose, of course, from the rise of Britain, France's nearest rival as a commercial empire and civilised monarchy. The perceived paradox which fascinated authors throughout the eighteenth century was how Britain, a nation inferior in size, population, and natural resources, in addition to being deemed to be less civilised, appeared to have become the superior state to France with respect to its ability to wage war.[43] Certain patriots

[40] Samuel Pufendorf, *An Introduction to the History of the Principal Kingdoms and States of Europe*, trans. Jodocus Crull, 5th edn (London, 1702 [orig. 1682]), p. 236. It is significant that in Pufendorf's *The Present State of Germany*, ed. M. J. Seidler, (Indianapolis, IN, 2007 [orig. 1667]), pp. 186–97, England is mentioned as a state without any relevance to German interests. Throughout the eighteenth century even the most patriotic British authors accepted that France was 'the most ancient and powerful civilized monarchy': see Charles Tweedie, *The Conduct of Great Britain, Vindicated Against the Calumnies of Foreign Enemies and Domestic Conspirators* (London, 1799), p. 12.

[41] Slingsby Bethel, *The Interest of Princes and States* (London, 1680), p. 268; Anon., *Discourses upon the Modern Affairs of Europe. Tending to Prove, that the Illustrious French Monarchy May be Reduced to Terms of Greater Moderation* (n.p., 1680), p. 5, and *The True Interests of the Princes of Europe in the Present State of Affairs: or Reflections upon a Pamphlet Written in French, Entituled, A Letter from Monsieur, to Monsieur, Concerning the Transactions of the Time* (London, 1689), p. 11; Charles Davenant, *An Essay upon Ways and Means of Supplying the War* (London, 1695), pp. 14–15, and *An Essay upon the Probable Methods of Making a People Gainers in the Ballance of Trade* (London, 1699), p. 280; Anon., *A Defence of the Right of the House of Austria to the Crown of Spain* (London, 1703); Anon., 'To the French King', *Poems on Affairs of State, from the Reign of K. James the First, to this Present Year 1703*, 2 vols ([London], 1703), vol. 2, pp. 313–14; Samuel Wesley, *Marlborough; or, The Fate of Europe: A Poem* (London, 1705), pp. 3, 9.

[42] Charles Dodd, *A Display of French Politicks* (London, 1739), pp. 45, 58; Anon., *The Progress of the French, in their Views of Universal Monarchy* (London, 1756), pp. 28–30; Dutot, *Political Reflections upon the Finances and Commerce of France; Shewing the Causes which Formerly Obstructed the Advancement of Her Trade* (London, 1739), p. 304; Philippe Minard, *La fortune du colbertisme: État et industrie dans la France des lumières* (Paris, 1998).

[43] Arthur Young, *Letters Concerning the Present State of the French Nation* (London, 1769), pp. 1–16, 394–425.

traced Britain's eminence to 'the true Protestant Religion' and God's providential plan.[44] Far more located its source in Britain's greater commerce and public credit. John Law, the Scots adventurer and finance minister in Regency France after the death of Louis XIV, summarised this position early in the century, praising the commitment of successive British ministries to 'treasure by foreign trade', entailing the meticulous payment of public debts, support for merchant companies across the globe, the levy of heavy duties upon foreign manufactures, and prohibitions on the export of raw materials such as wool.[45] Law was defining what became known as the mercantile system.[46]

There had always been uncertainty about the ability of the mixed government and church established at the Revolution to maintain civil peace and economic flourishing, and the consequences of the seventeenth-century republican legacy for the composite polity in the longer term.[47] Commentators were concerned about whether the mercantile system committed Britain to reason of state in international affairs, and whether the system itself corrupted trade.[48] If Britain's commerce was not founded, as John Law hoped France's could be made to rest, on a bedrock of natural resources exploited through trade then Britain's military greatness was a product of accident and fortune, and would collapse when the 'natural order' reasserted itself, corresponding to the size, cultivated land, mineral wealth, and population of each state. Britain, it was further argued, would decline and ultimately fall because of the conjoined forces

---

[44] See for example Robert Fleming, *Seculum davidicum redivivum; or, The Divine Right of the Revolution Evinc'd and Apply'd* (London, 1706), pp. 38, 82.

[45] John Law, *Money and Trade Considered* (Edinburgh, 1705), p. 59; 'Premier mémoire sur les banques' (1715–16), in E. Daire (ed.), *Économistes financières du XVIIIe siècle* (Paris, 1843), pp. 549–53.

[46] On the origins of the mercantile system, see Thomas Mun, *England's Treasure by Forraign Trade. or, The Ballance of Our Forraign Trade Is the Rule of Our Treasure* (London, 1664), pp. 20–4, 217–20.

[47] Louis Joseph Plumard de Dangeul, *Remarks on the Advantages and Disadvantages of France and of Great-Britain with Respect to Commerce* (London, 1754), pp. 110–37; Josiah Tucker, *An Essay on the Advantages and Disadvantages which Respectively Attend France and Great Britain, with Regard to Trade*, 4th edn (Glasgow, 1756), pp. 64–166, and *A Treatise Concerning Civil Government, in Three Parts. Part I. The Notions of Mr. Locke . . . Examined and Confuted. Part II. The True Basis of Civil Government Set Forth . . . Part III. England's Former Gothic Constitution Censured and Exposed* (London, 1781), pp. 207–59.

[48] David Hume, 'Of Commerce', in *Essays and Treatises*, pp. 156–63; Adam Smith, *An Inquiry into the Nature and Causes of the Wealth of Nations*, 3 vols (Dublin, 1776), vol. 2, pp. 339–40, 471–2, 501–2, 508; George Chalmers, *An Estimate of the Comparative Strength of Britain during the Present and Four Preceding Reigns; And of the Losses of Her Trade from Every War* (London, 1782), pp. 74–7.

of luxury and effeminacy. Such a perspective on imperial collapse was popularised by the innumerable readers of Fénelon's *Télémaque*.[49] As Lord Kames put it:

> The corruption of a court spreads through every member of the state. In an extensive kingdom, powerful above its neighbours, the subjects, having no occasion to exert themselves in defence of their country, lose their manhood, and become cowards. At the same time, great inequality of rank and fortune engender luxury, selfishness, and sensuality. The fine arts, it is true, gain ground, manufactures are perfected, and courtly manners prevail: but every manly virtue is gone; and not a soul to be found, who will venture his life to save his country. That disease is spreading in Britain; and the only circumstance that guards France from equal pusillanimity, is an established mode, that every gentleman must serve some campaigns in the army.[50]

Coupling a moral indictment of Britain's mercantile system with the anticipated collapse of Britain's political system became a dominant idiom between the 1730s and the 1750s. It marked political culture on both sides of the Channel through the writings of Bolingbroke, Hume, John Brown, and Montesquieu.[51] One issue that obsessed Britons was the extent to which the mercantile system entailed what Michael Sonenscher has recently called 'the command structure of absolute monarchy', and was therefore incompatible with the system of representative government established in 1688/9.[52]

The dilemma for French projectors was whether Britain would self-destruct as an empire, could be vanquished by military prowess, or might be challenged by the development of more moral and stable forms of commerce that were nevertheless capable of out-competing their

---

[49] Fénelon, *Telemachus*, ed. P. Riley (Cambridge, 1994), p. 297; Istvan Hont, 'The Early Enlightenment Debate on Commerce and Luxury', in M. Goldie and R. Wokler (eds), *The Cambridge History of Eighteenth-century Political Thought* (Cambridge, 2006), pp. 379–412.

[50] Henry Home, Lord Kames, *Sketches of the History of Man*, 4 vols (Dublin, 1774–5), vol. 2, p. 215.

[51] Henry St John, Viscount Bolingbroke, *Letters, On the Spirit of Patriotism: On the Idea of a Patriot King: And on the State of Parties, at the Accession of King George the First* (Dublin, 1749), pp. 164–6; John Brown, *An Estimate of the Manners and Principles of the Times. By the Author of Essays on the Characteristics*, 2nd edn (London, 1757), pp. 142–5. On Hume, see Hont, 'The Rhapsody of Public Debt: David Hume and Voluntary State Bankruptcy', in *Jealousy of Trade*, pp. 325–54. On Montesquieu, see Michael Sonenscher, *Before the Deluge: Public Debt, Inequality, and the Intellectual Origins of the French Revolution* (Princeton, NJ, 2007), pp. 95–173.

[52] Sonenscher, *Before the Deluge*, pp. 41–66, and Josiah Tucker, *A Brief Essay on the Advantages and Disadvantages, which Respectively Attend France and Great Britain, with Regard to Trade* ([London], 1749), pp. 53–6.

mercantile counterparts.[53] The alternative was that France became mercantile in the manner of the British, and developed a national debt to the same extent.[54] Contemporaries were, however, fearful that armies funded by credit would lead to the tyrannical rule of new Caesars. Bankruptcy caused by excessive credit was associated with popular rebellion headed by a latter-day Spartacus. Perhaps the most feared possibility was voluntary bankruptcy, whereby an absolute monarch expanded credit to strengthen the military capacities of the state, then sacrificed the creditors in the name of national survival or imperial glory, creating a potentially all-powerful polity inimical to liberty and addicted to war.[55] The deadly consequences of unintended national bankruptcy, or monarch-inspired planned bankruptcy, for the 'princes and states fighting and quarrelling amidst their debts, funds and public mortgages' were likened by David Hume to a cudgelling match in a china shop.[56] In an era of experiment with representative government and more general constitutionalism, another danger commonly identified was that the imperative of paying the national debt would lead wealthy creditors to control politicians and statesmen. Alternatively, high taxes would beggar the populace, or at the very least reduce commercial competitiveness, making rich states prey to their poorer neighbours.[57]

Such concerns made the eighteenth century an era of singular uncertainty for commercial empires. It was also an era of constant innovation with respect to conjectures intended to prevent economic decline and, in the cases of Britain and of France, to secure international supremacy. In

[53] One of the most influential speculations on these options was Jean-François Melon, *A Political Essay upon Commerce* (London, 1739), pp. 54–65, 348–51. On Melon's influence, see John Robertson, *The Case for the Enlightenment: Scotland and Naples 1680–1760* (Cambridge, 2005), pp. 360–80.

[54] François Véron de Forbonnais, *Elémens du commerce*, 2nd edn, 2 vols (Leiden and Paris, 1754), vol. 1, pp. 261–345, vol. 2, pp. 1–40, and Sonenscher, *Before the Deluge*, pp. 179–88.

[55] On all of these possibilities, see Hont, 'Rhapsody of Public Debt: David Hume and Voluntary State Bankruptcy', in *Jealousy of Trade*, pp. 325–54, and Michael Sonenscher, 'The Nation's Debt and the Birth of the Modern Republic: The French Fiscal Deficit and the Politics of the Revolution of 1789', *History of Political Thought*, 18 (1997), pp. 64–103, 267–325.

[56] David Hume, 'Of Public Credit', in *Essays and Treatises on Several Subjects*, 2nd edn (Edinburgh, 1753), vol. 4, p. 119.

[57] Hont, 'The "Rich Country—Poor Country" Debate in Scottish Political Economy', *Jealousy of Trade*, pp. 267–324, and 'The Rich Country—Poor Country Debate Revisited: The Irish Origins and French Reception of the Hume Paradox', in Margaret Schabas and Carl Wennerlind (eds), *Hume's Political Economy* (London, 2007), pp. 222–342; Sonenscher, 'Property, Community, and Citizenship', in *Cambridge History of Eighteenth-century Political Thought*, pp. 465–96, and *Before the Deluge*, pp. 34–94, 159–72, 179–222, 266–334.

the background for British and French authors was the constant fear of a new coinage, 'oriental despotism', foreseeing the fall of Europe's effeminate and exhausted monarchies before vast marauding slave-based armies from the East.[58] Many acute observers took an interest in the 'asiatic' or 'oriental' despotisms of the East, and pre-eminently Russia, which several authors, and Rousseau most famously in the second book of the *Contrat social*, believed would invade western Europe as soon as the commercial monarchies of France and Britain exhausted themselves in war or imploded via bankruptcy.[59] For Rousseau, as for so many eighteenth-century observers, the salient fact about civilised monarchies was that they were organised for war. The oft-repeated claim that in Britain's case the economy had grown to an 'unnatural' extent and in a dangerous direction, and that France's international status was not in accordance with its underlying power, meant that few authors were phlegmatic with regard to the future of these states.[60] The view was everywhere accepted that security was the product of economic success, even if, because of the advantages of poorer states, this success was unlikely to be permanent.[61] All of these factors together explained for contemporaries why the long eighteenth century saw near-constant war across Europe and in the colonies. In turn, this was why so many observers, however pessimistic they were about the future of the great commercial empires of Europe, were convinced that the independence of the smaller states was likely to be short-lived.[62]

[58] Nicolas-Antoine Boulanger, *Recherches sur l'origine du despotisme oriental* (Amsterdam, 1766), pp. 311–30.

[59] Jean-Jacques Rousseau, *The Social Contract and Other Later Political Writings*, ed. and trans. V. Gourevitch (Cambridge, 1997), p. 73, and *Émile; ou, De l'éducation*, 2 vols (Frankfurt, 1762), vol. 1, bk 3, pp. 59–60.

[60] For a summary of the arguments about Britain, see Thomas Paine, *The Decline & Fall of the English System of Finance* ([London], 1796) and the responses in Ralph Broome, *Observations on Mr. Paine's Pamphlet, entitled The Decline and Fall of the English System of Finance. In a Letter to a Friend* (London, 1796) and Joseph Smith, *An Examination of Mr. Paine's Decline & Fall of the English System of Finance, in a Letter to a Friend* (London, 1796).

[61] William Playfair, *An Inquiry into the Permanent Causes of the Decline and Fall of Powerful and Wealthy Nations, Illustrated by Four Engraved Charts. Designed to Shew How the Prosperity of the British Empire May Be Prolonged*, 2nd edn (London, 1807), p. 182: 'There is not any one thing in which a nation resembles an individual so much, as in mercantile transactions . . . The rich carry on an extensive trade, by means of great capital; the poor, a limited one, dependent chiefly on industry; but wherever the poor persevere in good conduct, they finish by getting the command of the rich, and then becoming their rivals.'

[62] Edmund Burke, 'Letters on a Regicide Peace', *The Works and Correspondence of the Right Honourable Edmund Burke*, 8 vols (London, 1852), vol. 5, p. 258, letter I.

V

In his essay 'Great and Small States Compared', Lord Kames wrote that 'patriotism is vigorous in small states; and the hatred to neighbouring states no less so: both vanish in a great monarchy'.[63] The exact opposite of this maxim characterised the ongoing bellicosity between Britain and France, during which national antagonism and patriotic warmongering reached new heights.[64] Kames was full of praise for small states, citing their immunity to despotism, their stability relative to the internal convulsions of monarchy, their ease of defence, the manliness, courage, modesty, frugality, and ardent unity of their citizens, and the uniformity of their manners. Their only disadvantages lay in their inability 'to execute great works', such as the pyramids of Egypt or the hanging gardens of Babylon, and their failure to produce good writers, because 'where there are few readers, there is no sufficient incitement to exert literary talents'.[65] Contemporary authors readily contradicted such opinion. Small states, and more particularly the small republics, considered their advantages to be meagre, because they could no longer guarantee their own security. The Roman view that luxury corrupted manners and weakened empires was widespread.[66] Certain writers focused on the incompatibility of commerce and the relative equality needed to sustain the popular governments of small republics. As Mercier put it, democracy was an enemy to emulation, which underpinned the growth of trade:[67]

> Polity [policy], being unable to establish a real equality in the fortune of the citizens, seems instinctively to reject a popular government. In vain have little republics imagined that the people would never cease to be free; there is an invincible progression, above all in modern states, where commerce so quickly modified the members of the same society . . . The poorer citizens necessarily come under the influence of the rich. And these little republics, after having raised some unsuccessful storms, fall into all the snares laid for them. It is the height of folly, in a Lilliputian state, to believe that it will recover by force what

[63] Kames, *Sketches of the History of Man*, vol. 2, p. 200.

[64] Linda Colley, *Britons: Forging the Nation, 1707–1837* (London, 1992), pp. 284–7, and Robert Tombs and Isabelle Tombs, *That Sweet Enemy: The French and the British from the Sun King to the Present* (London, 2006), pp. 119–233.

[65] Kames, *Sketches of the History of Man*, vol. 2, pp. 211–13.

[66] Niccolò Machiavelli, 'Discourses', bk 2, ch. 19, in *The Works of Nicholas Machiavel, Secretary of State to the Republic of Florence* (London, 1762), vol. 2, p. 248; see further Béla Kapossy, *Iselin contra Rousseau: Sociable Patriotism and the History of Mankind* (Schwabe, 2006), pp. 21–94.

[67] Mercier, *Fragments of Politics and History*, vol. 2, pp. 313–14.

has before been refused to its remonstrances . . . A poorer nation has no other weapons than the incessant complaints and lamentations it makes. It must tease and weary out its adversaries like beggars.[68]

Exceptions to the view that the small republics had declined could be found, and particularly with regard to Switzerland. The policy of neutrality that had served the cantons well historically was often praised.[69] Despite antagonism towards Catholicism, Swiss soldiers who were Protestant were said to maintain their valour by serving the king of France as mercenaries; they were allowed to bring their ministers to war and maintain their faith even in the midst of more general French persecution of non-Catholics.[70] Swiss success was described by the English visitor William Coxe in letters of 1779:

> . . . with such wisdom was the Helvetic union composed, and so little have the Swiss, of late years, been actuated with the spirit of conquest, that since the firm and complete establishment of their general confederacy, they have scarcely ever had occasion to employ their arms against a foreign enemy; and have had no hostile commotions among themselves, that were not very soon happily terminated. Perhaps there is not a similar instance in antient or modern history, of a warlike people, divided into little independent republics, closely bordering upon each other, and of course having occasionally interfering interests, having continued, in an almost uninterrupted state of tranquillity. The youth are diligently trained to all the martial exercises . . . a considerable number of Swiss troops are always employed in foreign services; and the whole people are enrolled, and regularly exercised in their respective militia. By these means they are capable, in case it should be necessary, of collecting a very respectable body of forces, which could not fail of proving formidable to any enemy who should invade their country, or attack their liberties. Thus, while most of the other states upon the continent are tending more and more towards a military government, Switzerland alone has no standing armies; and yet, from the nature of its situation, from its particular alliances, and from the policy of its internal government, is more secure from invasion than any other European power, and full as able to withstand the greatest force that can be brought against it.[71]

---

[68] Ibid., vol. 2, pp. 41–2.

[69] James Currie, *A Letter, Commercial and Political, Addressed to the Rt. Honble. William Pitt, in which the Real Interests of Britain, in the Present Crisis, are Considered, and Some Observations are Offered on the General State of Europe*, 3rd edn (London, 1793), p. 60.

[70] Joseph Addison, *Remarks on Several Parts of Italy, &c. in the Years, 1701, 1702, 1703* (London, 1753), pp. 289–90.

[71] William Coxe, *Sketches of the Natural, Civil, and Political State of Swisserland; in a Series of Letters to William Melmoth, Esq.* (London, 1779), pp. 517–19; for an earlier view, although more circumspect about the consequences of the growth of French power, see Temple Stanyan, *An Account of Switzerland, Written in the Year 1714* (Edinburgh, 1756), pp. 196–203.

Some authors conjectured that cantons like Berne might become a new Rome, particularly as they were unique in having avoided the practice of acquiring public debts.[72] But the few genuine believers in potentially neo-Machiavellian futures for small republics, such as Micheli du Crest at Geneva, found themselves persecuted by ruling magistrates, who were fearful of unrest and of antagonising larger neighbours.[73] France was to a greater and greater extent involved in Swiss politics, signing an alliance at Soleure in 1777. At Geneva, France was party to a 'guarantee' of the Genevan constitution, with the cantons of Zurich and Berne, which led to intervention to end popular disturbances in 1738 and 1768, and invasion to suppress revolution in 1782.[74] Proof that small republics could not stand against larger states came with the French Revolution, when French republican troops in 1798 subdued Switzerland, creating a new unitary republic, and annexed Geneva to France. As one British observer put it, 'Thus did the MONSTROUS REPUBLIC, fascinate and fix the little Republics, of Holland, Venice, Switzerland, &c. till they were swallowed up in succession.'[75] One English writer argued that it was the judgement of God upon Swiss socinians, their clergy having become 'atheists and fanatics'.[76]

That so many republicans believed themselves to be living through an age of crisis, during which the doctrine they espoused was likely to be proved so archaic as to be irrelevant to the modern age, might appear a surprising fact given recent historiographical trends. The impression is sometimes given that a republican baton was straightforwardly passed from early modern neo-Machiavellians to their North American and French cousins at the end of the eighteenth century, and thence into the

---

[72] Béla Kapossy, 'Neo-Roman Republicanism and Commercial Society: The Example of Eighteenth-century Berne', in Martin van Gelderen and Quentin Skinner, *Republicanism: A Shared European* Heritage, 2 vols (Cambridge, 2002), vol. 2, pp. 226–47.

[73] Jacques-Bartélemy Micheli du Crest, *Question politique, savoir s'il convient, en 1716, d'entreprendre un grand projet de fortification pour Genève*, Archives d'État de Genève, Pièces historiques, 4563 bis. no. 4; *Relation de tout ce qui c'est passé* (Cologne, 1731), pp. 10–31, and *Supplication avec supplément presentée aux loüable cantons de Zurich et de Berne* ([Basle], 1745), pp. 60–9.

[74] John Wilson, *The History of Switzerland* (Philadelphia, PA, 1832), pp. 225–33, and Heinrich Zschokke and Emil Zschokke, *The History of Switzerland, for the Swiss People* (New York, 1855), pp. 233–68.

[75] William Hales, *The Monstrous Republic: or, French Atrocities Pourtrayed* (London, 1799), pp. 5–6.

[76] John Wood, *A General View of the History of Switzerland; with a Particular Account of the Origin and Accomplishment of the Late Swiss Revolution* (Edinburgh, 1799), pp. 414–15.

nineteenth century to become 'a shared European heritage'.[77] It is difficult, however, to conceive of republican ideas as a tradition of argument
or pan-European ideology. The case of North America is distinctive in its
republicanism because it was among the only places in the world where,
at the foundation of the new state, commerce could be coupled with
land-ownership for every citizen who desired it.[78] In Europe many ardent
cosmopolitan patriots advocated republican ideas for small states, while
abhorring the prospect of the transformation of France or Britain into a
republic. It did not make sense to alter large monarchies, whose manners
were associated with luxury, and whose populace was drastically divided
both in status and wealth.[79] French republicanism in the 1790s was distinctive because advocating commercial republicanism in a large European
state that had been a monarchy reputedly for two millennia could only
minimally be indebted to a classical republican heritage, the North
American example, or Machiavelli's or Rousseau's anti-commercial
advocacy of Spartan virtue.[80] From the perspective of national security,
the disjunction between Europe's small republics and their larger counterparts was still greater. When France became a republican empire
seeking to develop its trade and to spread liberty, this translated into
traditional reason of state politics, as small state republicans like Mallet
Du Pan noted when writing about the invasion of Switzerland in 1798:

[77] The term comes from van Gelderen and Skinner, *Republicanism*, although what it means in
this context is uncertain, because the volumes lack a justificatory introduction and several of the
essays explicitly attack the notion of a single republican or shared European ideology. Quentin
Skinner, in *Liberty before Liberalism* (Cambridge, 1998), has sketched a neo-roman theory of
free states, and Philip Petit has defined a republican tradition in *Republicanism: A Theory of
Freedom and Government* (Oxford, 1997): neither has anything to say about differences between
republicans on the issue of maintaining small and large states. See further Manuela Albertone,
'Democratic Republicanism: Historical Reflections on the Idea of Republic in the Eighteenth
Century', *History of European Ideas*, 33, 1 (2007), pp. 108–30.
[78] On the distinctiveness of North American republicanism, see Manuela Albertone, 'George
Logan: un physiocrate américain', in Bernard Delmals, Thierry Demals, and Philippe Steiner
(eds), *La diffusion internationale de la physiocratie, Actes du Colloque International de Saint-
Cloud, 23–24 septembre 1993* (Grenoble, 1995), pp. 421–39, and 'Condorcet, Jefferson et
l'Amérique', in Anne-Marie Chouillet and Pierre Crépel (eds), *Condorcet: Homme des lumières
et de la révolution* (Paris, 1997), pp. 189–99.
[79] A good example here is Etienne Dumont, the Genevan republican who became Jeremy
Bentham's editor and translator. For Dumont's opposition to French republicanism, see Richard
Whatmore, 'Etienne Dumont, the British Constitution, and the French Revolution', *Historical
Journal*, 50, 1 (2007), pp. 23–47.
[80] Elizabeth Rawson, *The Spartan Tradition in European Thought* (Oxford, 1969), pp. 220–60,
and Judith N. Shklar, 'Rousseau's Two Models: Sparta and the Age of Gold', *Political Science
Quarterly*, 81, 1 (1966), pp. 25–51.

> This Directory punishes the Swiss for their neutrality . . . proclaims its respect
> for their independence, whilst with the fire of the canon it deprives them of
> their laws and their ancient Constitution . . . institutes republics against the will
> of republicans . . . which, in its destructive rage overturns all states, throws
> republics upon monarchies, neutral countries on belligerent ones, and mani-
> festly demonstrates to all countries, that the worst of all conditions is to be at
> peace with it, and to remain secure under the faith of treatises.[81]

Significantly, Mallet Du Pan ended his work with the statement, 'Now all
Europe is concentrated in England. Its salvation depends upon the fate of
that power!'[82]

VI

If republican patriotism was widely acknowledged no longer to guarantee the security of small states in the eighteenth century, the same was
also said of the traditional fellow strategies of neutrality and confederation. Samuel Pufendorf had recognised this at the beginning of the
period:

> A well composed Kingdom or Monarchy is certainly the most perfect Union,
> and the best fitted for duration or continuance; for as for Aristocrasies [*sic*] . . .
> they can scarce ever conveniently subsist . . . A System of many Cities united by
> a League, is much more loose in its conjunction, and may more easily be
> dissolved (which is the Case of the States of Holland).[83]

The marquis d'Argenson advised small-state republicans in the 1740s
of an alternative strategy, that in the modern world 'friendship with large
monarchies is most certain to sustain them'.[84] Emer de Vattel in his *Droit
des gens* (1758), the most popular and influential work on international

---

[81] Jacques Mallet Du Pan, *A Short Account of the Invasion of Switzerland by the French, in a
Letter from M. Mallet du Pan to M. de M* (London, 1798), pp. 18–19.

[82] Ibid., p. 28.

[83] Pufendorf, *Present State of Germany*, p. 200.

[84] René-Louis de Voyer, marquis d'Argenson, *Mémoires et journal inédit*, 5 vols (Paris, 1858), vol.
5, pp. 299–300; see also *Mémoires du marquis d'Argenson, ministre sous Louis XV avec une notice
sur la vie et les ouvrages de l'auteur: publiés par René d'Argenson* (Paris, 1825), pp. 366, 376, 383,
and the comment at p. 112: 'Quelle belle idée . . . que celle d'une république protégée par un Roi,
et qui se gouverne d'autant mieux qu'elle est mieux protégée!' Rousseau made a similar point
when advising the Genevans not to adopt democratic reforms for fear of antagonising France,
against whom they could not stand: see letters to François Coindet and François-Henri
D'Ivernois, 9 February 1768, in R. A. Leigh (ed.), *Correspondance complète de Rousseau*, 51 vols
(Oxford, 1963–94), vol. 35, pp. 91–108.

law of the second half of the eighteenth century, was one of the first authors to accept d'Argenson's point of view, and advise the Swiss in consequence that they had to rely upon Britain's empire for their survival. Vattel was a native of Neuchâtel, a principality ruled by the kings of Prussia, and served the elector of Saxony as a civil servant for much of his life, but the premise of his writing was that 'A dwarf is as much a man as a giant; a small republic is no less a sovereign state than the most powerful kingdom.'[85] Vattel reiterated the old trope that Switzerland had survived because of the valour of its citizens, which was maintained by their service as mercenaries in the armies of monarchies, in addition to the policy of neutrality.[86] He was also a staunch advocate of leagues and confederations of republics against over-powerful sovereigns. At the same time, he recognised that schemes to keep peace by equalising the political power of states, which he ascribed to Henri IV of France, or of perpetual peace by the dominion of a single power, which he associated with the abbé de Saint-Pierre, were inferior to the operation of the balance of power.[87]

Vattel was confident that Europe was in a better condition than formerly in that the residence of ambassadors across states, and the attention of sovereigns to international politics, 'make of modern Europe a kind of republic, of which the members—each independent, but all linked together by the ties of common interest—unite for the maintenance of order and liberty'.[88] Supporting the political balance meant that states had to be willing to go to war if necessary to prevent one state becoming over-powerful. Vattel argued that the small states had to help Britain to do this, because this state alone was in a position to act as guarantor of Europe's ongoing security:

> It is a more simple, an easier, and a more equitable plan, to have recourse to the method . . . of forming confederations in order to oppose the more powerful potentate, and prevent him from giving law to his neighbours. Such is the mode at present pursued by the sovereigns of Europe. They consider the two principal powers, which on that very account are naturally rivals, as destined to be checks on each other; and they unite with the weaker, like so many weights

---

[85] Emer de Vattel, *The Law of Nations, and the Duties of Citizens, or Principles of the Law of Nature Applied to the Conduct and Affairs of Nations and Sovereigns* (London, 1797), p. lxiii.

[86] Ibid., p. 89, bk 1, ch. 14, s. 180; p. 298, bk 3 , ch. 2, s. 13; bk 3, ch. 3, s. 314; p. 340, bk 3, ch. 7, s. 118.

[87] Isaac Nakhimovsky, 'Vattel's Theory of the International Order: Commerce and the Balance of Power in the *Law of Nations*', *History of European Ideas*, 33, 2 (2007), pp. 157–73.

[88] Vattel, *Law of Nations*, p. 312, bk 3, ch. 3, s. 47.

thrown into the lighter scale, in order to keep it in equilibrium with the other. The house of Austria has long been the preponderating power: at present France is so in her turn. England, whose opulence and formidable fleets have a powerful influence, without alarming any state on the score of its liberty, because that nation seems cured of the rage of conquest,—England, I say, has the glory of holding the political balance. She is attentive to preserve it in equilibrium.[89]

The operation of the balance of power rested upon Britain's willingness to go to war, and this in turn, for Vattel, rested on Britain's commercial might: 'it is chiefly commerce that places in her hand the balance of Europe'.[90] Vattel was convinced that Britain was a different kind of empire to the larger European monarchies. Britain had in the past sought the return of French lands, and in consequence had been like its neighbours in seeking a land-based empire, and potentially European dominion. It had also acted as a crusader for Protestantism, and mistakenly been willing to allow religious belief to influence foreign policy. All of this had changed by the time of the War of the Austrian Succession (1740–8), which Vattel referred to as 'the last war'. Mercantile empire might entail monopoly and corruption, but it did not, in Vattel's view, entail reason of state. In becoming a commercial empire, Britain had lost the 'rage for conquest'. Developing commerce meant that Britain had both an interest in, and also the means, to prevent a universal monarchy or a universal republic from developing in Europe. Vattel was equally convinced that the development of trade across Europe would ultimately result in a new economic balance of power, with wealthy states large and small adverse to war but with greater means of self-defence. Until that point was reached, the small states were reliant upon Britain's willingness to defend and protect them.

These themes were taken up by republicans in the following generation, and particularly at Geneva. Many Genevan citizens had long argued that their state had become a French protectorate. This was confirmed in 1782 when the French foreign minister Vergennes orchestrated the banishment of several republican reformers who were calling for the establishment of a democratic republic.[91] The Genevans who were forced to leave included many individuals who subsequently became prominent in

---

[89] Vattel, *Law of Nations*, p. 312, bk 3, ch. 3, s. 48; see also p. 7, bk 1, ch. 2, s. 24; p. 34, bk 1, ch. 7, s. 76.

[90] Ibid., p. 37, bk 1, ch. 8, s. 85.

[91] On Vergennes's view, see Otto Karmin, *Sir Francis D'Ivernois* (Geneva, 1920), p. 65, and Pierre-Victor Malouet, *Mémoires*, 2 vols (Paris, 1874), vol. 1, p. 180.

the French Revolution, such as Etienne Clavière, and in British politics, such as Sir Francis D'Ivernois. None of the exiled Genevans abandoned their desire to remove the French 'guarantee' of Geneva's constitution, which in their view prevented genuine independence. All of them accepted that for this to occur change was necessary in the relationship between small republics and large empires. When some of the exiles together composed a history of the Genevan rebellion, which was published in the name of D'Ivernois, they blamed Britain for failing to become involved in Genevan affairs when invited by the democrats from the 1760s onwards: 'England ought to have declared that she would watch over that independence, and cover the liberty of this small state with her powerful protection.'[92] Their argument was not a moral one, but rather founded on the need for Britain to protect commercial centres from falling under French dominion, which would allow their commerce to be controlled within a French mercantile system; this was, of course, exactly what happened with Napoleon's Continental System.

For Clavière, Britain's failure to protect small republics like Geneva was due to the mercantile system itself, which committed it to reason of state, as evinced by its treatment of Ireland. Clavière accepted Turgot's prediction, in his letter to Richard Price of 1782, that because of its lesser debt and greater natural resources, France was more likely to emerge victorious from the turmoil of conflict between the two empires, and that Britain would soon collapse, by civil war or by bankruptcy.[93] In consequence, Clavière believed that the surest future for small republics lay under the protection of a France reformed domestically and espousing the liberty of trade. France could be armed against British mercantile power through a commercial alliance with the USA, establishing an international division of labour that would allow France to achieve its economic potential by rapid export growth of manufactures, supplying resources to defeat Britain if war arose.[94] Moral commerce fostered by free trade was anticipated, once monopolies in France and America had been removed, and corrupt practices abolished, including aristocracy and

---

[92] Francis D'Ivernois, *An Historical View of the Constitution and Revolutions of Geneva in the Eighteenth Century* (London, 1784 [orig. 1782]), pp. 238–9.

[93] Gabriel-Honoré de Riquetti, comte de Mirabeau, *Considerations on the Order of Cincinnatus; to which are added, as well several original papers relative to that institution, as also a letter from the late M. Turgot, . . . to Dr. Price, on the constitutions of America; and an abstract of Dr. Price's Observations on the importance of the American Revolution* (London, 1785), pp. 153–73.

[94] Etienne Clavière and Jacques-Pierre Brissot de Warville, *Considerations on the Relative Situation of France and the United States of America* (London, 1788), pp. xi–xvi, 35–40, 99–100, 153–6.

slavery.[95] In the early years of the Revolution, Clavière was in the van-guard of those who considered it essential that France defeat Britain economically in order to prevent mercantile wars from breaking out.[96] When France became a republic, he was accused of advocating republican empire as the surest means to put an end to Britain's involvement in European politics.[97]

Clavière's friend and compatriot Francis D'Ivernois espoused exactly the opposite view. D'Ivernois followed Vattel in believing that Britain's mercantile system was open to reform as commerce grew, and had become a global power with a more general interest in peace rather than war. D'Ivernois also sought to combat Turgot's opinion, and those of many other projectors, that France's fundamental wealth was greater and more stable than that of Britain. In the context of the French Revolution, when accusations of British weakness were more vociferous than ever, D'Ivernois published a stream of works dedicated to showing that peace in Europe was dependent upon Britain preventing the growth of a French empire.[98] D'Ivernois became a major critic of the revolution in France, but his broader goal was to reveal a link between the moderation of Britain's domestic politics, which he traced to a constitution that demanded regular acts of compromise, and a pacific British foreign policy.[99] Like Vattel, he saw Britain as a new form of empire, and dedicated to the balance of power: 'The inhabitants of these islands are not children in the school of politics ... sound judgement has convinced them that they must, at any risk, prevent the aggrandisement of France, and leave nothing undone to preserve the balance of power in Europe.'[100] France was, both in its revolutionary guise and under Bonaparte, the greatest aspirant in modern times to the status of a new Rome.[101] As a tyranny, France was declining economically, and this meant that war was the only

---

[95] Clavière and Brissot de Warville, *Considerations*, pp. 246, 272–4.

[96] Clavière to Dumont, 19 July 1792, in Otto Karmin, 'Trois lettres inédites de Clavière à Etienne Dumont (1791–1792)', *Revue historique de la révolution française*, 5 (1914), pp. 11–17; 'De la conjuration contre les finances', *Chronique du mois*, January 1792, pp. 132–3.

[97] Clavière, *Correspondance du Ministre Clavière et du Général Montesquiou* (Paris, 1792).

[98] Francis D'Ivernois, *A Cursory View of the Assignats; And of the State in which the Convention Leaves the Finances to Their Successors (September 6, 1795)* (London, 1795), pp. iv–v, 19.

[99] D'Ivernois, *Des révolutions de France et de Genève* (London, 1795), pp. 473, 404–9, and *Réflexions sur la guerre: En réponse aux Réflexions sur la paix, adressées à Mr. Pitt et aux français* (London, 1795), pp. 121–57.

[100] D'Ivernois, *Reflections on the War* (London, 1795), p. 121.

[101] D'Ivernois, *Historical and Political Survey of the Losses Sustained by the French Nation, in Population, Agriculture, Colonies, Manufactures, and Commerce* (London, 1799), pp. 410–36.

policy capable of maintaining the French Republic or Empire.[102] The duty and interest of Britain was to prevent France from success, with the deadly consequences of French policy revealed in the treatment of Europe's small republics.[103] Once France was subdued, a more general economic balance could be established, in which all nations recognised their interest in peace and the benefits that would then accrue to all through trade.[104] In case Britain was taken for a state with imperial pretensions towards small states, D'Ivernois took particular care to explain the desire of the Irish to form a union with Britain, and the prosperity that quickly resulted from the Union of 1800.[105]

VII

Several of Europe's small states lost their independence in the aftermath of the French Revolution, including Venice, Genoa, and a large number of German principalities; several annexations or redistributions of land were confirmed by the leading European powers during the Vienna Settlement. This led James Mackintosh to condemn post-1815 international relations as the opposite of a balance of power, being a 'repartition of power' in foreign secretary Castlereagh's phrase, or concert of large European states against the small and weak:

> In the new system, small states are annihilated by a combination of great ones: — in the old, small states were secured by the mutual jealousy of the great . . . When the Noble Lord [Castlereagh] represents small states as incapable of self-defence, he in truth avows that he is returned in triumph from the destruction of that system of the Balance of Power, of which indeed great empires were the guardians, but of which the perfect action was indicated by the security of feebler commonwealths. Under this system no great violation of national

---

[102] Ibid., pp. iii–xi; *Exposé de la situation de l'empire français, et des comptes de finances publiés à Paris, en février et mars 1813*, 2nd edn (Paris, 1814), pp. 175–83.

[103] D'Ivernois, *A Short Account of the Late Revolution in Geneva; and of the Conduct of France towards That Republic, from October 1792, to October 1794* (London, 1795), *The Five Promises: Conduct of the Consular Government toward France, England, Italy, Germany, and especially Switzerland* (London, 1803), pp. 101–69, and *Immenses preparatifs de guerre qui eurent lieu en France d'abord après le traité d'Amiens. Fragment d'un exposé historique* (London, 1804).

[104] D'Ivernois, *Tableau historique et politique: Des pertes que la révolution et la guerre ont causées au peuple français, dans sa population, son agriculture, ses colonies, ses manufactures et son commerce*, 2 vols (London, 1799), vol. 2, pp. 278–312.

[105] D'Ivernois, *Effects of the Continental Blockade upon the Commerce, Finances, Credit and Prosperity of the British Islands* (London, 1810), pp. 70–147.

independence had occurred from the first civilisation of the European states till the partition of Poland. The safety of the feeblest states, under the authority of justice, was so great, that there seemed little exaggeration in calling such a society the 'commonwealth of Europe'. Principles, which stood in the stead of laws and magistrates, provided for the security of defenceless communities, as perfectly as the safety of the humblest individual is maintained in a well-ordered commonwealth. Europe can no longer be called a commonwealth, when her members have no safety but in their strength.[106]

From the perspective of the republics that had returned to a state of independence after experience of revolution and empire, Mackintosh's view was mistaken. Genevans had become Swiss when the city state became a canton in 1815, and patriots like D'Ivernois were convinced that neutrality could now be practised under a British guarantee.[107] Britain's constitution, for foreign observers, was linked to the remarkable commercial system, which together formed a new kind of empire. Remarkably, Britain seemed to have discovered a means to channel the republican patriotism of its public culture towards trade rather than towards war, although a more military patriotism was always retained for times when necessity dictated, and when commerce could be relied upon to underpin national security. Voices could still be heard anticipating the imminent collapse of Britain.[108] Most domestic commentators, however, for the first time since the Glorious Revolution, were confident about the survival of both the political and the commercial systems, however great the national debt, the population, and pauperism.[109] Britain was clearly committed to permanent involvement in mainland Europe, not as a potential conqueror, but as the power willing to prevent modern versions of universal monarchy from arising once again. This entailed defending the weak against the strong, which became a vital component of the liberal conception of empire.

---

[106] Sir James Mackintosh, 'Speech on the Annexation of Genoa to the Kingdom of Sardinia, delivered in the House of Commons on the 27th of April, 1815', in *The Miscellaneous Works of the Right Honourable Sir James Mackintosh*, new edn, 3 vols (London, 1854), vol. 3, pp. 349–50; for a related view, see Alexander Hill Everett, *Europe: or, A General Survey of the Present Situation of the Principal Powers: With Conjectures on Their Future Prospects* (Boston, CT, 1822).

[107] Karmin, *Sir Francis D'Ivernois*, pp. 545–60, 607–15, 657–63.

[108] Henry Schultes, *Reflections upon the Progressive Decline of the British Empire, and the Necessity of Public Reform*, 2nd edn (London, 1815) and Jean-Baptiste Say, *De l'Angleterre et des Anglais* (Paris, 1815).

[109] William Alexander Mackinnon, *On the Rise, Progress and Present State of Public Opinion in Great Britain and Other Parts of the World* (London, 1828), pp. 202–6.

Note.   I would like to thank the British Academy, the Arts and Humanities Research Council, and the School of Humanities Research Fund at the University of Sussex for supporting this research. Thanks also go to Duncan Kelly, Knud Haakonssen, and Ruth Woodfield for helpful comments.

4

Virgil and the British Empire, 1760–1880

PHIROZE VASUNIA

> . . . and when gradually, though not yet thirty years of age, I found myself
> helping to rule Millions in their hundreds of towns and thousands of villages,
> the lines of Virgil came back to me:
> 'Tu regere imperio populos, Romane, memento;
> Hae tibi erunt artes; pacisque imponere morem,
> Parcere subjectis, et debellare superbos.'
>
> Robert Needham Cust[1]

VIRGIL WILL NEVER CEASE TO BE the poet of empire. In speaking about his
new translation of the *Aeneid*, Robert Fagles observes that the Latin epic
is '[a]bout the terrible ills that attend empire—its war-making capacity,
the loss of blood and treasure both. But it's all done in the name of the
rule of law, which you'd have a hard time ascribing to what we're doing
in the Middle East today.'[2] The most celebrated American version of
the preceding generation contained a memorable postscript in which the
translator Robert Fitzgerald recalled the time when he first read the
Aeneid. The year was 1945, and, in the final months of the war, Fitzgerald
was stationed with US armed forces on an island in the Pacific Ocean
when he read through the Latin text in its entirety. 'Our navy's Actium
had been fought long before at Midway . . . There we were on our island
in fresh khakis, laundered and pressed, the little bars gleaming on our

---

[1] *Memoirs of Past Years of a Septuagenarian* (Hertford, 1899), p. 17. Cust, who lived from 1821
to 1909, was a member of the Indian Civil Service, and was quoting from book 6 of the *Aeneid*;
see the translation of these lines by Dryden below. For a biography, see Peter Penner, *Robert
Needham Cust, 1821–1909: A Personal Biography* (Lewiston, ME, 1987). For the role played by
Greek and Latin in the ICS entrance examinations, see Phiroze Vasunia, 'Greek, Latin, and the
Indian Civil Service', *Cambridge Classical Journal: Proceedings of the Cambridge Philological
Society*, 51 (2005), pp. 35–71.
[2] See Charles McGrath, 'Translating Virgil's Epic Poem of Empire', *New York Times*, 30 October
2006, section E, p. 1.

Proceedings of the British Academy **155**, 83–116. © The British Academy 2009.

collars and caps, saluting the old admiral with his snowy Roman head . . .
The scene could not have been more imperial or more civilised.'[3] *More
imperial or more civilised*: Fitzgerald was commenting on the ruthless effi-
ciency of the American war machine and the military elegance of his
compatriots on an outpost in the Pacific even as he spoke about Virgil's
ability to make his readers think deeply about empire and civilisation in
their own times. Fagles and Fitzgerald belong to a lengthy tradition that
connects the *Aeneid* to a contemporary imperial milieu.

In my essay, I reflect on uses and readings of Virgil in British imperial
contexts, namely in the eighteenth and nineteenth centuries. British
interest in Virgil acquired a particular resonance in the middle of the
eighteenth century, around the time when Britain began to acquire its
Second Empire. In the age of Elizabeth I and Shakespeare, Virgil had
been deployed to great effect by writers in a variety of imperial situations.
In the mid-eighteenth century, writers such as Edward Gibbon turned to
Virgil not to promote monarchical imperialism but to evaluate the workings of empire, to question its durability, and to explore its limits and contradictions. These issues needed to be worked out not just in connection
with the emergent British nation or the American colonies, but also in the
light of the mercantile imperialism of the East India Company. Much
later, in Victoria's reign, when the empire in India seemed to many Britons
to be long-lasting, several prominent figures, Tennyson among them,
highlighted the prophetic and providential interpretations of Virgil and
speculated about an empire that was divinely ordained and had no limit.
What follows is an attempt to trace these themes from Gibbon to the
Victorians and to describe the intersecting patterns and relationships that
connect the reception of Virgil and the history of empire.[4]

---

[3] *The Aeneid: Virgil* (New York, 1990), p. 414. Fitzgerald's experience can be compared to that
of Noel Currer-Briggs, a Bletchley Park operative who was on duty at an old Foreign Legion fort
at Constantine in eastern Algeria: 'Fort Sid M'Cid was built in true Beau Geste tradition on top
of a hill above the astonishing gorge which bisects the city of Constantine. It may have looked
romantic, but it was the filthiest dump imaginable . . . I also recall, with more pleasure, reading
Virgil on the battlements. Hardly typical of military life but in the true tradition of BP [i.e.
Bletchley Park]' (quoted in Michael Smith, *Station X: The Codebreakers of Bletchley Park*
(London, 1998), p. 106). I am grateful to Llewelyn Morgan for this reference.

[4] For reasons of space, this essay does not consider responses to Virgil from sources outside
Britain and, therefore, omits figures such as Michael Madhusudan Datta, in India, or T. J.
Haarhoff, in South Africa, among others. On the former, see the forthcoming work of Alexander
Riddiford; and on the latter, see Grant Parker, 'Heraclitus on the Highveld: The Universalism
(Ancient and Modern) of T. J. Haarhoff', in S. Stephens and P. Vasunia (eds), *Classics and
National Cultures* (Oxford, forthcoming).

I

'No critic after 1715', Daniel L. Selden has reminded us recently, 'seriously questions Homer's precedence and Vergil's relative inferiority',[5] and indeed the writings of such men as Joseph Addison, Alexander Pope, and Samuel Johnson effectively confirmed this hierarchy for contemporaries and generations of subsequent readers. In Britain, the reasons for the eighteenth century's objections to Virgil were political no less than literary, as scholars have argued, and were connected to the poet's alleged relationship with Augustus. Just as the early seventeenth century celebrated the poet's royalist associations and the close connection between court and letters, the early eighteenth century was already witness to writers' anxieties about Augustus' gory rise to power, destruction of the republic, and tyrannical rule. These later writers pointed out that Augustus' usurpation was not a model, and they emphasised the ruthless ambition that propelled him to the highest position after a series of bloody wars. More importantly, Augustus was regarded by numerous Britons as the destroyer of republican liberty and virtue, and critics of royalism found little to praise in the Augustan restoration or in the poets who appeared to champion his regime. It is true that both Virgil and Augustus had their defenders in the eighteenth century, but, equally, a significant number of published authors were critical of the ruler and were troubled by what they perceived as Virgil's support for him. By 1764, for example, John (Estimate) Brown wrote of Virgil that 'the *strongest Lights, and highest Colourings* of his Pencil are prostituted to the *Vanity* of the *ruling Tyrant*', and, in 1785, John Pinkerton chastised him for placing 'superstitious offerings on the altar of slavery'.[6]

Edward Gibbon is a remarkable exception to this 'historical perspective, and emotional commitment', as Tony Harrison puts it, 'which brings Virgil into odium along with a now tyrannical emperor'.[7] The largely disdainful attitude he adopts toward Octavian's rise does not translate into disavowal of Virgil; ingeniously, Gibbon finds the poet to be still a

---

[5] Daniel L. Selden, 'Vergil and the Satanic Cogito', *Literary Imagination*, 8 (2006), pp. 345–85, at p. 347.

[6] Quoted in Howard D. Weinbrot, *Augustus Caesar in 'Augustan' England: The Decline of a Classical Norm* (Princeton, NJ, 1978), pp. 127, 128.

[7] T. W. Harrison, 'English Virgil: The *Aeneid* in the XVIII Century', *Philologica Pragensia*, 10 (1967), pp. 1–11 and 80–91, at p. 4.

republican at heart and ready 'to punish as well as to resist a tyrant'.[8] Virgil's appeal to writers such as Gibbon requires further attention and is rendered intelligible within certain conceptions of empire. Gibbon's letters indicate that he often agreed with those who denied rights to the American colonies, and that, as he stated in a letter of 1775, 'having supported the British I must destroy the Roman Empire'.[9] But, as Gibbon knew and implied in his letters, developments in India compensated for the loss of the American colonies. He owned bonds in the East India Company, and several of his letters are concerned with his finances and the affect of those bonds on his personal income. In 1783 he remarked that the vices of the Company 'were manifold and manifest' and that 'an Empire with thirty millions of Subjects was not to be lost for trifles'.[10]

In his *Essay on the Study of Literature* (1761), which was first published in French, Gibbon discusses Virgil at length and admires 'the art and address of the poet'.[11] He writes, 'I constantly draw my examples from Virgil.'[12] The association with Augustus should not provoke censure, he argues in the *Essay*, and readers of the *Georgics* would appreciate that Virgil's poetry helped turn his restless veterans from violent unrest to 'a quiet life'.[13] Here the Tacitean interpretation that was to leave so deep an impress on chapter 3 of the *Decline and Fall of the Roman Empire* comes to the surface, for Gibbon speaks of Augustus as a 'sanguinary tyrant' who 'soon made those republicans forget they had ever been free', but the ruthless pragmatism of the ruler was not to obscure Virgil's skill at verse and his handling of a great theme.[14] Nevertheless, Gibbon's point in the *Essay* is less about Virgil's service to the political restoration achieved by Augustus, as we shall see, and more about a truly historical understanding of the poet's relationship to the ruler.

'The history of empires is that of the miseries of humankind', Gibbon writes in his *Essay on the Study of Literature*; 'the history of the sciences

[8] Edward Gibbon, *Critical Observations on the Sixth Book of the Aeneid* (London, 1770), in Patricia B. Craddock (ed.), *The English Essays of Edward Gibbon* (Oxford, 1972); also quoted in Harrison 'English Virgil', p. 6.

[9] Letter to J. B. Holroyd (15/5/75), in J. E. Norton (ed.), *The Letters of Edward Gibbon*, 3 vols (London, 1956), no. 303.

[10] Letter to Lord Sheffield (20/12/83), in *Letters of Edward Gibbon*, no. 609.

[11] Edward Gibbon, *An Essay on the Study of Literature* (London, 1764), p. 32; references to the *Essai* are to this English edition.

[12] Ibid., pp. 35–6.

[13] Ibid., p. 45.

[14] Ibid., p. 155.

is that of their splendour and happiness'.[15] As the *Essay* progresses, it blurs the distinction between those two histories, and makes a case for reading literature in its political, social, and philosophical contexts, thereby implying that the history of the sciences and the arts cannot be understood outside of wider frameworks:

> It is impossible to comprehend the design, the art, the circumstantial beauties of Virgil, without a perfect knowledge of the history, the government, and the religion of the Romans; of the geography of ancient Italy; the character of Augustus; and of that particular and singular relation he bore to the Senate and the people. Nothing could be more striking, or interesting to this people, than the contrast between Rome, with its three thousand citizens living in hovels thatched with straw, and the same Rome the metropolis of the universe, whose houses were palaces, whose citizens Princes, and whose provinces were extensive empires. As Florus has remarked this contrast, it is not to be thought Virgil was regardless of it. He has struck it off in a most masterly manner.[16]

In other words, the history of the arts and sciences is inseparable from the history of empires, and to understand the one, it is necessary also to understand the other. The reader who takes from Virgil's poetry a deracinated sense of beauty and structure, Gibbon argues, is gaining only a partial appreciation of the verse and missing its connectedness to the world. As J. G. A. Pocock has written:

> The words *histoire* and *historien* recur in its text; but more importantly, the study of literature becomes more and more a matter of anchoring texts in their historical contexts, as we should say; the contexts of past states of society and culture, recovered by philosophy and erudition, the exercise of the imagination and the judgment. Without this texts can barely be understood; with its aid their understanding is enriched, and the mind knows itself better in its capacity so to understand them . . . It was necessary to situate oneself in the world of Virgil and Augustus—*se donner les yeux des anciens*—in order to understand how the *Aeneid* and the *Georgics* had been written, heard or read by inhabitants of that world.[17]

Significantly, Gibbon is calling on his audience to contextualise or historicise its readings of Virgil and to see that his poetry gains in meaning and resonance through such work. Virgil's poetry reflected the circumstances of its composition, when thatched huts and palaces, citizens and

[15] Ibid., p. 1.
[16] Ibid., pp. 30–1.
[17] J. G. A. Pocock, *Barbarism and Religion*, Vol. 1: *The Enlightenments of Edward Gibbon, 1737–1764* (Cambridge, 1999), p. 238; see also pp. 222–4.

princes, metropolis and provinces, connected with each other within the frame of the empire.

But Gibbon sets out as well here a further invitation to his audience, that it read Gibbon's own work within its contexts and grasp his own intent and programme. Given that invitation, it seems legitimate to look, proleptically, at the history of the Roman Empire that appeared in the decade after the *Essay*.[18] To think of the *Decline and Fall* in these terms, however, and to read it within the world of the late eighteenth century is immediately to locate it within contemporary imperial contexts; it is to understand the contrasting elements that constitute the multi-ethnic, multiracial, sea-borne British Empire. If, by paying considerable attention to those parts of the empire that lie beyond Rome and Italy, the *Decline and Fall* suggests that the future of the empire is determined, in part at least, by its provinces, then the implication of Gibbon's work must be that the future of the British Empire, too, lies in its colonies and that the Empire's longevity, or collapse, turns on the way in which Britain manages its relationship with its overseas possessions. Nevertheless, there is a second possibility that the youthful Gibbon comprehends from Virgil as well, and it lies in the contrasts between hovels and palaces that the poet grasped through his own genius. For Gibbon, this interplay between the two Romes, between the most low and the most high, had several interpretive possibilities—there was the possibility that they were dependent on each other, and even, or especially, that the one Rome might become the other. Jupiter had prophesied in book 1 of the *Aeneid* that he set no limits in space or time for the Romans and that he gave them empire without end; but one lesson that Virgil himself offered was that Rome, the metropolis of the universe, could turn into the city of 3,000 citizens living in hovels thatched with straw. Without making any explicit comparison, Gibbon implies that the possibility of decline and fall hovers over the British Empire and that Britain, too, might some day find itself bereft of its imperial possessions.

Gibbon returned to Virgil not just in his journals but also in his *Critical Observations on the Sixth Book of the Aeneid* (1770), his first

---

[18] Pocock, *Barbarism and Religion*, vol. 1, pp. 272–4, offers an evocative reading of Gibbon's journal for December 1763 in which he shows how Gibbon was already formulating a historical conception of the *Decline and Fall* by that date. Gibbon's observations of 1763 turn on a contrast between the Rome of Virgil's era and that of Claudius Rutilius Namatianus, by which time Alaric and the Goths had sacked the city. See *The Miscellaneous Works of Edward Gibbon Esq. With Memoirs of His Life and Writings, Composed by Himself: Illustrated from His Letters, with Occasional Notes and Narrative*, 5 vols, ed. John Sheffield (London, 1814), vol. 5, pp. 436–8.

English publication, and a vehement repudiation of William Warburton's argument in *The Divine Legation of Moses* that Aeneas' visit to the underworld was an allegory for the hero's initiation into the Eleusinian mysteries. The details of Gibbon's refutation of the religious perspective taken by Warburton need not detain us here. Significantly, the portrait of Augustus that Gibbon offers in the *Critical Observations* diverges somewhat from the shape it will assume in the *Decline and Fall*, and the author commends the ruler for his 'prudence and felicity' and for his 'cautious Policy' in war.[19] Thus, Virgil was right to support such a ruler, and, in any case, he showed by the story of Mezentius in book 8 of the *Aeneid* that he was no friend of tyrants. Virgil was a closet Republican, and even if 'the Republic was subverted . . . the minds of the Romans were still Republican'.[20] Virgil was not a sycophant and naive admirer of Augustus: 'he was too judicious to compliment the Emperor, at the expence of good sense and probability'.[21] Nevertheless, Gibbon seems less interested in delivering a eulogy for Virgil than in making the case for a historical evaluation of politics and religion, an evaluation that remains sensitive to the social context and alive to the connections that tie the poet of the *Aeneid* to the fabric of the world around him.

As Gibbon flies rapidly over several disconnected points in his effort to denounce Warburton's theories, moreover, he regards Virgil's poem as being consistent with the values of the legendary society in which it was set. The epic was about a hero who could found an empire at a time far removed from first-century Rome, and it did not make Aeneas anachronistically follow the same code of honour as would have applied to Augustus. The *Aeneid* was even more important than the story of the discovery of the new world or Columbus who sailed to the Americas 'with three sloops and ninety sailors', for it told of 'a virtuous Prince saved from the ruins of his country, and conducting his faithful followers through unknown seas and through hostile lands'. More importantly, and perhaps uniquely, Aeneas 'had conducted to the Banks of the Tyber a Colony from which Rome claimed her origin'.[22] But this is not to say that

---

[19] I refer to the text in Craddock (ed.), *English Essays of Edward Gibbon*, pp. 131–62, at p. 157.
[20] Ibid., p. 139; cf. *Encyclopaedia Britannica*, 2nd edn (1778–83), vol. 10, p. 8723: 'But the monarchical form of government must naturally displease the Romans; and therefore Virgil, like a good courtier, seems to have laid the plan of his poem to reconcile them to it. He takes advantage of their religious turn, and of some old prophecies that must have been very flattering to the Roman people, as promising them the empire of the whole world.'
[21] Gibbon, in Craddock (ed.), *English Essays*, p. 143.
[22] Ibid., p. 138.

Aeneas was a 'lawgiver' or the inventor of a system of politics.[23] Aeneas was a hero of justice, piety, and valour, and the poem judged his actions according to the spirit of his times.[24] And while it was true that the *Aeneid* told about 'the establishment of an empire', Virgil ended his story at the moment that the hero's difficulties were over, and he felt no compulsion to wax poetic about 'the sober arts of peace' or the institution of laws and government since these were formalised only at a later date and were irrelevant to Virgil's theme.[25]

Not long after Gibbon began to publish the first volumes of the *Decline and Fall*, Edmund Burke also made a turn to Virgil in an imperial context, namely during the trial of Warren Hastings. Hastings, who was the first governor-general of Bengal, had served for two long periods in India and had returned to England each time with a substantial fortune (he squandered the first). Although he was received well in England after he returned for the second time, his enemies pursued him relentlessly on charges of murder and extortion, and he was impeached in parliament by the Board of Control in 1786. The trial was a sensation, and lasted from 1788 until 1795, when Hastings was acquitted despite the vehemence and oratorical brilliance of Burke, who was the leading prosecutor. Gibbon wrote in his *Memoir*, 'It is not my province to absolve or condemn the Governor of India', at which point the memoir's editor remarks that Gibbon departed from Burke, with whom he concurred about the dangers of the French revolution, in considering 'the *persecution* of that highly respectable person to have arisen from party views'.[26] Nevertheless, we are reminded about the overlapping imperial milieus in which Gibbon and Burke were operating by the presence of the former at the impeachment proceedings, and by the fact that he was a contemporary of Hastings at Westminster. In his book on the Hastings trial and other 'scandals' of empire, Nicholas B. Dirks suggests that Gibbon's *Decline and Fall* served as a model for such contemporary accounts of British overseas activities as the *History and Management of the East India Company* (1779), by

---

[23] Gibbon, in Craddock (ed.), *English Essays*, pp. 141–2.

[24] Ibid., pp. 138–40.

[25] Ibid., p. 142.

[26] Edward Gibbon, *Memoirs of My Life and Writings, Illustrated from His Letters, with Occasional Notes and Narrative, by the Right Honourable John, Lord Sheffield*, bicentenary edn, eds A. O. J. Cockshut and Stephen Constantine (Keele, 1994), p. 207. The revolution did little to revive Virgil's fortunes in imperial Britain, though it did prompt a reappraisal of Roman republicanism and its potential for anarchic excess; see Harrison, 'English Virgil', p. 10.

James Macpherson, who was renowned and vilified as the source of Ossian by the time he came to be involved with India.[27]

Like Gibbon, Burke also used Virgil to caution against untrammelled empire, but where Gibbon largely restricted his published comments to the Roman Empire, and only indirectly evoked the British Empire, Burke addressed the issue of contemporary empire very directly. He used the occasion to warn his audience about the violent corruption of the East India Company, and claimed to be acting zealously for the principle of justice, the people of India, and the honour of Great Britain.[28] There was a sense during the proceedings that Britain's very mode of being an imperial power was on trial. Burke was saying to his contemporaries that greed, exploitation, and the disregard of British law would surely bring about the dissolution of empire. On this point, he would have been in agreement with Gibbon, and he might well have said that the behaviour of Hastings in India was a symptom of the kind of factors that lead to an empire's decline and fall.

Burke's admiration of Virgil went back to his university days in Dublin, when he preferred Virgil to Homer, and Plutarch to all other writers. His partiality to Virgil moved Burke to compose a translation of the last sections of book 2 of the *Georgics*, and his writings, from the essays on the sublime to the political tracts and speeches, are replete with allusions and references to the Latin text as well as to Dryden's translation. One editor of his collected works was so embarrassed by this judgement that he found it necessary to defend the young Burke's estimation and wrote that Burke 'was at least true to the tastes and habitudes of his own mind'.[29] Burke's admiration of Plutarch was part of his interest in the philosophy of human nature, the editor wrote, and if he preferred Virgil to Homer, 'can we wonder at it in a mind so highly distinguished by its elegance, possessed of a taste so polished, and so exquisitely alive to the more refined beauties of composition?'[30] If the editor's emphasis on aesthetics is interesting, it is also typical of much contemporary criticism, which sought to deflect attention away from what was presumed to be the poet's political sympathies to his artistic skill and to his command of a language redolent of the sublime and the melancholy.

---

[27] Nicholas B. Dirks, *The Scandal of Empire: India and the Creation of Imperial Britain* (Cambridge, MA, 2006), p. 264.

[28] Edmund Burke, *The Works of the Right Honourable Edmund Burke*, new edn (London, 1822), vol. 14, pp. 89–90.

[29] *Works of the Right Hon. Edmund Burke* (London, 1834), vol. 1, p. iv.

[30] Ibid.

In Burke's case, however, Virgil figures not just in the essay on the sublime but also in his more spectacular performances at Hastings's trial on the charge of high crimes and misdemeanours. The speech on 30 May 1794 compares Hastings to Turnus, who, in book 12 of the *Aeneid*, desperately tries to escape from death at the hands of Aeneas:

> Thank God, my Lords, men that are greatly guilty never are wise men, that they do not know how to order their defence in such a way that, when they attempt to escape in one way they, like the Ghosts mentioned in the tragedy of Virgil, when they attempt to fly out at [one evasion], his contradiction stops him. If he attempts to escape at one door, there a criminal allegation of one kind stops him. If he attempts to escape at another, the facts and allegation for another wicked purpose stare him in the face.[31]

If the hapless Turnus is unable to avoid being killed by Aeneas, as the last lines of the *Aeneid* suggest, then so must Hastings be unable to flee from the many charges and accusations that are piled up against him. The ancient author had already figured in the impeachment proceedings, for earlier Burke had directed his audience to another part of the *Aeneid* when he described the behaviour of Hastings on a visit to the village of Murshidabad:

> We upon our feasts light up this whole capital city; we in our feasts invite all the world to partake them. Mr. Hastings feasts in the dark; Mr. Hastings feasts alone; Mr. Hastings feasts like a wild beast; he growls in the corner over the dying and the dead, like the tigers of that country, who drag their prey into the jungles. Nobody knows of it, till he is brought into judgment for the flock he has destroyed. His is the entertainment of Tantalus; it is an entertainment from which the sun hid his light.[32]

As Philip Ayres says, Hastings's 'natural habitat is the Virgilian underworld . . . The imagery is from the sixth book of the *Aeneid*, the phrasing and rhythms from the Gothic novel.'[33]

Burke's use of Virgil is part of a broader Roman frame that he often invokes in his speeches against Hastings. Thus, Virgil is not the only ancient author to be quoted by Burke during the trial, nor is he among the most frequently mentioned names. On several occasions, Burke

---

[31] *The Writings and Speeches of Edmund Burke*, Vol. 7: *India: The Hastings Trial, 1789–1794*, ed. P. J. Marshall (Oxford, 2000), pp. 307–8. The words 'one evasion' are supplied by earlier editions. For the Virgilian reference, see *Aeneid* 12.913–14; for another Virgilian reference in the same speech, see *Writings and Speeches of Edmund Burke*, vol. 7, p. 302.

[32] Burke, *Works of the Right Honourable Edmund Burke*, new edn, vol. 14, p. 41.

[33] Philip J. Ayres, *Classical Culture and the Idea of Rome in Eighteenth-century England* (Cambridge, 1997), pp. 43–4.

implied that he himself was Cicero and that Hastings was Verres, the pro-praetor of Sicily who was brought to trial in 70 BCE, and, in fact, the comparisons between Cicero and Burke were made not just by the latter in his speeches but also by contemporary observers of the trial.[34] But the identification that Burke was also attempting to foster in his audiences was between the British Empire in India and Rome of the first century BCE. Roman conceptions of virtue, liberty, and law were models to be defended and upheld by the British as they sought to extend and maintain their own empire. The wealth and corruption of the east were to be feared and avoided, for their certain consequences were the decay of Britain and the demise of its imperial power. That power had already taken a beating with the loss of the American colonies in the 1770s, and now appeared to be at risk again thanks to the rapacious behaviour of the East India Company and its colonial administrators. In such a scenario, Burke remarked, in 1786, what was needed was 'the mode adopted by Rome as to the Government of the distant provinces, so long as a spark of patriotism and public virtue remained in her bosom'.[35] Montesquieu, who died in 1755, had already seen that Rome's greatness was 'the product of military and civic *virtù*' and its decline the result of 'the corruption of *virtù* under the burdens of the empire it had won'.[36] Burke, too, was clear that the merchants and soldiers of the East India Company would precipitate the decay of republican liberties if their power was allowed to remain unchecked and their excesses not called to account.[37]

The acquisition of the Indian Empire was not just about a struggle between the 'force of money', on the one hand, and the 'preservation of our manners—of our virtues', on the other.[38] In his thinking about the growth of the East India Company, Burke was troubled by the way in which it was combining political and mercantile powers and blurring the distinction between sovereign and merchant. In other countries, he claimed at the opening of impeachment, on 15 February 1788, 'a political body that acts as a Commonwealth is first settled, and trade follows

---

[34] See H. V. Canter, 'The Impeachments of Verres and Hastings: Cicero and Burke', *Classical Journal*, 9 (1914), pp. 199–211; G. Carnall, 'Burke as Modern Cicero', in *The Impeachment of Warren Hastings: Papers from a Bicentenary Commemoration*, eds G. Carnall and C. Nicholson (Edinburgh, 1989), pp. 76–90; and *The Writings and Speeches of Edmund Burke*, Vol. 6: *India: The Launching of the Hastings Impeachment, 1786–1788*, ed. P. J. Marshall (Oxford, 1991), p. 29.
[35] *Writings and Speeches of Edmund Burke*, vol. 6, p. 105.
[36] Pocock, *Barbarism and Religion*, vol. 1, p. 88.
[37] See e. g. *Works of the Right Honourable Edmund Burke*, new edn, vol. 14, p. 277, and *Writings and Speeches of Edmund Burke*, vol. 6, p. 63.
[38] Quoted in *Writings and Speeches of Edmund Burke*, vol. 6, p. 34.

as a necessary consequence of the protection obtained by political power. But there the affair was reversed. The constitution of the Company began in commerce and ended in Empire.'[39] Given the superior strengths of Europeans in the arts, laws, and war, and given the weak state of governments and military discipline in Asia, the India Company was bound to turn its commercial advantages to political gain, and thus, after the Battle of Plassey, in 1757, it had become 'a great Empire carrying on subordinately (under the public authority), a great commerce. It became that thing which was supposed by the Roman Law so unsuitable, the same power was a Trader, the same power was a Lord.'[40] This was a highly anomalous situation, and it illustrated a problem that lay at the heart of early capitalist imperialism: by its 'peculiar' nature, the British presence in India was making it difficult for contemporaries to offer cogent or coherent definitions of the nation state.[41] What was this Company that could send vast sums of money to England, rule over millions, maintain a standing army, and follow its own system of justice? On this point Burke could be both clear and obscure. 'The East India Company in India is not the British Nation', he said. 'The Company in India does not exist as a Nation. Nobody can go there that does not go in its Service. Therefore the English Nation in India is nothing but a seminary for the succession of Officers. They are a Nation of placemen. They are a Republic, a Commonwealth without a people.'[42] A seminary, a nation of placemen, a republic, a commonwealth without people—the Company had refused to follow the precedents of Roman history and Roman Law, as Burke understood them, and confounded political entities that ought to have been kept distinct; the result was an obscene and monstrous hybrid, which needed to be tamed and subjected to the norms of civil society.[43]

If ancient Rome was part of the lineage of empire for Gibbon and Burke, Virgil and his *Aeneid* lay at the very heart of this genealogy. But, then as now, not all readers saw that the epic offered a straightforward affirmation of empire, and several remarked on the ambiguities and contradictions that, in their view, complicated any poetic justification for

---

[39] *Writings and Speeches of Edmund Burke*, vol. 6, p. 283.
[40] Ibid.
[41] Ibid., p. 285.
[42] Ibid.
[43] In another use of Virgil in a political scenario, Burke wrote in a letter of 1796 that the French revolutionaries and their sympathisers exceeded the harpies of Virgil in their monstrosity and that even so inventive a poet would have been unable to describe the revolting features of those modern-day beasts. See *Works of the Right Hon. Edmund Burke* (London, 1834), vol. 2, p. 262.

empire building or imperial expansion. In particular, Aeneas' desertion of Dido in Carthage posed a problem because, among other things, it suggested potential defects in the hero's character and opened up the possibility, however briefly, that he might neglect his imperial duty for the love of a woman. Norman Vance has drawn our attention to Pietro Metastasio's libretto *Dido abandonnata*, which found a wide audience and was staged with relative frequency in a number of countries in the eighteenth century and after. When performed at the court of Spain, Metastasio's opera ended not with the death of Turnus, but of Dido, which was then supplemented by a further *Licenza* where the god Neptune delivered a prophetic utterance. 'Like Virgil in the *Aeneid*, Metastasio moves beyond the immediate situation to open up a grand historical vista, setting this particular episode in the larger and rather more positive political context of international tranquillity and ultimate peace on earth, the famous *pax Romana* to be achieved by Aeneas' descendants.'[44]

It was, of course, this providential quality of Virgil's poetry that was adopted by exponents of empire in the eighteenth century and at other times. In a real sense, this feature of the Virgilian reception was opposed to Gibbon's hesitation about the permanence of empire and Burke's clarion call for imperial reform. The prophecies of the *Aeneid* and the Fourth Eclogue were often interpreted as promises of a time when the successors of Aeneas would extend their dominion over land and sea and establish *imperium* over the whole world. As far back as the Roman Empire, the emperor Constantine had claimed that Virgil had foreshadowed the advent of Christ in the Fourth Eclogue and that the virgin of the poem was none other than the Virgin Mother.[45] While that messianic understanding of Virgil never ceased to find willing followers, it was often conjoined with a universalist imperialism, and this combination of ideas was used as a justification to create on earth an empire of men and women no less than an empire of God. In the seventeenth century, for instance, among the sources on which the virginal queen Elizabeth I drew in order to promote the 'imperial theme' were the very poems of Virgil, and the Fourth Eclogue exerted a powerful appeal with its prophecy of a new golden age and the return of the virgin: 'iam redit et virgo, redeunt

---

[44] Norman Vance, 'Imperial Rome and Britain's Language of Empire, 1600–1837', *History of European Ideas*, 26 (2000), pp. 211–24, at p. 221.

[45] See Constantine, *Oratio ad sanctorum coetum*, ch. 19 (J.-P. Migne (ed.), *Patrologiae cursus completus, series graeca*, p. 20, cols 1290–1), which also refers to Virgil's use of the Sibyl and Sibylline prophecy.

Saturnia regna'.[46] Quoting that line from Virgil, Frances Yates writes, 'Those are words which have never been forgotten in the history of the West.'[47] In fact, as Yates has shown brilliantly, several authors and artists exploited Virgilian prophecy and the symbol of the virgin queen to explore or promote Tudor imperialism with its 'blend of nascent nationalism and surviving medieval universalism'.[48]

Nearly 200 years after the death of Elizabeth, and during the years of the Hastings trial, another version of Metastasio's libretto re-enacted the message of Virgilian prophecy in relation to Dido and Aeneas. By that time, Deborah Fisk and Jessica Munns claim, 'Dido's story had become a straightforward justification for the expansion of the British Empire.'[49] In the account by Fisk and Munns, earlier versions of the Dido episode, and notably the opera *Dido and Aeneas* of Purcell and Tate, which was first performed in the 1680s, questioned the benefits of empire and under-played the gravity of Aeneas' imperial duty, but the performance of *Dido, Queen of Carthage* in 1792 was 'a virtual paean to Empire'.[50] Certainly, there is much in the later opera, which was adapted by Prince Hoare and featured music by Stephen Storace 'with selections from the most cele-brated works of' other composers, that conforms to such a description, though equally striking is the work's Orientalism. After Aeneas opens the opera with a reference to heroic glory, the king Iarbas tries to steal Dido away from her lover. Iarbas' entry is accompanied by an extravagant parade of 'an ostrich led by a young slave, two soldiers, chief slave, a camel led by a slave, getulian officer, two Getulian soldiers, elephants' teeth carried by slaves, two soldiers, chief of the band, Lond drum, two triangles, two tambours, two cymbals, a slave, an elephant conducted by a cornac riding on his neck, a Mauritanian officer', followed by Iarbas, who arrives 'under a sumptuous palanquin, carried by eight slaves'.[51]

---

[46] Virgil, *Eclogues* 4.6.

[47] Frances Yates, *Astraea: The Imperial Theme in the Sixteenth Century* (London, 1975), p. 33.

[48] Ibid., p. 87. David Armitage, 'The Elizabethan Idea of Empire', *Transactions of the Royal Historical Society*, 14 (2004), pp. 269–77, on p. 274, emphasises the importance of the First Eclogue over the Fourth to Elizabeth's imperial ideology and points to lines 'more frequently cited by contemporaries' where Virgil mentions the isolation of the Britons from the rest of the world; see *Eclogues* 1.66.

[49] Deborah Payne Fisk and Jessica Munns, '"Clamorous with War and Teeming with Empire": Purcell and Tate's Dido and Aeneas', *Eighteenth-century Life*, 26 (2002), pp. 23–44, at p. 39.

[50] Ibid., p. 39.

[51] *Dido, Queen of Carthage; An Opera. With the Masque of Neptune's Prophecy . . . [By Prince Hoare.] The music principally new, and composed by Mr. Storace; with selections from the most celebrated works of Sacchini, Salieri, Andreozzi, Giordaniello, Cimarosa, Sarti, Rompini, Schüster, and Par* (1792), p. 5.

Vance reminds us as well that the opera 'can be seen against the general background of imperial glory and the continuing success of British arms in India in 1792: the first performance was on 23rd May and on 25th February of the same year Lord Cornwallis had defeated Tippoo Sultan of Mysore and compelled him to concede half his territories'.[52] Although India is not mentioned in the opera, it is possible to imagine the figure of Tipu Sultan lurking behind the despotic Iarbas, who is repeatedly characterised as 'Afric' as well as a 'barbarian' and a 'haughty Moor'.

While the Virgilian sense of providence emerges most starkly in the 'Masque' of Neptune that concludes the opera, the imperial line that commences with Aeneas proceeds not to Rome but to England. Venus, who follows Neptune on stage, makes a declaration of the gods' interest in Aeneas and the imperial benefits that await him:

> Æneas, hail! the Gods present thee
> All the richest of their treasures,
> Lasting peace and festive pleasures—
> Joys of empire to content thee.[53]

Then Neptune returns and sings to Aeneas and his son Ascanius about the power that will be transferred to Brutus, and from him to Britain:

> Immortal kings, a godlike race,
> From thee their bright descent shall trace;
> Third from thy Sire shall Brutus rise,
> Who, far beneath yon western skies,
> Ordain'd to empire yet unknown,
> On Albion's coast shall fix his throne,
> And, crown'd with laurels, spoils, and fame,
> Shall change to Britain Albion's name.[54]

And, as the opera concludes, a chorus of sea gods and nymphs proclaims:

> Renown, thy trumpet loudly sound!
> From pole to pole proclaim around
>   Great Albion's name,
>   The theme of Fame;
> Record her glory,
> Record her glory to the wond'ring ear,
> And swell th' immortal story
> With songs of Gods, and fit for Gods to hear![55]

---

[52] Vance, 'Imperial Rome', p. 222.
[53] *Dido, Queen of Carthage*, p. 39.
[54] Ibid., p. 41.
[55] Ibid., p. 42.

The Masque's conception of empire follows the legend in which Brutus (Brut, Brute, Brutus the Trojan), a grandson of Aeneas, makes his way as an exile from Italy to the British Isles, where he establishes New Troy and changes the name of Albion to Britain. While these lines bring together the great themes of nationalism and 'sacred imperialism' in proximity to Virgilian prophecy, the opera struggled to find an audience and closed, to mixed reviews, after only five performances.[56]

The production of 1792 failed to connect with audiences for reasons that are not fully clear, but it seems that the blend of imperialism and Orientalism was not worked through by the production to the satisfaction of the English audience. According to one critic, an explanation may lie 'with the subjects of a constitutional monarchy often indifferent to or positively uneasy about expensive conquests'.[57] However, that theory does not quite square with the continued support given by many of those same subjects to the expansion of the East India Company and the acquittal of Hastings or with the lukewarm support given to Burke. A plausible explanation lies in the mismatch of form and content since the Orientalist fancy of the opera may have been realised in cardboard rather than with actual animals or elaborate props, and therefore produced spectacular disappointment among audiences. The words, too, were barely audible, according to one reviewer, and as for the style in which the opera was presented, sung 'recitative' was not favoured by English audiences in the eighteenth century, with another Eastern fantasia inspired by Metastasio, the *Artaxerxes* (first performed in 1762) of Thomas Arne, being the major exception.[58]

II

In his essay on Virgil in Victorian classical contexts, Frank M. Turner has argued that, by the end of the eighteenth century, 'several factors combined to displace Virgil in critical estimation' and that his 'reputation in

---

[56] The term 'sacred imperialism' is from Yates, *Astraea*, p. 87. On the failure of the opera, see Jane Girdham, *English Opera in Late Eighteenth-century London: Stephen Storace at Drury Lane* (Oxford, 1997), pp. 54–5, with the reviews in the *Morning Chronicle*, *Public Advertiser*, and *The Times* of 24 May 1792.

[57] Vance, 'Imperial Rome', p. 222.

[58] See Roger Fiske, 'The Operas of Stephen Storace', *Proceedings of the Royal Musical Association*, 86 (1959–60), pp. 29–44, esp. pp. 40–1. Arne, the composer of 'Rule, Britannia', was also responsible for a masque called *Dido and Aeneas* that ran for seventeen performances in the 1730s.

England suffered'.[59] We cannot enter here into all the reasons for the putative decline in the poet's status in England in the first half of the eighteenth century. Some of the reasons go back to the seventeenth century and earlier—the charge that Virgil was derivative and largely inferior to Homer, for instance, or that he was the servile court poet of Augustus, himself a despot. However, views of Virgil's unpopularity should not be taken to mean that little was written about him in the early Victorian period or that there were no translations of his works: translations of his poetry continued to be published throughout the nineteenth century at a rate that seems almost astonishing today.[60] For all the claims about the Romantics' resistance to epic, moreover, it should be recalled that William Wordsworth attempted a translation of large parts of the *Aeneid*. Nevertheless, it is true that the poet was subjected to hostile criticism in the first half of the nineteenth century by writers such as B. G. Niebuhr, who was especially condemnatory of the *Aeneid*, which he notoriously called 'a complete failure' and 'an unhappy idea from beginning to end', and who also said that Virgil's was 'a remarkable instance of a man mistaking his vocation: his real calling was lyric poetry'.[61] At any rate, Turner has suggested that a revaluation against the likes of Niebuhr was set in motion with John Conington's edition of Virgil, begun in the early 1850s, the fourth volume of Charles Merivale's history of Rome, published in 1856, and the review of Conington by H. A. J. Munro in 1859.[62] It is in

---

[59] Frank M. Turner, 'Virgil in Victorian Classical Contexts', *Contesting Cultural Authority: Essays in Victorian Intellectual Life* (Cambridge, 1993), pp. 284–321, quotations on p. 291. For the Victorian background, see also R. D. Williams, 'Changing Attitudes to Virgil: A Study in the History of Taste from Dryden to Tennyson', in D. R. Dudley (ed.), *Virgil* (London, 1969), pp. 119–38, on pp. 128–37; Norman Vance, *The Victorians and Ancient Rome* (Oxford, 1997), ch. 6; and Stephen Harrison, 'Victorianising Vergil: Some 19C Translations of the Aeneid', a paper read at the annual meeting of the Classical Association (Birmingham, 2007).

[60] See Elizabeth Nitchie, *Vergil and the English Poets* (New York, 1919), pp. 236–44. Cust, who was at Haileybury College (the training institution for civil servants of the East India Company) in the 1840s, translated parts of the *Aeneid* into Sanskrit verse; see Vance, *Victorians and Ancient Rome*, pp. 13–14.

[61] B. G. Niebuhr, *Lectures on the History of Rome, from the Earliest Times to the Fall of the Western Empire*, ed. Leonhard Schmitz, 2nd edn, with every addition derivable from Dr Isler's German edition, 3 vols (London, 1850, 1849), vol. 3, pp. 134, 137.

[62] Conington's commentary was a detailed philological study of Virgil's poetry and renewed appreciation of the poet's Latin among English readers. Munro wrote a grudging review of the first volume but lauded Conington's hard work and linguistic precision: see *Journal of Classical and Sacred Philology*, 4 (1859), pp. 267–86. Merivale, who studied at Haileybury, wrote a glowing account of Julius Caesar and a more careful appraisal of Augustus in his widely read history of the Roman Empire. His reading of the *Aeneid* is consonant with the religious and providential interpretations of the poem. See e.g. Charles Merivale, *A History of the Romans under the*

the context of this revaluation, and of sympathetic readings of Virgil from prior periods, that Tennyson's poetry should be situated.

In a study published in 1901, Andrew Lang followed what had by then become a critical commonplace and called Tennyson 'the most Virgilian' of poets.[63] Tennyson's work is heavy with allusions to Virgil as well as other Greek and Roman sources, and already by 1880 critics such as H. D. Rawnsley and John Churton Collins were comparing Tennyson to Virgil by name.[64] If there is no need to document again the many direct and indirect evocations of Virgil that appear in Tennyson's work, it would be nonetheless instructive to look briefly at some of the passages from his work that bear on empire. In this respect, the reader's task is made easier thanks to a coruscant essay by Victor Kiernan about imperialism in *Idylls of the King* and in Tennyson's other works. Kiernan draws attention to the many British wars and military expeditions that occurred in Tennyson's lifetime and in which he was sometimes implicated through family ties.[65] These foreign campaigns enhanced Britain's far-flung empire, and made it 'something tangible and vast, which could be admired from every point

---

Empire, 7 vols (London, 1850–64), vol. 4, pp. 578–9: 'But the pious sentiment of Virgil receives its highest development in the monument he has erected to the glories of his countrymen, and of their tutelary saint Augustus. The grand religious idea which breathes throughout his Æneid, is the persuasion that the Romans are the sons and successors of the Trojans, the chosen race of heaven, of divine lineage and royal pretensions, whose destinies have engaged all the care of Olympus from the beginning, till they reach at last their consummation in the blissful regeneration of the empire. It maintains the existence of Providence as the bond of the Roman commonwealth. *Yes! there are Gods*, it proclaims, and the glories of the Romans demonstrate it. Yes! there are Gods above, and the Romans are their children and their ministers upon earth, exercising in their name a delegated sovereignty, sparing those who yield, but beating down the proud. This is the mission of the race of Assaracus, to vindicate the ways of God to man, to impose upon him the yoke of an eternal peace, and bring all wars to an end for ever!'

[63] Andrew Lang, *Alfred Tennyson* (Edinburgh, 1901), p. 197; cf. Wilfred P. Mustard, 'Tennyson and Virgil', *American Journal of Philology*, 20 (1899), pp. 186–94, and Nitchie, *Vergil and the English Poets*, ch. 10.

[64] A. A. Markley, *Stateliest Measures: Tennyson and the Literature of Greece and Rome* (Toronto, 2004), p. 8.

[65] See Victor Kiernan, 'Tennyson, King Arthur, and Imperialism', in R. Samuel and G. S. Jones (eds), *Culture, Ideology and Politics: Essays for Eric Hobsbawm* (London, 1982), pp. 126–48. Kiernan lists the following wars and campaigns: 1839–42, the opium wars in China; 1840s, wars against South African Kaffirs and New Zealand Maoris and the conquest of Punjab; 1854–6, Crimean war; 1854, conquest of lower Burma; 1856–60, second China war; 1857, attack on Persia; 1857–8, Indian 'mutiny'; 1865, Governor Eyre case in Jamaica; 1866, Abyssinian expedition; 1870, repulse of Fenian expansion in Canada; 1871, Maori resistance destroyed; 1874, campaign against Ashantis in west Africa; and 1882, conquest of Egypt. On the relationship between these events and Victorian writers, see Edward W. Said, *Culture and Imperialism* (New York, 1993), pp. 105–6.

of view from commercial to moral, and was coming to be seen almost as God's final bequest to humanity, the labour of His eighth day. It had, of course, the warrant of Roman precedent, and of Virgil and Horace, whose poetry he had at his fingertips.[66] In connection with the empire, we know as well from his son's account that the Indian uprising of 1857 'stirred him to the depths' and that a 'brother of his friend [Benjamin] Jowett died in India, the second to do so, in 1858'.[67] The violent unrest in India, like the Morant Bay rebellion in Jamaica in 1865, disturbed him for the impression it gave of 'barbarism revolting against Christian civilisation, a land only narrowly prevented from "reeling back into the beast" like Arthur's Britain'.[68]

I do not suggest, and Kiernan does not suggest, that Tennyson was an imperialist poet in any simple or straightforward manner.[69] His poetry is too complex and layered to allow for such an interpretation. Kiernan himself observes that Tennyson's homage to Virgil—Lang found him never 'more Virgilian than in this unmatched panegyric'[70]—'dwells mostly on peaceful themes, common humanity' and he appears to detect empire in this short poem only at the moment where the Victorian says that Virgil's 'ocean-roll of rhythm/ sound forever of Imperial Rome':

> Roman Virgil, thou that singest
>   Ilion's lofty temples robed in fire,
> Ilion falling, Rome arising,
>   wars, and filial faith, and Dido's pyre;
>
> . . .
>
> Thou that seest Universal
>   Nature moved by Universal Mind;
> Thou majestic in thy sadness
>   at the doubtful doom of human kind;
>
> Light among the vanished ages;
>   star that gildest yet this phantom shore;
> Golden branch amid the shadows,
>   kings and realms that pass to rise no more;
>
> Now thy Forum roars no longer,
>   fallen every purple Cæsar's dome—

---

[66] Kiernan, 'Tennyson, King Arthur, and Imperialism', p. 131.

[67] Ibid., p. 136.

[68] Ibid.

[69] See also Lang's defence of the poet, in his *Alfred Tennyson*, pp. 225–8.

[70] Lang, *Alfred Tennyson*, p. 198.

> Though thine ocean-roll of rhythm
>   sound forever of Imperial Rome—
>
> Now the Rome of slaves hath perished,
>   and the Rome of freemen holds her place,
> I, from out the Northern Island
>   sundered once from all the human race,
>
> I salute thee, Mantovano,
>   I that loved thee since my day began,
> Wielder of the stateliest measure
>   ever moulded by the lips of man.[71]

While at one level a tribute to an ancient figure, the poem also thematises Tennyson and the British Empire as the heirs to Virgil and the Roman Empire. Significantly, Tennyson refers several times to the Virgilian past that has been lost, whether in relation to 'kings and realms that pass to rise no more', the 'Forum that roars no longer', the domes of the Caesars that have 'fallen', or 'the Rome of slaves' that 'hath perished'. Virgil knows that Rome, like other cities, will decay, and his foresight leads to him write poetry that is melancholy and leaves him 'majestic in . . . sadness at the doubtful doom of human kind'. Tennyson's own poetry was often melancholy and elegiac, and he, too, composed a great epic in verse, and he was seeking to associate his own name with Virgil's. Thus, the poem, which was composed at the request of the city of Mantua for the nineteenth centenary of Virgil's death, is a claim by Tennyson to the ancient poet's status and legacy; and the ambiguous syntax of the last two lines mean that not just Virgil but also Tennyson can be wielders 'of the stateliest measure/ ever moulded by the lips of man'. Moreover, just as the transfer of power etched out in these lines proceeds from Virgil to Tennyson, so also it moves from Rome to Britain, that 'Northern Island/ sundered once from all the human race'. If in the *Aeneid* there was 'Ilion falling, Rome arising', at a later stage it was the turn of the Roman Empire to be falling, and another *imperium* to be arising. In the world of this poem, that other power is the British Empire.

Where Jupiter had once prophesied in the *Aeneid* that Rome's empire would have no end in time, Tennyson suggests here that Virgil's verses will forever echo the might of imperial Rome and hence predicts no end in time for the fame of the *Aeneid* and of its subject, the Roman Empire. The infinite future that Jupiter prophesies for Rome is transferred by

---

[71] From 'To Virgil' in Christopher Ricks (ed.), *The Poems of Tennyson* (London, 1969), pp. 1312–13 (omitting stanzas 2 to 5).

Tennyson to the infinite renown of Virgil and his subject matter. In this poem, Tennyson notably does not explicitly extend the concept of endless dominion to the British Empire but reserves it for Virgil and Rome. Elsewhere, however, he broaches the theme directly. In 'To the Queen', the poem that closes *Idylls of the King*, Tennyson speaks dismissively of those who are calling for a separation of Canada from the Empire and reminds his readers of a Britain that is becoming 'wealthier—wealthier' with every hour and of 'Our ocean-empire with her boundless homes/ For ever-broadening England, and her throne/ In our vast Orient'.[72] Hardly apologetic about imperialism, 'To the Queen' was openly an oath of loyalty to Victoria (soon to be crowned empress of India), a rallying cry for British subjects everywhere, and an exhortation to Britons to overcome their fears and not succumb to '[t]he darkness of that battle in the West' where Arthur once fought.[73] A. A. Markley is scarcely exaggerating, then, when he says, 'There is no denying that as Poet Laureate, and even before his appointment to that post, Tennyson was a devoted supporter of the interests of the crown.'[74]

Markley also writes that, for Tennyson, Virgil was 'a poet of both great patriotism and great sensibility', and Vance refers to *Idylls of the King* as 'the noblest tribute of the nineteenth century to the high seriousness of the *Aeneid*'.[75] If there are many echoes of Virgil in *Idylls of the King*, as Vance has written, the passing of Arthur appears to be 'essentially Virgilian' and also hints at 'a sense of future possibility and a new day dawning'.[76] The tone and language of the poem are reminiscent of book 6 of the *Aeneid* and the messianic Fourth Eclogue:

> Then from the dawn it seemed there came, but faint
> As from beyond the limit of the world,
> Like the last echo born of a great cry,
> Sounds, as if some fair city were one voice
> Around a king returning from his wars.
>
> Thereat once more he moved about, and clomb
> Even to the highest he could climb, and saw,
> Straining his eyes beneath an arch of hand,
> Or thought he saw, the speck that bare the King,
> Down that long water opening on the deep

---

[72] Ibid., p. 1755.
[73] Ibid., p. 1756.
[74] Markley, *Stateliest Measures*, p. 8.
[75] Ibid., p. 8; Vance, *Victorians and Ancient Rome*, p. 152.
[76] Vance, *Victorians and Ancient Rome*, p. 149.

> Somewhere far off, pass on and on, and go
> From less to less and vanish into light.
> And the new sun rose bringing the new year.[77]

When Bedivere throws Excalibur into the waters, on the king's instructions, he signals the end of the Arthurian era, and we hear 'the last echo born of a great cry' that recalls the king as if he were a warrior returning home from the war. But the speck of Arthur receding into the distance is balanced by 'the new sun' that rises 'bringing the new year'. From his vantage point, Bedivere observes a beginning as well as an end, and the poem holds out the possibility 'of historical succession'.[78]

Like many Victorian contemporaries who placed much value in the concept of progress, Tennyson was trusting to the future, and specifically to the imperial future, for deliverance from the present. It was in this time to come, guided by the principles of a true English Christianity, that Tennyson found a haven from the turmoil of the present and from the crass materialism of his own people. The seeds of this prospective moment were being sown in his own time by the Knights of the Round Table, now reborn as the administrators of empire, so that 'the Residency at Lucknow stood, and would stand, like Horace's Rome', even though Arthur's world was lost forever.[79] A similar vision of coming events is also offered to Percival earlier, in the poem entitled 'The Holy Grail', after he mistakenly believes that he has found the Grail. In counterpoint to the ruined city of Camelot, Percival sees a vision of the heavenly city, 'the spiritual city and all her spires/ And gateways in a glory like one pearl'.[80] Nor is this impression of a divinely supported anticipation far removed from 'On a Mourner', written by Tennyson to mourn the early death of his friend Arthur Henry Hallam, where the poet recalls 'Faith' and 'Virtue, like a household god/ promising empire; such as those/ Once heard at dead of night to greet/ Troy's wandering prince'.[81]

Not all critics read the *Idylls* as a straightforward expression of hope for a better destiny, or at least not all found an exact correspondence with the *Aeneid* on this point. In his essay of 1876, 'Aeneas: A Vergilian Study', John Richard Green accepted that the *Aeneid* was throughout 'a song of

---

[77] *Poems of Tennyson*, p. 1754.

[78] Vance, *Victorians and Ancient Rome*, p. 150.

[79] Kiernan, 'Tennyson, King Arthur, and Imperialism', p. 145.

[80] 'The Holy Grail', ll. 524–32 in *Poems of Tennyson*, pp. 1676–7; see Vance, *Victorians and Ancient Rome*, p. 151.

[81] *Poems of Tennyson*, p. 559.

Rome' and read it as 'a song of the future rather than of the present or past, a song not of pride but of duty'.[82] Green directed his readers to the temporal situation of the hero when he remarked that 'Aeneas is the reflection of a time out of joint', by which he meant that good Romans of the Augustan era found it hard to reconcile their own sense of morality and rightness with the violent experiences of the civil wars and Octavian's rise to power.[83] No doubt because of Tennyson's success with his own poem, the author notably also compared Aeneas with Arthur, for he declared that 'Aeneas is the Arthur of the Vergilian epic'.[84] But for Green the two poems offered different dreams of the future:

> We close it [i.e. the *Aeneid*] as we close the Idylls with the King's mournful cry in our ears. But the Roman stoicism is of harder and manlier stuff than the chivalrous spiritualism of Arthur. The ideal of the old world is of nobler, sterner tone than the ideal of the new. Even with death and ruin around him, and the mystery of the world darkening his soul, man remains man and master of his fate. The suffering and woe of the individual find amends in the greatness and welfare of the race. We pity the wandering of Aeneas, but his wanderings found the city. The dream of Arthur vanishes as the dark boat dies into a dot upon the mere; the dream of Aeneas becomes Rome.[85]

In Green's interpretation, the *Aeneid* recognises that its hero's dream will be realised in due course, whereas *Idylls of the King* leaves the reader with no optimistic ending since Arthur's boat vanishes into the mist and light. Even if Green's reading leaves out important details from both poems, his analysis underlines the point that for many Victorians the *Aeneid* was clearly a providential poem in which the fate of the city was proclaimed by the gods to Aeneas.

Tennyson's inventive refashioning of Virgil in *Idylls of the King* identified two important strains in the Victorian engagement with the Latin poet: the first was religious, as signified by the quest for the Holy Grail, and the second, temporal, as signified by the last line of the 'Passing of Arthur'. Both these features of the Virgilian reception were considered by Frederic William Henry Myers, the writer and psychical researcher. As a young man in Cambridge, Myers had submitted an entry for the Camden medal in which he included lines from prize-winning Latin compositions written by others in Oxford. Although he said he was only following

---

[82] John Richard Green, 'Aeneas: A Vergilian Study', in *Stray Studies from England and Italy* (London, 1876), pp. 257–86, at pp. 260, 261.
[83] Ibid., p. 284.
[84] Ibid., p. 265.
[85] Ibid., p. 286.

Virgil's practice, and even quoted the passage in Donatus' *Life* where Virgil proclaims, 'I am collecting gold from Ennius' dung' (*aurum colligo e stercore Ennii*), he got into trouble over the copied lines and had to resign the prize.[86] However, the early scandal did not prevent him from writing what the eleventh edition of the *Encyclopaedia Britannica* would refer to as 'the most famous English essay on Virgil'.[87] This essay, which was republished in his book *Essays Classical*, joined together Virgil and Christianity, and reckoned the poet to be 'the earliest and the official exponent of the world-wide Empire of Rome, the last and the closest precursor of the world-wide commonwealth of Christ'.[88] Victorian commentators were, of course, well aware that Virgil for centuries had been connected to Christianity: they knew of his appeal to the early Church fathers and of the prophetic strains of the Fourth Eclogue, and they perceived that the poet's countrymen prepared the ground for the birth of Christ. Myers, too, noticed the religious dimensions of Virgil's work, but he argued vividly that the object of his worship was nothing other than Rome itself:

> However variously expressed or shrouded, the religion of the Romans was Rome. The destiny of the Eternal City is without doubt the conception which, throughout the long roll of human history, has come nearest to the unchangeable and the divine. It is an idea majestic enough to inspire worship, and to be the guide of life and death. This religion of Rome, in its strictest sense, has formed no trifling factor in the story of the Christian church . . . But nowhere, from Ennius to Mazzini, has this faith found such expression as in Virgil's Aeneid. All is there. There is nothing lacking of noble reminiscence, of high exhortation, of inspiring prophecy. Roman virtue is appealed to through the channel by which alone it could be reached and could be restored; it is renewed by majestic memories and stimulated by an endless hope. The Georgics had been the psalm of Italy, the Aeneid was the sacred book of the Religion of Rome.[89]

In Myers's reading, Virgil's greatness was to perceive, more clearly than his contemporaries, the destiny of Rome as the eternal city and to understand the central place it would occupy both in Christian history and Christianising interpretations of the poet. Rome was of Virgil's time and also beyond it; it was the capital city of the Roman Empire and also

---

[86] See Alan Gauld, 'Myers, Frederic William Henry (1843–1901)', in H. C. G. Matthew and Brian Harrison (eds), *Oxford Dictionary of National Biography* (Oxford, 2004), vol. 40, pp. 59–62, at p. 60.

[87] *Encyclopaedia Britannica*, 11th edn (1910–11), s.v. 'Virgil', p. 116.

[88] F. W. H. Myers, 'Virgil', in *Essays Classical* (London, 1883), pp. 106–76, at p. 146.

[89] Ibid., pp. 152–3.

the capital of the world; it was the city that Augustus found brick and turned into marble and also the city of God that would eventually come to encompass the earth. Virgil's inspired poetry allowed him to express this dual aspect of the city, and it would endow millions, in his day and afterward, with 'an endless hope' for the almost mystical realisation of the kingdom of heaven on earth. To quote Charles-Augustin Sainte-Beuve, he had 'divined at a decisive hour of the world what the future would love'.[90]

Myers's book was published in 1883, at which time promoters of empire were increasingly turning to Virgil for inspiration and support. In that same year, John Seeley compared the founders of 'Greater Britain' with Aeneas and Abraham, while, some years later, James Bryce called Virgil 'the national poet of the Empire', and Lord Cromer referred to him as 'an enthusiastic imperialist'.[91] According to the Scottish classical scholar William Young Sellar, who died in 1890, Virgil was quoted more often than any other ancient or modern poet in the English Parliament.[92] Throughout the nineteenth century, in fact, Anchises' advice to Aeneas in book 6 of the *Aeneid* had echoed in the speeches and writings of figures such as John Henry Newman, Lord John Russell, and Sir Robert Peel. In John Dryden's famous translation, which was widely quoted by Victorians, Virgil's vision was laid out in heroic couplets:

> Let others better mold the running Mass
> Of Mettals, and inform the breathing Brass;
> And soften into Flesh a Marble Face:
> Plead better at the Bar; describe the Skies,
> And when the Stars descend, and when they rise.
> But, *Rome*, 'tis thine alone, with awful sway,
> To rule Mankind, and make the World obey;
> Disposing Peace, and War, thy own Majestick Way.

[90] Quoted in *Encyclopaedia Britannica*, 'Virgil', p. 112. Sainte-Bueve's *Étude sur Virgile* (Paris, 1857), an influential study, was based on the author's proposed course of lectures at the Collège de France. However, Sainte-Beuve was so tainted by his association with Napoleon III and the revived empire that French liberals interrupted the lectures, and he never finished giving them. See Ruth E. Mulhauser, *Sainte-Beuve and Greco-Roman Antiquity* (Cleveland, OH, 1969), esp. pp. 60–6, 201–2, and Vance, *Victorians and Ancient Rome*, pp. 139–40.

[91] John Seeley, *The Expansion of England* (London, 1883), p. 135; James Bryce, 'The Roman Empire and the British Empire in India', in *Studies in History and Jurisprudence*, 2 vols (Oxford, 1901), vol. 1, p. 72—for Bryce, the comparison is between the Roman Empire, which has a national poet, and India, which lacks a 'national literature' and a Virgil who 'inspires an imperial patriotism' (p. 73, cf. Bryce, *Studies*, vol. 2, pp. 78–9); Lord Cromer, *Ancient and Modern Imperialism* (London, 1910), p. 14.

[92] See W. Y. Sellar, *The Roman Poets of the Augustan Age: Virgil*, 3rd edn (Oxford, 1897), p. 422.

> To tame the Proud, the fetter'd Slave to free;
> These are Imperial Arts, and worthy thee.[93]

'It would have been hard indeed for an Englishman in the last century to read these words', Richard Jenkyns says, 'and not think of his own country . . . to the English providence had assigned another task, to take up the splendors and burdens of empire. The British combined an arrogance about their empire and institutions with a feeling of inferiority about their powers of taste and intellect; it was naturally fascinating to them to find a Roman expressing a similar mixture of emotions.'[94]

But no less important to the late Victorian political programme was the infinitesimal frame given to the theme of imperial mission and national destiny by Jupiter when he prophesied to Venus, in book 1:

> To them, no Bounds of Empire I assign;
> Nor term of Years to their immortal Line.
> Ev'n haughty *Juno*, who, with endless Broils,
> Earth, Seas, and Heav'n, and *Jove* himself turmoils;
> At length atton'd, her friendly Pow'r shall joyn,
> To cherish and advance the *Trojan* Line.
> The subject World shall *Rome*'s Dominion own,
> And, prostrate, shall adore the Nation of the Gown.
> An Age is ripening in revolving Fate
> When *Troy* shall overturn the *Grecian* State,
> And sweet Revenge her conqu'ring Sons shall call,
> To crush the People that conspir'd her Fall.
> Then *Caesar* from the *Julian* Stock shall rise,
> Whose Empire Ocean, and whose Fame the Skies
> Alone shall bound. Whom, fraught with *Eastern* Spoils,
> Our Heav'n, the just Reward of Human Toyls,
> Securely shall repay with Rites Divine;
> And Incense shall ascend before his sacred Shrine.[95]

As if in anticipation of Edward Gibbon's history of the decline and fall, Jupiter defers into eternity the end of empire and indicates that the date of its fall lies outside of time and hence outside of history. 'With this definition of empire', Duncan F. Kennedy notes, 'an event such as the sack of Rome by Alaric in 410 CE marks not the demise of empire, but opens up the discursive opportunity to speak of Rome as a historical episode

---

[93] John Dryden, *Aeneis* 6.1168–77.
[94] Richard Jenkyns, 'Late Antiquity in English Novels of the Nineteenth Century', *Arion*, 3, 3 (1996), pp. 141–66, at p. 155.
[95] *Aeneis* 1.378–95.

within the continually and ever-receding horizon of empire'.[96] In that sense, Rome functioned as a figure of empire, and it was available to those who wished to transfer *imperium* to themselves and claimed the authority to speak for empire in their own time. Of course, *translatio imperii* was what lay at the heart of the comparison between the Roman and British empires. One point of the comparisons was that the 'authentic' imperial experience of the ancient Romans was now available to the British. But underlying the *translatio imperii* at work in Jupiter's declaration was the promise of a dominion unbounded in time and space, and it was the sense of an expanding, global empire that appealed to British imperialists.

Against the authors who thrilled to the Virgilian sense of an imperial mission extending into the future one needs to set the many Victorians who were more grudging in their praise of the Latin poet, and who were unwilling to elevate him above Homer. Most of their criticisms were not original but reworkings from a contemporary perspective of comments made by writers at earlier times. In a lecture given at Oxford, in 1857, Matthew Arnold was clear that Greek literature was 'even for modern times, a mighty agent of intellectual deliverance; even for modern times, therefore, an object of indestructible interest'.[97] Arnold found the Dido episode to be 'the most interesting portion of the Aeneid' but implied that Virgil suffered in comparison with the greatest of the Greek poets such as Aeschylus and Sophocles. While Virgil was a delicate and sensitive poet, he was also not equal to the task of explaining and describing the contemporary Roman world. 'This suffering, this graceful-minded, this finely-gifted man is the most beautiful, the most attractive figure in literary history; but he is not the adequate interpreter of the great period of Rome.'[98] Thus, Arnold resumed an old strain of Virgilian criticism, though one diametrically opposed to the point of view taken by Gibbon in his essays.

---

[96] Duncan F. Kennedy, 'A Sense of Place: Rome, History and Empire Revisited', in Catharine Edwards (ed.), *Roman Presences: Receptions of Rome in European Culture, 1789–1945* (Cambridge, 1999), pp. 19–34, at p. 26. My discussion in this paragraph is borrowed from my essay 'Greater Rome and Greater Britain', in Barbara Goff (ed.), *Classics and Colonialism* (London, 2005), pp. 38–64.

[97] Matthew Arnold, 'On the Modern Element in Literature', in Fraser Neiman (ed.), *Essays, Letters and Reviews* (Cambridge, MA, 1960), pp. 3–19, at p. 5.

[98] Arnold, 'On the Modern Element', p. 17. W. R. Johnson calls this 'the kiss of death' for Virgil, and adds, 'Nor should we take occasion to wax merry over the follies of British imperialism; it is hardly the place of an American to castigate another nation's dreams of glory': see *Darkness Visible: A Study of Vergil's 'Aeneid'* (Berkeley, CA, 1976), p. 5.

More fierce than Arnold in his criticism of Virgil was William Ewart Gladstone, the sometime prime minister, author of several works on Homer, and friend of Tennyson. Frank Turner characterises Gladstone's polemic as the 'harshest directed against any figure in the ancient world by a Victorian commentator', and even a brief consideration shows that Gladstone's critique, which occurs in his studies of Homer, is a virulent denunciation of Virgil and the *Aeneid*.[99] One of the main charges against Virgil was that he was a court poet of Augustus and therefore incapable of offering anything other than panegyric to the emperor. For Gladstone, the entire poem was a failure, and the failure sprang primarily from the faulty conception of the hero Aeneas:

> ... this crying vice of the Aeneid, the feebleness and untruth of the character of Aeneas, was due to the false position of Virgil, who was obliged to discharge his functions as a poet in subjection to his dominant obligations and liabilities as a courtly parasite of Augustus. As the entire poem, so the character of its hero, was, before all other things, an instrument for glorifying the Emperor of Rome.[100]

For Gladstone, Virgil did not draw on true sources of 'religion, patriotism, and liberty', but rather composed the most untruthful if elaborate verse for 'fear of stumbling upon anything unfit for the artificial atmosphere of the Roman court'.[101] Virgil was found wanting in almost every point of comparison with Homer by Gladstone, who indicated that much of the blame rested on the circumstances in which the Roman composed his work. Virgil lived 'among a people always matter-of-fact rather than poetical, in an age and a court where the heart and its emotions were chilled, where liberty was dead, where religion was a mockery, and the whole material of his art had passed from freshness into the sear and yellow leaf'.[102] Gladstone, who was not an enthusiastic imperialist in his political life, was uneasy at the thought of a court poet singing the praises of a royal patron and granting legitimacy to bloody conquests. In addition, he, like many other Victorians, sought to draw a distinction between the Romans and his fellow countrymen, even if he also assiduously cultivated comparisons between past and present. Both gentlemanly and capitalist in its self-definition, British imperialism was different in kind from any other, and Gladstone could not have been drawn to the image

---

[99] Turner, 'Virgil in Victorian Classical Contexts', p. 296.
[100] W. E. Gladstone, *Studies on Homer and the Homeric Age* (Oxford, 1858), vol. 3, p. 509.
[101] Ibid., p. 512.
[102] Ibid., p. 534.

of an imperial court that consisted of minstrels and flatterers who earned their keep through songs for hire. This relationship between Virgil and Augustus, so close to the kind stereotypically attributed to Oriental courts with their despots and sycophants, was contrary to the ideals of parliamentary democracy or liberal empire, and unacceptable to the reformist Gladstone on political grounds. On another level, the *Aeneid*'s conception of unbounded empire failed to impress the statesman who seldom championed imperial expansion and conquest and who publicly argued, often unsuccessfully, that further expansion diverted Britain from its most suited political and economic path.

One of those who came to Virgil's defence was the scholar T. L. Papillon, who, in the 'Introduction' to his edition of Virgil, referred to the reproaches levelled against the poet. Papillon said that the attitude of poets such as Virgil and Horace to Augustus 'was a genuine popular sentiment, the outcome of a variety of feelings—a mixture of the old Greek hero-worship, of Eastern monarchical sentiment, and of the revived national enthusiasm for the "Imperium Romanum", and the destiny of the Eternal City'.[103] Augustus was no ordinary king but the man responsible for the restoration of peace and order in Rome, the defender of the old mores and values, and the bulwark against Marcus Antonius, his Egyptian queen, and the barbarism of the East. The Roman emperor had earned the gratitude of a nation, so that poems such as the *Aeneid* and the *Georgics*, 'however repugnant to modern taste', were 'neither unnatural nor derogatory to Virgil's poetic fame'. Virgil was a 'national' poet, Papillon wrote, and his poetry expressed 'the thoughts not of a courtier, but of a nation'.[104]

It is precisely the nation and 'national sentiment' (an idea that goes back at least to Niebuhr in the early nineteenth century) that Sellar emphasised in his influential writings about Virgil, from the 1870s onward. Sellar was responsible for a series of articles on Roman poets in the ninth edition of the *Encyclopaedia Britannica*, and the substance of his article on Virgil was largely maintained into the influential eleventh edition (1910–11), where it was supplemented by T. R. Glover. Stressing the importance of line 33 from book 1, *tantae molis erat Romanam condere gentem* ('so great a task was it to found the nation of Rome'), Sellar called this the 'true keynote' of the poem and he added that the action of

---

[103] T. L. Papillon, *P. Vergili Maronis opera: Virgil with an Introduction and Notes* (Oxford, 1882), vol. 1, p. xxvii.
[104] Ibid.

the poem was based on the 'great part played by Rome in the history of the world, that part being from of old determined by divine decree, and carried out through the virtue of her sons. The idea of universal empire is thus the dominant idea of the poem.'[105] According to Sellar, this universal empire was based on characteristically national beliefs, religious observances, 'the feeling of local attachment', 'reverence for old customs and for the traditions of the past'. Feeling the need, as others did, to respond to Gladstone, Sellar conceded that the *Aeneid* was inferior to the *Iliad* and the *Odyssey*, but denied that Virgil showed 'servile adulation' of Augustus and claimed that the poet made a strong case for why Augustus was the right ruler for Rome at that moment in its history. Thus, Sellar thematised important features of the Virgilian reception in late Victorian Britain, a reception that may be said to culminate in the article written for the eleventh edition of the *Encyclopaedia Britannica*: first, Sellar rejected the notion that Virgil was the court poet of a tyrannical emperor; second, he emphasised the value of nation-building and national unity and the process that might lead from these values to universal empire; and, third, he argued that Virgil held up in Aeneas 'an ideal of pious obedience and persistent purpose—a religious ideal belonging to the ages of faith combined with the humane and self-sacrificing qualities belonging to an era of moral enlightenment'.[106] These elements of one critic's engagement with Virgil can undoubtedly be discerned at other moments in the history of Virgilian interpretation, but it is nonetheless clear that they find a particular valence in the contexts of late nineteenth-century imperial Britain.

III

Several scholars have discussed Virgil's use of past and present in relation to the question of *imperium* as it is figured in the *Aeneid*. Even at a basic level of textual analysis, the reader recognises the significance of various inset narratives, flashbacks, and predictive utterances that Virgil deploys throughout the poem. Perhaps the most widely discussed of these are the prophetic passages that move forwards from the present-time of the narrative into a future-time when Rome is established as a city. Such passages, in which an extraordinary or supernatural force prophesies the

---

[105] *Encyclopaedia Britannica*, 'Virgil', p. 114.
[106] Ibid., p. 115.

future history of the city, include Jupiter's speech to Venus in book 1, Anchises' remarks to Aeneas in book 6, and the shield forged by Vulcan in book 8. While characters such as Aeneas are mostly incapable of seeing fully into the years ahead, the gods have a foresight that allows them to recognise the significance of present actions and to predict their consequences into a distant time to come. Since Jupiter predicts empire without end in space and time for the descendants of Aeneas, as Kennedy says, '[i]t is the explicit representation in the person of Jupiter within the narrative of the view "forwards" . . . that has made the *Aeneid* the paradigm of teleological narrative. The association of the view "forwards" with the god Jupiter makes the view, in the fullest sense of the term, providential.'[107] In this sense, history is already known to the divinity, but may be disclosed to select human agents when they have the capacity for such understanding.

If readers in Virgil's own day took Augustan Rome as the end point of that providential narrative, readers after Augustus have deferred into the future the *telos* of this 'suprapersonal, providential order of history'.[108] Christian readers took it to refer to the establishment of the empire of God on earth, while others have interpreted it in terms of various monarchies or kingdoms at particular times and places. Few British readers explicitly identified the Virgilian *imperium* as the empire of their own time, but the authors whom we have considered here illustrate how their conceptions of the empire foreshadowed in Virgil's verse could be rendered consistent with an understanding of the British Empire. 'Virgil is rarely deployed explicitly by Victorian translators to justify the Empire', writes Colin Burrow, 'since such an appropriation would weaken their repeated claims to fidelity, but the vocabulary with which they describe the act of translation shows that they regard the conquest of Virgil as the ultimate display of Anglo-Saxon strength.'[109] It was not just Virgil who was liable to be conquered, and there are two points that I would underline in connection with this issue. First, there is the actual expansion of the British Empire that went into high speed in the late Victorian period and reached one significant point in the early twentieth century when the Empire covered almost a quarter of the earth's surface. This late

---

[107] Duncan F. Kennedy, 'Modern Receptions and Their Interpretive Implications', in Charles Martindale (ed.), *The Cambridge Companion to Virgil* (Cambridge, 1997), pp. 38–55, at p. 47.
[108] Ibid.
[109] Colin Burrow, 'Virgil in English Translation', in Martindale, *Cambridge Companion to Virgil*, pp. 21–37, at p. 34.

Victorian imperialism is also connected to changing attitudes towards imperialism: whereas Britons might earlier have viewed the term 'emperor' with suspicion and ascribed it to political regimes in France or Germany, after the 1870s, Britain, too, would have its empress and the concept of imperialism would shed some of its negative connotations. At this time, one also discerns a rehabilitation of Augustus and of his reputation as an efficient administrator, a rehabilitation related to political developments in Britain and overseas and facilitated by sympathetic histories of Rome such as those written by Merivale.

Second, there is the conception of imperial 'trusteeship'. According to this idea, which goes back to Burke in 1783, Britain was entrusted with the rule of its colonies and was, in theory, only ruling other peoples and places as a trustee since the native rulers were incapable of ruling their own lands and were therefore 'guilty of a dereliction of the highest moral trust which can devolve upon a nation'.[110] Thomas Macaulay and John Stuart Mill both claimed to welcome the day when India would be free and self-governed; since that time had not yet arrived, however, they sanctioned British rule as the best possible governance for the region. While this policy brought several improvements to the colonies, in practice it deferred self-rule into a distant future. No Victorian in the middle of the nineteenth century expected that the colonies would be independent at any foreseeable point, despite what a Macaulay or a Mill might say in public. In this sense, trusteeship was the ostensible antitype to the idea of an *imperium* without end, but in reality both visions held out the promise of an empire on which the sun would never set.

Even when the empire's demise came to seem an imminent reality, the providential meaning of Virgil's poetry continued to find sympathetic readers. In his presidential address delivered to the Virgil Society in 1944, the year before Fitzgerald in the Pacific found himself glued to the poet's 'descriptions of desperate battle, funeral pyres, failed hopes of truce or peace', T. S. Eliot overcame his early reluctance about Virgil, whom he once called 'a sychophantic [*sic*] supporter of a middle-class imperialist dynasty', and placed him squarely 'at the centre of European civilisation'. For Eliot, who was born in 1888, Europe had a special relationship with the Roman Empire and with Latin, and, especially at a time when Europe appeared to be forgetting its debt to the civilised past, 'the poet in whom

[110] Ronald Hyam, 'Bureaucracy and "Trusteeship" in the Colonial Empire', in J. M. Brown and W. Roger Louis (eds), *The Oxford History of the British Empire*, Vol. 4: *The Twentieth Century* (Oxford, 1999), pp. 255–79, quotation by Mill on p. 265.

that Empire and that language came to consciousness and expression [was] . . . a poet of unique destiny'.[111] Not all contemporary poets agreed with Eliot, however. One of the sharpest English-language criticisms of Virgil's conception of empire came from W. H. Auden, in the 1950s, a decade after Eliot's address. In 'Secondary Epic', a post-war sensibility, suspicious of claims made in the name of empire, nation, and people, emphatically rejects the political affectations of Virgil's epic from its very first line:

> No, Virgil, no:
> Not even the first of the Romans can learn
> His Roman history in the future tense,
> Not even to serve your political turn;
> Hindsight as foresight makes no sense. . . .
>
> Cooked up in haste for the drunken enjoyment
> Of some blond princeling whom loot had inclined
> To believe that Providence had assigned
> To blonds the task of improving mankind.[112]

Auden expresses his dismay ('the weeping of a Muse betrayed') at the version of history offered by the epic, and refers in his poem to places and peoples that he thinks Virgil fails to emphasise: the hostile Germans, the Goths, and 'plundered Greece', for instance. Tellingly, he covers not just moments of Roman history that he feels Virgil has brushed aside too conveniently, but also those critical episodes that have occurred after the death of Virgil. Just as Virgil looks forward into Roman history after the age of Aeneas, so Auden casts forward to events that take place after the death of Virgil. In a concluding twist, Auden turns the far-sighted anticipation of the epic on its head and, in lines corrosive and ironic ('Surely, no prophet could afford to miss/ No man of destiny fail to enjoy/ So clear a proof of Providence as this'), mentions the 'Catholic boy/ whom Arian Odovacer will depose'. Readers of Edward Gibbon will recall that it was Odovacer who dethroned a young ruler and, by that action, 'extinguished the Roman Empire in Italy and the West'.[113]

---

[111] Fitzgerald, *The Aeneid: Virgil*, p. 414; Eliot's reluctance, in Theodore Zielkowski, *Virgil and the Moderns* (Princeton, NJ, 1993), p. 124 (quoting from *Criterion*, January 1933); and T. S. Eliot, 'What Is a Classic?' in *On Poetry and Poets* (New York, 1957), pp. 52–74, at pp. 70–1. See also Eliot's essay 'Virgil and the Christian world', pp. 135–48.
[112] From W. H. Auden, 'Secondary Epic', in *Collected Shorter Poems, 1927–1957* (London, 1966), pp. 296–7, at p. 296.
[113] In 'Antiquities of the House of Brunswick', *English Essays*, p. 460; Gibbon placed the date 476 here in his text. See also *The Decline and Fall of the Roman Empire*, ch. 36.

Note. Earlier versions of this essay were presented at Cape Town, Liverpool, and London. I am grateful to the audience on each occasion for constructive criticism. I am indebted to Richard Alston, Stephen Harrison, Tom Harrison, and Llewelyn Morgan for help and advice; to Miriam Leonard for her valuable comments on a draft; and to Duncan Kelly for the invitation to contribute to this volume.

5

Edmund Burke and Empire

IAIN HAMPSHER-MONK

THIS ESSAY, LIKE THE MOST CELEBRATED imperial provinces, is divided into three parts. The first sketches the background to the concept of empire as it was available to Burke and his contemporaries. The second focuses on the way in which the emergence of political economy affected thinking about empire, and in particular the tension, highlighted recently by Istvan Hont, between political reason of state, and what were increasingly claimed by some to be the imperatives of the international trading system. The final part assesses Burke's position within this controversial nexus.[1]

I

Empire is an ambivalent substantive. As a term, it hovers between designating a particular (absolute) quality of rule, and calling to attention the diversity of the peoples and territories over which that rule is exercised. Those of us who grew up in schoolrooms with world maps, large parts of which were coloured pink, might naturally think of it in terms of the latter. Yet for much of its life the word tended to designate the rule, and only by consequence that over which it would be exercised; its history paralleling (and complexly intertwined with) that of the 'state' which possessed a similar ambivalence between the state or sway of the prince— and the impersonal apparatus through which it increasingly came to be exercised—and the latter's geographical reach.[2]

---

[1] Istvan Hont, *Jealousy of Trade* (Harvard, MA, 2006), 'Introduction', *passim*.
[2] Quentin Skinner 'The State', in Terence Ball, James Farr, and Russell Hanson (eds), *Political Innovation and Conceptual Change* (Cambridge, 1989). The nineteenth-century political scientist Seeley called attention to the 'imperial' characteristics of most modern states, and David Armitage remarked on the 'relationship between state-formation and Empire-building that historians have yet to investigate comprehensively'. See J. R. Seeley *The Expansion of England*

Proceedings of the British Academy **155**, 117–136. © The British Academy 2009.

Edmund Burke was involved with three British empires in the pink sense. The so-called first British Empire, lost in the American War of Independence, and the second, which was emerging in India during his lifetime. But he was also concerned with aspects of that half-hidden *internal* empire accumulated by the English Crown over the Welsh, the Irish, and the Scots. Like his contemporaries he wrestled with the problem of how to describe the political relationship between parts and whole, centre, and periphery, and with the dynamic between the economic and moral properties of empire, and its prospects for survival.

Imperium is the name given to the rule of the highest Roman magistrates, supposedly collected together at the downfall of the Republic under the *lex regia* and exercised by the *Princeps*, on behalf of the people.[3] It becomes identified with the emperor himself, in whom was concentrated, according to the Roman Jurists who influenced late medieval and Renaissance thought, the authorities to legislate, command, and judge. *Imperium* was not incompatible with inferior jurisdictions— such as those exercised by city magistrates within the Empire—or an individual citizen's rights, including property rights. But because of its associations with the post-republican period no less than its juridical preeminence, it was equivocally related to liberty. It is, at least in the sense of its unrestricted character, modern sovereignty.[4]

This quality of rule is not unrelated to the diversity of that which is ruled. For in any entity larger than a city, and in the absence of the unified, functionally integrated state of modernity, *imperium* was almost always exercised over internally differentiated political communities. These could be separate realms with different juridical regimes happening to share a single monarch, as in the case of the complex and composite monarchies of Spain, and of England and Scotland between 1603 and 1707. Or they could be subordinate jurisdictions within a single or combined monarchy, as in the case of England itself, which was an internal mosaic of sovereignties, of Ireland, Wales, the Isle of Man and the

---

(London, 1883), *passim*, and the discussion in David Armitage, *The Ideological Origins of the British Empire* (Cambridge, 2000), pp. 19–20.

[3] 'Quod principi placuit, legis habet vigorem: utpote cum lege regia, quae de imperio eius lata est, populus ei et in eum omne suum imperium et potestatem conferat'; see *Digest of Justinian*, ed. T. Mommsen and P. Kruger, trans. and ed. A. Watson, 4 vols (Philadelphia, PA, 1985), vol. 1, 1. 4. 1.

[4] John Procope, 'Greek and Roman Political Theory', in J. H. Burns (ed.), *The Cambridge History of Medieval Political Thought* (Cambridge, 1997), pp. 30–1, and the implications in the later middle ages, discussed by J. P. Canning, 'Law, Sovereignty and Corporation Theory, 1300–1450', ibid., pp. 454 ff.

Channel Islands, and Scotland after the Act of Union.[5] What became the British Crown was therefore, like almost all early modern European dynastic states, a composite one.[6] Like many of them, and even before it acquired transoceanic colonies, it was *aboriginally* an empire in the sense of being a single domain, within which internal jurisdictions were differently related to the centre.[7]

This was a conception of empire with which Burke entirely concurred. 'My idea of an Empire', he claimed in his speech on conciliation 'is that an Empire is the aggregation of many states under one common head whether this head be a monarch or a presiding republick.' The 'subordinate parts' may, and probably should, 'have many local privileges and immunities' and the political problem of imperial rule consisted precisely of finding the 'extremely nice' correct balance between them.[8] To rule an empire required conforming government to the 'character and circumstances of the several people who compose this mighty and strangely diversified mass'; he added that he was never 'wild enough to conceive that one method would serve for the whole ... that the natives of *Hindostan* and those of *Virginia* could be ordered in the same manner'.[9] Burke also happily applied the term 'Empire' indifferently to the constituent parts of the United Kingdom and to its overseas territories. Writing of the phlegmatic quality of the English he notes how it contrasts with 'our neighbours on the continent', but goes on: 'It even appears remarkable among the several tribes which compose the great mass of the British Empire. The heat of the Welch, the impetuosity of the Irish, the Acrimony of the Scots, and the headlong violence of the Creoleans, are national temperaments very different from that of the native genuine English.'[10]

---

[5] J. G. A. Pocock has pioneered this conception of the political identity of the British Isles: see the essays now collected in J. G. A. Pocock *The Discovery of Islands: Essays in British History* (Cambridge, 2005), esp. part 3, 'Empire and Rebellion in the First Age of Union'.

[6] H. G. Koenigsberger, 'Composite States, Representative Institutions and the American Revolution', *Historical Research*, 62, 148 (June 1989), pp. 135–53.

[7] The *OED* lists this as the fifth meaning, but with the earliest of all recorded usages: '5. an extensive territory (*esp.* an aggregate of many separate units under the sway of a supreme ruler; also an aggregate of subject territories ruled over by a sovereign state.' Its first use is dated to 1297.

[8] Edmund Burke, 'Speech on Conciliation', in *The Writings and Speeches of Edmund Burke*, Vol. 3: *Party, Parliament, and the American War, 1774–1780*, ed. W. M. Elofson and J. A. Woods (Oxford, 1996), p. 132. This edition hereafter cited as *W&S*.

[9] Edmund Burke, 'Letter to the Sheriffs of Bristol', *W&S*, vol. 3, p. 316.

[10] 'Mnemon to the *Public Advertiser*', *W&S*, Vol. 2: *Party, Parliament and the American Crisis, 1766–1774*, ed. P. Langford (Oxford, 1981), p. 76.

It is these two features of empire—its pre-eminence and its hetero-
geneity—that were picked out by Firth in possibly the first modern scholarly paper on the concept of empire.[11] It was, according to Firth, Henry
VIII who, in rejecting papal authority, first claimed that 'this realm of
England was an Empire'. And in glossing the contemporary meaning of
empire he gave (wittingly or not, but without acknowledgement) almost
word for word Bartolus' classic definition of a free state: 'a country of
which the sovereign owes no allegiance to any foreign superior'.[12] Firth
claimed that it was in the pamphlet literature around the union of the
crowns that the term empire came to be used of the dual monarchy.
Whatever authorities and jurisdictions existed under the joint monarch—
as he or she continued to be until 1707—it was his or her empire which
bound them together. So originally empire came to be used within the
British Isles to designate the nature of the rule holding together the
diverse parts of the whole, *and so also* the collection of communities so
ruled.

At least in part because that collection of communities comprised an
archipelago, the exercise of sovereignty over its many parts came to presuppose, or at least to seem to require, *imperium* over the seas in which
they were set, as David Armitage has made clear. The most extravagant
version of this claim was also one of the earliest—that made by John
Dee, who asserted, in Latin, Elizabeth's *imperium* over all the islands of
the north Atlantic, and, in English, her 'sea jurisdiction' over the ocean
for 100 miles around the English coast, western Scotland, and 'a mighty
portion of the Ocean between Scotland and North America'.[13] In his time
Dee's claim was not only extravagant (it included Iceland and
Greenland), but also eccentric (even without the Arthurian pedigree he
claimed for it), and contrary to the general British policy (advanced
against the Spanish) of a blue water claim to the freedom of the seas, a
version of *mare liberum*. But James's accession brought with it the preferred Scottish strategy of claiming *mare clausum* in adjacent waters.
When John Selden came to refute Hugo Grotius' *Mare liberum* with his

---

[11] C. H. Firth 'The British Empire', *Scottish Historical Review*, 15, 59 (April, 1918), pp. 185–9;
see too Walter Ullmann, 'This Realm of England is an Empire', *Journal of Ecclesiastical History*,
30 (1979), pp. 175–203.

[12] Firth, 'British Empire', p. 185. Bartolus' claim is that 'Civitates tamen quae principem non
recognoscunt in dominum et sic equum pupulus liber est' in such a situation 'civitas sibi princeps
est'. This is glossed by Canning, 'Law and Corporation Theory', in *Cambridge History of
Medieval Political Thought*, p. 471.

[13] John Dee, 'Brytanici imperii limites' (22 July 1576) cited in Armitage, *Ideological Origins*, p. 106.

Mare clausum in 1618, he did so in part by reiterating Dee's claim that the Ancient Britons had enjoyed lordship over the 'northern sea' so that 'the sea and the land comprised the single body of the British Empire' and that in subsequent history 'empire of the waters always followed dominion of the island'.[14] A claim of empire over the adjacent seas—on Selden's authority—played a part in deciding the case of Ship Money in favour of the Crown,[15] and was to become increasingly common from the Commonwealth on. That accommodating publicist Marchamont Nedham, hired to translate Selden's work, dedicated it to the first true emperor of the seas and archipelago of the British Isles, the (awkwardly republican) Oliver Cromwell.

In the eighteenth century this situation was complicated in two dimensions. First, the increasing identification of sovereignty as the King-in-Parliament made it more difficult to articulate the relation of the parts to the whole via a freestanding Monarch as opposed to an already internally complex 'Crown'. The *persona* of the Monarch in relation to his parliament was certainly different in England, Scotland, Ireland, and Wales (which had none). Second, with the growing importance of communities of transatlantic Englishmen—and indeed Welsh, Irish, and Scots—the issue of the kind of rule through which the various parts were to be connected became a notorious point of controversy. How then was empire within the British kingdoms (wherever this was located in relation to the archipelagic realms) related to its *imperium* over its overseas colonies?

One further issue should be noted. John Pocock has rightly pressed the point that the assertion of *imperium* in Henry's Act in Restraint of Appeals was made not against another secular ruler but against the pope.[16] And, if we accept this as the original of British *imperium*, then it was as much an ecclesiastical as a political claim. The logic of this argument, which was borne out in the wars of the three kingdoms as we must learn to call the English Civil War, is that English, and eventually British sovereignty as it emerges from the turmoil of the seventeenth century is of the King in Parliament with an established (though tolerant) church. American colonies dislocated this logic in not one but two important ways. The separation of the monarch from parliament has already been

---

[14] John Selden, *Mare clausum seu de dominio maris* (London, 1635), ss 12, 14, 29, cited in Armitage, *Ideological Origins*, p. 113.
[15] See Armitage, *Ideological Origins*, p. 116; see too Mónica Brito Vieira, '*Mare liberum* vs. *Mare clausum*: Grotius, Freitas, and Selden's Debate on Dominion over the Seas', *Journal of the History of Ideas*, 64, 3 (2003), pp. 361–77.
[16] Pocock, *Discovery of Islands*, pp. 136–8.

canvassed. But the other dimension derived from this ecclesiastical *imperium* exercised by the monarch. There was no established imperial church in America—even episcopalian Virginia's bishops were not royally appointed. Collectively America was congregational. The structure of British *imperium* there—as in Ireland—was doubly fractured.

If, as most earlier writers suggested, the Empire comprised the realm of the newly united monarchy of England and Scotland and the decidedly lower-status province of Ireland, then the transatlantic settlements could be thought of as ruled in a kind of eminent domain as subordinate imperial possessions; a transatlantic conception of empire. On the other hand, if all of the parts related equally and similarly to the whole, a pan-Atlantic conception of empire became possible in which the British Empire simply was all the peoples and settlements linked through language, allegiance, and descent—but mostly through commerce—to Britain. These different conceptions of empire carried important ideological freight. It is only in the eighteenth century that empire comes to be commonly and specifically used of the territories held by the Crown *beyond* the British archipelago, nor is it generally so used until the middle of that century. Although the distinction between empire as *rule* and empire as *territory* is perhaps not always as clear as one might like, there is no doubt that the issue becomes highly politicised. Again, as Armitage shows, the emergence of this concept of empire was driven by the ideological needs of those deploying it. He writes:

> The concept of the British Empire as a congeries of Territories linked by their commerce, united with common interests and centred politically on London was . . . the product above all of a group of colonial administrators, merchants and politicians, for whom an appeal to a common interest with Britain was a necessary strategy to encourage equal treatment for their compatriots whether under the terms of the Navigation Acts or the Constitutional framework of the United Kindom. Their concept of the British Empire, projected from the provinces back to a metropolitan audience, was both the expression of their own interest and the means to develop a coincident appreciate of a common interest among their British audiences.[17]

The famous claim by Thomas Pownall, returned loyalist governor of Massachusetts articulates the pan-Atlantic in explicit opposition to the transatlantic. Great Britain, he claimed, was no more a kingdom with many 'appendages of provinces, colonies, settlements and other extraneous parts'. It was instead to be considered as:

---

[17] Armitage, *Ideological Origins*, pp. 181–2.

... a grand marine dominion consisting of our possessions in the Atlantic
and in America united into a one empire in a one centre, where the seat of
government is.[18]

Pownall was of course not just arguing about definition. Committed as he
was to maintaining the links between America and Britain, redefining the
Empire as the whole rather than as the British archipelago with external
possessions was a classical rhetorical move with political intent. It was
designed to make dismemberment more difficult.

However, the very diversity, noted by Burke, not only of the peoples
but of the institutional links within the Empire made the argument for
imperial homogeneity a difficult one to sustain. Moreover the character
of one of the commonest institutional vehicles of British expansion –the
chartered trading company—posed problems of its own. Commercial
companies may possess property, and even exert dominion, but neither
form of rule comprised *imperium*, even if, as we shall see, the relationship
between *imperium* and property was to pose difficulties for theorising the
relationship between the metropolis and the province. This chartered
status (as trading companies or corporations) seemed to link them
directly to the king—as granter of the charter—rather than to the British
sovereign: the King in Parliament—a fact that some sought to exploit in
appealing to him against Parliament's taxation of them. This further
seemed to imply that their local assemblies stood in the same relation to
the king as the local assembly of Britain (the Westminster Parliament)
did.[19] Granville Sharp pointedly reminded his readers (with Ireland as
much as America in mind) that 'the making laws for the subjects of
any part of the British Empire, *without their participation and assent*, is
INIQUITOUS, and therefore *unlawful*'. [20] The question of whether liberty
was consistent with the local metropolitan legislature exercising sovereignty over the provincial ones (and whether empire was consistent with
its not doing so) was the heart of the matter and would continue to
exercise commentators for another 100 years and more.[21] But there was a

---

[18] Thomas Pownall, *The Administration of the Colonies* (London, 1764), p. 9, cited in Peter N.
Miller, *Defining the Common Good: Empire, Religion and Philosophy in Eighteenth-century
Britain* (Cambridge, 2004), p. 211.

[19] See Richard Koebner, *Empire* (Cambridge, 1961) pp. 206 ff.

[20] Granville Sharp, *A Declaration of the People's Natural Right to a Share in the Legislature;
which is a Fundamental Principle of the British Constitution of State* (1775), pp. 11–12.

[21] The conceptual difficulties encountered in the late nineteenth century are canvassed in D. Bell,
'The Victorian Idea of a Global State', in D. Bell (ed.), *Victorian Visions of Global Order*
(Cambridge, 2007), pp. 159–85, and they recur in an inverse kind of way in the vexed 'East
Lothian Question'.

more radical claim to be made, and those who wished to resist imperial demands, Jefferson among them, stated it clearly. It was an argument that 'America was conquered and her settlements made and firmly established at the expense of individuals, and not of the British public'. That colonisation was undertaken by natural individuals and not by, or even under, the Crown, presupposed a very different relationship with the country of origin, one that 'cannot give a title to that authority which the British Parliament would arrogate over [them]' (for the colonies had their own) but related only through a decision to 'submit to the same common sovereign, who was thereby made the central link connecting the several parts of the empire thus newly multiplied'.[22]

II

The idea of trade has already been introduced and from there it is but a step to the commercial empire, but before focusing on that, the overwhelmingly important set of economic reverberations of empire in the early modern mind must be sketched.

Empire, in the sense of extent of territories, was notoriously both the reward of the successful polity and the seeds of its downfall. The competitive state environment of early modern Europe mirrored that endured in Italy and the Mediterranean by classical Rome, the paradigmatic status of which in early moderns' understanding of the dynamics of political success, growth, corruption, and downfall is attested by the number and fame of works claiming to analyse that process, from Machiavelli right through to Montesquieu, Hume, Smith, and Gibbon in Burke's own time. The topos of decline and fall had already acquired a massive presence (and literature) even before Gibbon's culminating effort.[23] Correlatively, the topos of survival required military effectiveness. Military success entailed expansion. Imperial expansion led with varying degrees of inexorability, to luxury, moral and political corruption, loss of *virtú* in the metropolis, susceptibility to military coups, and consequent decline. Implicit for modern monarchies subscribing to this analysis no less than for republics was the loss of liberty. The political economy of early

---

[22] Thomas Jefferson, *A Summary View of the Rights of British America* (Williamsburg, 1774), repr. in *Jefferson, Political Writings*, ed. Edward Dumbald (Indianapolis, IN, 1955), pp 17–18.
[23] For an exhaustive reconstruction of this particular topos, see J. G. A. Pocock, *Barbarism and Religion*, Vol. 3: *The First Decline and Fall* (Cambridge, 2003).

modernity was built on a recognition of the ultimately self-defeating character of ancient, extensive empire based on territorial expansion, its subsequent pillage, and the importation of treasure and precious metals— a truth currently being illustrated by the relative decline of Spain. But awareness of this classic trajectory and the aspiration to evade it did not of itself guarantee success in doing so. One of the paths from which political economy emerges in the eighteenth century is trying to puzzle through a dynamic by which classic decline and fall could be evaded. Commerce was increasingly thought to be the key to the answer. In particular the *commercial empire*, it was claimed, simply did not generate the baneful properties of terrestrial expansion. Once worries about the intrinsic evils of luxury were assuaged, trade provided a means to wealth and, via the monetary sinews of war, a means to military security that avoided the pursuit of wealth through conquest. *Maritime empire* possessed even further advantages, removing residual worries about the threat that standing professional armies posed to liberty. Standing navies, unlike standing armies, could not be used to coerce citizens. If the promise of commerce could be realised, wrote John Oldmixon at the dawn of the eighteenth century, 'the Arguments brought from Antiquity will be of no use to the Enemies of Colonies'.[24]

Burke's writings on empire demonstrate a rich familiarity with the conceptual field just sketched, and his policies in relation to empire operate under the kind of constraints and assumptions implied by it. Even, perhaps in some less familiar places. The internal politics of Great Britain, he insisted, were entangled in, and endangered by, institutional features consequent on the fact of its possessing an internal imperial character.

In his speech introducing a 'Bill for Economical Reform' he pointed out how much of the cost of the Crown's administration was consequent on its emergence from what was originally the royal household, and the fact that that household was replicated in the different domains that made up the diverse and composite monarchy under which Great Britain was now governed. Superficially England *looked* like a unitary monarchy, but in fact the status of the monarch changed as he moved around the country:

> Cross a brook and you lose the King of England; but you have some comfort in coming again on his majesty, now no more than the Prince of Wales. Go to the North and you find him dwindled to a Duke of Lancaster; turn to the West

---

[24] John Oldmixon, *The British Empire in America*, 2 vols (London, 1708), vol. 1, pp. xxxv–xxxvi, cited in Armitage, *Ideological Origins*, p. 175.

... and he pops upon you in the humble character of Earl of Chester. Travel a few miles on and the Earl of Chester disappears; and the king surprises you again as the Count Palatien of Lancaster. If you travel beyond Mt Edgcombe you find him once more in his incognito and he is the Duke of Cornwall ... every one of these principalities has the apparatus of a Kingdom.[25]

Burke's proposal for abolishing the replication of oeconomies (in the sense of royal households with all their offices) was not, of course, simply a matter of economising. The fundamental issue, though perhaps not the mechanism, would have been familiar to any follower of the classical neo-Harringtonian aetiology of empire, namely the undermining of liberty through executive control of imperial revenue or patronage. With the possible exception of Cornwall, all these offices 'exist solely for the purpose of multiplying offices and extending [the] influence' of the Crown, the reduction of which was, of course, Burke's object.

But these issues were not entirely political and constitutional, as Burke himself signalled in his vain attempt to save British America by claiming Britain's declaratory sovereignty whilst yielding, in practice and on consequentialist considerations, the rights that would have followed from America's claims to independence and sovereignty. Indeed, these consequentialist considerations drew increasingly on debates about the supposed properties of national and international political economy, as Istvan Hont has suggested. Within such debates the notion of empire plays an important if muted role. Although Burke plays only a very minor role in the analysis given in *Jealousy of Trade*, the rest of this essay aims to locate him within this discussion.

One way of characterising Hont's claim that jealousy of trade comprised a continuing topos amongst early modern publicists is to say that it raised the question of the relative primacy of the political and the economic in state policy-making. As these two topoi became disentagled in analysts' minds and the relative autonomy of the economic asserted, political economy could re-enter policy-making with imperatives of its own. This raised, but did not settle, the question of whether economics could be subordinated to political ends, without ultimately disastrous political consequences.

A political economy perspective for example, illuminated the fact that a burgeoning internal economy tended to raise domestic wage rates. This perhaps need not worry smaller trading states such as Venice and Genoa whose economies were based on the specialist carrying trade. But no great

---

[25] Edmund Burke, 'Speech on the Economical Reform', *W&S*, vol. 3, pp. 497–8.

state—with the noted exception of the Dutch—had yet based its economy purely on trade; and in agricultural or manufacturing economies, where wages were a major component of prices, wealthier producer-states, perhaps still aiming at universal land monarchy within Europe, would tend to become uncompetitive in the international market. This had suggested to the French under Colbert a policy of a protected internal free market, combined with a militaristic suppression of competitors as tactics leading to universal empire. This would render tractable the problem of terms-of-trade imbalance produced through growth by dislocating the internal from the international market. Whilst critics with a neo-Machiavellian moralistic bias such as Fénélon attacked this policy on traditional grounds (it undermined *virtú* and destabilised the political order), another view (that of St Pierre) suggested abolishing the military dimension altogether and seeking a European confederation united by trade but eschewing dominion—at least over each other.

If Colbert had gone wrong, suggested others including Montesquieu, it was not in seeing the problem in terms of political economy, it was in thinking that political ends could be achieved by subordinating the economy to the independently construed demands of realpolitik. The way for modern European states to subsist was to reject the confused mix of monarchical and republican principles, and with them the itch for empire, and to pursue simply the development of trade, which would make them all both wealthy and peaceable, resolving any tension between economy and politics. Montesquieu even insinuated an economic version of the rhetoric and dynamic of the Machiavellian causal chain by which harsh *necessità* led to *virtú* and *virtú* to glory in the rise of great empires. The political economy parallel that Montesquieu pointed to was the rise of great commercial entrepôts such as Marseilles which, being founded in an inhospitable marsh, exposed its inhabitants to the necessity of improvising a trading way of life as the only means of survival; this was a kind of commercial *virtú*.[26] On this view, trade and luxury, from being a cause of the downfall of states could be seen as the motor, both of their own growth, and of peaceful co-existence. And, moreover, this could come about piecemeal, without the need for utopian confederation or authoritative enforcement.

But *le commerce* was not necessarily *doux*. Given unequal terms of trade, national interest, or even survival, might require trade wars, and

---

[26] Montesquieu, *The Spirit of the Laws*, ed. A. Cohler et al. (Cambridge, 1989), bk 20, chs 4–5, pp. 340–1.

trade itself could be made an instrument of state aggrandisement. A sufficiently well placed nation 'could choose to hinder the economic growth of its direct competitors whilst assisting the development of those countries that presented no threat to its commerce'.[27]

It was into this nexus of argument that Adam Smith inserted his discussion of trade and the wealth of nations. Smith insisted that the subordination of economic thinking to political interest was ultimately mistaken. It was in the (economic and political) interests of all nations to live amongst and trade with wealthy neighbours. For those nations that beggared their neighbours in military (or indeed economic) war would ultimately only be undercut by their low costs of production in time of peace.

III

So how do we locate Burke in relation to this Smithian argument about commercial empire?[28] Despite the famous and persistent claim (based on a hearsay report by Bisset in his early life of Burke)[29] that Smith had told Burke that 'he was the only man, who, without communication, thought on [political economy] exactly as he did', the truth—at least in terms of the political economy of empire—turns out to be rather different. Burke, it is true, shared a presumptive commitment to Smith's belief in the local operation of the market as benign, and the desirability of allowing prices to move in line with demand as the best way both to clear markets and elicit sufficient supplies of at least agricultural commodities.[30] However, when it came to the political economy of empire Burke was considerably more cautious than Smith in allowing policy to be driven by what was, after all, on its way to becoming an abstract speculative theory.[31] Neither

---

[27] Hont, *Jealousy of Trade*, p. 32, glossing Jean-Francois Melon, *Political Essay upon Commerce* [1735], trans. Dublin, 1739.

[28] This section draws on Donald Winch, *Riches and Poverty* (Cambridge, 1996), pp. 137 ff.

[29] Robert Bisset, *Life of Edmund Burke* (London, 1800).

[30] Those who wish to recruit Burke as a principled economic libertarian are forced to generalise from his very specific argument about grain stocks made in *Thoughts and Details on Scarcity*, and choose to ignore his strictures on the irresponsibility of 'moneyed men', the destructive effects of market-driven economic changes, and a free market in credit in *Reflections on the Revolution in France*.

[31] Burke seems to address Smith's argument against allowing merchants to control markets in his 'Speech on Fox's East India Bill': 'I do not presume to condemn those who argue *a priori* against the propriety of leaving such extensive political powers in the hands of a company of merchants.

in the case of America nor in the case of India did Burke follow the implications—specifically drawn by Smith in both cases—of the new commercial political economy, that is to say of resisting the temptation to subordinate commerce to imperial political control.

In the case of America, Smith ultimately saw two possibilities: separation, or a consolidated ('pan-Atlantic') imperial union in which the centre might well, he thought, move to America. It was, of course, precisely between these two alternatives that Burke chose to steer a path. Burke not only argued for the retention of the Navigation Acts, by which England controlled trade into and out of the American colonies, but he did so on the distinctly un-Smithian and very Burkean grounds of custom, and with a political rather than an economic rationale: 'Be content to bind America by laws of trade: you have always done it. Let this be your reason for binding their trade. Do not Burthen them with taxes; you were not used to do so from the beginning. Let this be your reason for not taxing.'[32] Moreover he argued that this self-denying ordinance ('abandoning the practice of taxation') was perfectly compatible with the Declaratory Act, which asserted ultimate British authority over the colonies. Thus, 'I look . . . on the imperial rights of Great Britain, and the privileges which the Colonists ought to enjoy under these rights, to be just the most reconcilable things in the world.' Parliament related to its extensive empire, he claimed, in 'two capacities: one as the local legislature of this island [Great Britain—Ireland possessing its own] . . . the other, and nobler capacity is what I call her *imperial character*; in which, as from the throne of heaven, she superintends all of the several inferior legislatures, and guides, and controls them all, without annihilating any. . . . She is never to intrude into the place of the others, whilst they are equal to the common ends of their institution. But in order to enable parliament to answer all the ends of provident and beneficent superintendence, her powers must be boundless.'[33] Parliament, for Burke, in its second persona, here performed the role hitherto ascribed to the *princeps* or monarch in accounts of empire, binding together, but not destroying or usurping, the

---

I know much is, and much more may be said against such a system. But, with my particular ideas and sentiments I cannot go that way to work. I feel an insuperable reluctance in giving my hand to destroy any established institution of government, upon a theory, however plausible it may be.' See Edmund Burke, *W&S*, Vol. 5: *India: Madras and Bengal, 1774–1785*, ed. P. J. Marshall (Oxford, 1981), pp. 386–7.

[32] Edmund Burke, 'Speech on American Taxation', *W&S*, vol. 2, p. 458.

[33] Ibid., pp. 459–60.

competences of the subordinate legislative (tax-raising) and administrative entities.

In Smith's view, however, although Britain's colonial policy was preferable to that of other European nations and indeed gave her a comparative advantage, in comparison with a free trade policy, 'Britain derived nothing but loss from the dominion she assumes over her colonies.'[34] The artificial trading monopoly enjoyed by merchants distorted their economic decision-making and directed investment into the Atlantic trade, 'from which the returns [were] slow and distant' compared with others, with resulting opportunity costs to other possible investments.[35] And, whilst the trade monopoly increases the total revenue to the UK and, arguably, the tax returns of the exchequer, the benefits of monopoly flow to 'one particular order of men'[36](merchants) who cannot be differentially taxed, and this constitutes a relative loss to the rest of the population who would otherwise enjoy cheaper prices. The case for a monopolistic trading regime was, in modern terms, an act of rent-seeking by the merchant class. Finally, the cost of securing the sea routes and guaranteeing the integrity of the colonies falls on the metropolitan centre: only if the benefit of holding the colonies outweighed these costs (which Smith denied) was commercial empire at all an economically sensible proposition.[37]

Here is the nub of Smith's argument (which he conceded was, for reasons of national pride, unlikely to be implemented)[38] for either imperial integration or dissolution. Smith thought that imposing taxation on the American colonies (*or* Ireland) was, in principle, 'not contrary to justice', but it could be effected only if there were an integrated imperial parliament (which he was by no means the first to suggest).[39] But if that was not to be, empire should be given up and the costs born equally but separately by each freely trading nation.[40]

---

[34] Adam Smith, *An Inquiry into the Nature and Causes of the Wealth of Nations* (1776), ed. R. H. Campbell and A. Skinner (Indianapolis, IN, 1976), bk 4, vii, c. 65, p. 616, summarising the result of his discussion from p. 591 onwards.

[35] Ibid., vii, c. 55, p. 610.

[36] Ibid., vii, c. 61, p. 613.

[37] Ibid., vii, c. 66–7, pp. 617 f.

[38] Ibid., vii, c. 66, pp. 616 f: 'To propose [such a move] . . . Would be to propose such a measure as never was, and never will be adopted, by any nation in the world.' Such measures, he thought, 'though they might frequently be agreeable to the interests, are always mortifying to the price of every nation, . . . and . . . always contrary to the private interests of the governing part of it'.

[39] See citation of [Hugh Chamberlen], *The Great Advantage to both Kingdoms . . .* (London, 1702) and other references in Armitage, *Ideological Origins*, p. 162.

[40] Smith, *Wealth of Nations*, book 4, vii, a. pp. 556 ff; bk 4, vii, c. pp. 593 f.

The positions of Smith and Burke on the political economy of empire each possessed internal consistency but they were mutually contradictory. Burke presupposed the existence of a continued imperial link based on custom and shared culture but considered imperial representation at Westminster impractical. He did hint that other constitution structures were available, such as the status of the marcher counties palatine, and suggested that responsibility for taxation to defray the costs of imperial protection could ordinarily pass to the colonial assemblies.[41] The earls (and, in Durham's case, the bishop) of counties palatine—Chester, Durham, and Lancaster—had, because of their marcher status, enjoyed greater jurisdictional independence, and did not return members to Parliament. Blackstone defined them as possessing '*jura regalia* as fully as the king hath in his palace', and as a result 'All writs and indictments ran in their names as in other counties the king's; and all offences were said to be done against their peace, and not as in other places, *contra pacem domini regi*'.[42] Burke probably knew from his researches into the history of the colonies that the Maryland Charter specifically mentioned the Durham palatinate as the model for the authorities originally granted to 'the baron of Baltimore'.[43] Palatinate independence (of any degree) was jurisdictional, not fiscal—and it's not clear that Burke's allusion presses that closely on the case.[44]

Be that as it may, the right to tax, he thought, whilst asserted, should not be used. His reference to the 'Laws of trade' that bound the colonies to Britain was surely to the existing mercantile regulations, not to the more abstract conclusions of political economy appealed to by Smith, which suggested, on the contrary, trading relations *un*-hampered by political, legislative interference. For Smith, conversely, if empire were to be

---

[41] Edmund Burke, 'Speech on Conciliation with America', 22 March 1775, in *W&S*, vol. 3, pp. 146–52.

[42] Sir William Blackstone, *Commentaries on the Laws of England*, 1st edn (Oxford, 1765–9), bk 1, Introduction, s. 4, p. 114. Blackstone is citing Coke and Selden, and this was hardly the situation that obtained in the eighteenth century. As well as this, modern historians (to whose insights of course Burke was not privy) contest even the original status of the palatinates. See James W. Alexander, 'New Evidence on the Palatinate of Chester', *English Historical Review*, 85, 337 (October 1970), pp. 715–29.

[43] Tim Thornton, 'The Palatinate of Durham and the Maryland Charter', *American Journal of Legal History*, 45, 3 (2001), pp. 235–55.

[44] Given that the Durham palatinate was exercised by the bishop, it is tempting to suggest that Burke may, in suggesting the palatinate as a model, have had in mind the re-integration of the confessional element of imperial sovereignty originally claimed by Henry in his break with Rome, and so signally lacking in the northern American colonies, but this, I think, would be a mistake.

maintained, then imposing taxes to defray its costs was the least that
should be done, but he also accepted that the implication of this was true
political integration, and if that was denied (or thought impossible), then
dissolution was the logical outcome. In the case of the American colonies,
Burke thus departs significantly both from Smith's policies and the
grounds for advancing them.

The comforting argument that a trading empire evaded classical worries was even more imperilled in the case of India. The acquisition of
India again contravened the logic of Smith's argument that economic
considerations should not give way to misleading perceptions of political
interest. A free trade in carrying, it could be argued, indeed required no
more than ships, avoiding the temptations of terrestrial empire. But a
monopoly trade such as Burke supported required, at the very least, trading stations to collect and disperse the goods and from which to enforce
the monopoly. From such stations expansion, either directly or by proxy
through local rulers, had proved irresistible. Britain began as one of a
number of competing foreign trading powers in India, which included,
Burke insisted, the Moslems. The situation replicated that of Rome,
whose success in outwitting, coercing, or absorbing her competitors led
irresistibly to the acquisition of empire. It was not a process Burke had
endorsed, nor was he more than acquiescent in the result. The Indian
Empire was a trust, delivered 'by an incomprehensible dispensation of
Divine providence into our hands'.[45] For later, nineteenth-century inheri-
tors of empire this providential status inspired confidence in their rule,
but Burke quaked. He confessed himself 'not . . . very favourable to the
idea of our attempting to govern India at all. But there we are; we are
placed by the Sovereign Disposer; and we must do the best we can in our
situation.'[46] These obligations were to be discharged to our best understanding of our duty, and ability. Deeply critical as he was of the treatment of Indians, both Moslem and Hindu, it was the drawing of Britain's
commercial empire into a land commitment that had changed the pattern
of empire and re-evoked for Burke the spectre of the fate of Ancient
Rome for Britain itself.

In India the empire was no longer a trading relationship but one of
pillage conducted by successive cohorts of transient foreigners uncon-
nected with and uncaring of the society whose life blood they sucked.

---

[45] Edmund Burke, *The Correspondence of Edmund Burke*, ed. T. W. Copeland et al., 10 vols
(Cambridge and Chicago, IL, 1958–78), vol. 9, pp. 62–3.
[46] Ibid., p. 404.

Burke's analysis combined his moral outrage with keen insights into the sociological properties of successful polities. In India, 'young men, boys almost ... govern there, without society and without sympathy with the natives ... Animated with all the avarice of age, and all the impetuosity of youth, they roll in, one after another, wave after wave.' Thus, the natives have nothing but 'an endless prospect of new flights of birds of prey and passage with appetites continually renewing for a food that is continually wasting'.

But it is not just moral outrage at the treatment of India at the hands of the nabobs that concerns him for, he adds chillingly, 'Their prey is lodged in England.' These young men with 'all the vices by which sudden fortune is acquired' return home, he warns the Commons, and then 'They marry into your families, they enter your senate, they ease your estates by their loans; they raise their value by demand.' As a consequence, 'there is scarcely a house in the kingdom that does not feel some concern and interest that makes all reform of our eastern government appear officious and disgusting'.[47] Indian money was buying political power, and in the eighteenth century as now, it was, of course, only certain *kinds* of money that were supposed to influence elections. The nabobs were to Burke the modern equivalents of Roman provincial governors, returning home glutted with spoils, which they will spend inflating prices and corrupting domestic politics. That Burke has Rome in mind here is re-enforced by one of his relatively rare references to 'Tacitus and Machiavel' which is close to the passages just cited, and which is followed shortly by a quotation from Cicero against Verres, the corrupt governor of Sicily. There is now a small scholarship discussing Burke's increasing identification with Cicero (in fact he applied the Ciceronian epithet *novus homo* to himself during the impeachment of Warren Hastings, another supposedly corrupt homecoming provincial governor).[48] But the more dramatic implications for Burke's conception of the times in which he lived have not always been drawn.[49] If Hastings was to Verres as Cicero was to Burke,

---

[47] Burke, 'Fox's India Bill', *W&S*, vol. 5, p. 404; he returns to this theme in his peroration, esp. pp. 443 ff.

[48] Burke cites Cicero, e.g. 'Fox's India Bill', *W&S*, vol. 5, p. 416, and invokes him—particularly the Verrine orations against Verres, the returning corrupt governor of Sicily—from the beginning to the end of the prosecution of Warren Hastings: 'Motion for papers on Hastings'. So persistent was the identification that it could easily be exploited by cartoonists. See Burke as Verres in James Sayers, *The Impeachment*, 17 March 1786, and John Boyne, *Cicero against Verres*, 17 February 1787, both in Nicholas K. Robinson, *Edmund Burke, A Life in Caricature* (New Haven, CT, 1996), pp. 82, 92.

[49] See the discussion of this scholarship in Chapter 4 by Phiroze Vasunia in this volume.

then England and English liberty stood in the same perilous relationship to empire as Rome and Roman liberty did at that time. 'The downfall of the greatest empire this world ever saw, has been, on all hands agreed upon to have originated in the mal-administration of its provinces.'[50] It was not merely a question of justice, for self-interest was involved. Benign rule and political integrity at home had to be combined. Neither Britain nor India must be the loser. In sum: 'If we are not able to contrive some method of governing India *well*, which will not, of necessity become the means of governing Great Britain *ill*, a ground is laid for their eternal separation. But none for sacrificing the people of that country to our constitution.'[51]

The difficulty in contriving such a method lay partly in another awkward feature of the modern commercial empire—the property rights of the stockholders in the companies that were the effective imperial agents overseas. The destructive rule of the East India Company was grounded in its chartered rights established by Parliament. Burke recognised this and sought to deal with any objections that might flow from it at the start of his speech. Once again Smith turns out to be at odds with Burke. Smith observed: 'The government of an exclusive company of merchants is, perhaps, the worst of all governments for any country whatever.' For they have 'not only the power of oppressing them, but the greatest temptation to do so'. And in specific reference to the East India Company, they are 'incapable of considering themselves as sovereigns even after they have become such' preferring 'on all occasions the little and transitory profit of the monopolist to the great and permanent revenue of the sovereign'. Government by merchant monopolists places jealousy of trade squarely back in the political arena, for it 'tends to make government [of the province] subservient to the interests of monopoly, and consequently to stunt the natural growth of some parts at least of the surplus produce of the country to what is barely sufficient for answering the demand of the company'.[52] But, notwithstanding any moral considerations, might imperial rule via economic corporation not suit the political interests of the metropole by dislocating in Colbertian fashion domestic economic gains from imperial impoverishment, by holding political consequences at

---

[50] Burke, 'Motion for the Papers', *W&S*, Vol. 6: *India: The Launching of the Hastings Impeachment, 1786–1788*, p. 63.

[51] Burke, 'Fox's India Bill', *W&S*, vol. 5, p. 383.

[52] Smith, *Wealth of Nations*, bk 4, vii, b. 11, p. 570; bk 4, vii, c. 103, pp. 637 f.

arm's length? Could one gain on the imperial economic swings without losing on the domestic political roundabouts?

Once again, as in the case of America, Burke was prepared to temporise. He acknowledged, if not by name, Smith's position, referring to 'those who argue a-priori, against the propriety of leaving such extensive political powers in the hands of a company of merchants'.[53] But, once again for him political considerations overruled political economy, which was after all only an abstract ('a priori') theory. He expressed an 'insuperable reluctance in giving [his] hand to destroy any established institution of government, upon a theory, however plausible it may be'.[54] Burke respected the property rights of the shareholders in the East India Company (which, it has to be said, included his 'kinsman' William Burke), but the Bill he presented proposed vesting effective oversight of the company's agents in India in two parliamentary commissions, one political and one economic. Burke denied the East India Company's appeal against parliamentary control to what he conceded might be called the natural rights of mankind enshrined in such documents as Magna Carta, rights which restrain power and destroy monopoly. The Company's rights under its charter were, he claimed, the very opposite of these: they were rights to monopoly and power. All power exercised over men ought to be exercised for their benefit and is essentially a trust. In this case the trustees are answerable to Parliament. The very rights by which East Indiamen plead immunity from parliamentary interference are held, Burke points out, under the very charter 'which at once gives a title and imposes a duty on us to interfere with effect, wherever power and authority ... are perverted from their purpose and become instruments of wrong and violence'.[55]

Thus Burke's place within the developing language of the political economy of empire underscores significant differences with Smith. He is far more ready to maintain the primacy of the political, and to subordinate to it those economic considerations which, Smith urged, constituted the true reasons of states. In the process he comes, however reluctantly, to acquiesce in the loss of the American colonies rather than concede trade on equal terms; and to defend not the nature, indeed, but the fact of terrestrial empire in India and its attendant responsibilities. His reasons for doing these things are thoroughly Burkean, and illustrate a desire to

[53] Burke, 'Fox's India Bill', *W&S*, vol. 5, pp. 386–7, and the quotation in n. 31 above.
[54] Ibid., p. 387.
[55] Ibid., p. 385.

depart as little as possible from practices and institutions that have proved themselves, however flawed, to have worked and an unwillingness to deploy the conclusions of deductive a priori theory, however plausible, in the making of practical policy.

6

British India as a Problem in Political Economy: Comparing James Steuart and Adam Smith

ROBERT TRAVERS

THE CONSOLIDATION OF POLITICAL ECONOMY as a distinct branch of the science of politics was contemporaneous, in the third quarter of the eighteenth century, with a dramatic expansion and diversification of European overseas empires. Historians of the new political economy have recently emphasised its distance from and unease with the enterprise of imperial expansion. The physiocrats and Scottish political economists, pre-eminently Adam Smith, offered trenchant critiques of the mercantile system of restricted colonial trades and monopoly corporations.[1] According to a recent study by Jennifer Pitts, Adam Smith cultivated a sense of Europe at the vanguard of commercial society, while also remaining 'skeptical about European claims to superiority and the expansion of European political power around the globe'.[2] Pitts argues that it was only in the nineteenth century that liberal thinkers in Britain and France took an imperial turn, imagining European empires as a means of diffusing the self-evident truths of the science of legislation across the world.

There remains, however, an interesting disconnect between the intellectual history of political economy, and the history of imperial

[1] Donald Winch, *Classical Political Economy and Empire* (Suffolk, 1965); Emma Rothschild, 'Global Commerce and the Question of Sovereignty in the Eighteenth Century Provinces', *Modern Intellectual History*, 1 (2004), pp. 3–25; Sankar Muthu, 'Adam Smith's Critique of International Trading Companies: Theorizing Globalization in the Age of Enlightenment', *Political Theory*, 36 (2008), pp. 185–212.

[2] Jennifer Pitts, *A Turn to Empire: The Rise of Imperial Liberalism in Britain and France* (Princeton, NJ, 2005), pp. 25–6. Pitts's highly nuanced account of Smith's thought acknowledges that his 'theory of development may have left an ambivalent legacy', and that his view of historical progress which placed 'European commercial societies at the position of greatest development' would be 'deployed by others to justify civilizing imperial rule'.

Proceedings of the British Academy **155**, 137–160. © The British Academy 2009.

ideologies. A crucial case in point is the early history of British India. On the one hand, writers as diverse as Thomas Pownall, Adam Smith, and Diderot, applied the principles of political economy to denounce the mercantile sovereignty of the English East India Company after its conquest of the province of Bengal in the 1750s and 1760s. On the other hand, British empire builders soon began to reference the latest theories of political economy in organising and justifying the East India Company state in Bengal. Ranajit Guha argued several decades ago that British land policy in Bengal was informed by physiocratic conceptions of security of property as a spur to agricultural development, and also how British ideologues were, by the 1790s, imagining the British Empire as an agent of economic improvement on broadly Smithian lines.[3] In 1806, the East India Company founded the first British chair of political economy at its East India College at Haileybury, appointing Thomas Malthus to the post. The major textbook in Malthus's teaching into the 1830s remained Smith's *Wealth of Nations*, which had famously criticised the East India Company's government in India as corrupt and oppressive.[4]

Such ideological appropriations of philosophical arguments are not surprising or unusual in themselves, nor do they necessarily undermine the value of eighteenth-century political economy as a vital element in what Sankar Muthu has termed the 'enlightenment against empire'.[5] Yet it remains important to think through how and why languages of political economy played such an important role in the ideological renewal of the British Empire in the late eighteenth century. In doing so, we should be careful not to impose an anachronistic, post-facto coherence to the notion of eighteenth-century political economy as if it were analogous to a modern academic discipline. As Emma Rothschild has written, political economy was a 'vast and fluctuating enterprise', and 'the economy was not yet delineated as a distinct side or territory of human experience'.[6]

---

[3] Ranajit Guha, *A Rule of Property for Bengal: An Essay on the Idea of Permanent Settlement* (Paris, 1963, repr. New Delhi, 1982). See also, more recently, Sudipta Sen, *Empire of Free Trade: The East India Company and the Making of the Colonial Marketplace* (Philadelphia, PA, 1998), and Sudipta Sen, 'Liberal Government and Illiberal Trade: The Political Economy of "Responsible Government" in Early British India', in Kathleen Wilson (ed.), *A New Imperial History: Culture, Identity and Modernity in Britain and the Empire, 1860–1840* (Cambridge, 2004), pp. 136–54.

[4] Keith Tribe, 'Professors Malthus and Jones: Political Economy at the East India College, 1806–1858', *European Journal for the History of Economic Thought*, 2 (1995), pp. 327–54.

[5] Sankar Muthu, *Enlightenment Against Empire* (Princeton, NJ, 2003), p. 33.

[6] Emma Rothschild, 'The English Kopf', in P. K. O'Brien and Donald Winch (eds), *The Political Economy of British Historical Experience, 1688–1914* (Oxford, 2002), p. 33.

Yet, I would argue that it was exactly the opportunity to explore certain questions of economic justice as distinct from ideas of 'ancient constitutions' and republican-derived notions of political virtue that made writings on political economy an appealing resource for British empire builders in India.

In particular, works on political economy spoke to two pressing dilemmas of imperial politics in relation to India. First, the East India Company's growing empire scarcely fit with conventional notions of a British 'empire of liberty', that was imagined (in David Armitage's formulation) to be 'Protestant, commercial, maritime and free'.[7] Rather, Company rule was often lambasted by its British critics as a particularly virulent form of 'Asiatic despotism', conjuring stereotypes of lawlessness and arbitrary plunder. The problem of despotism was one area where theories of political economy offered possible solutions. Famously, the physiocrats advocated an absolute form of sovereignty as the best way to reinforce the eternal rules of nature through vigorous positive legislation; Quesnay had gone so far as valorising the empire of China, often understood as a quintessential despotism, for its masterful espousal of natural laws.[8] Meanwhile, David Hume insisted that the absolute monarchy of France was a regular form of government, directly countering the tendency of English Whigs to insist on the unique virtues of the ancient English constitution.[9] In a similar vein, Sir James Steuart subtitled his huge treatise on political economy as an 'essay on the science of domestic policy in free nations'; but his concept of 'free nations' was very different from 'vulgar whig' notions of liberty. 'By a people's being free', Steuart wrote, 'I understand no more than their being governed by general laws, well-known, not depending upon the ambulatory will of any man, or any set of men, and established so as not to be changed, but in a regular and uniform way'.[10] The model of freedom as dependent on 'regular law' was obviously far more easily adaptable to the British regime of

---

[7] David Armitage, *The Ideological Origins of the British Empire* (Cambridge, 2000), p. 198.

[8] Terence Hutchison, *Before Adam Smith: The Emergence of Political Economy, 1662–1776* (Oxford, 1996), pp. 282–4.

[9] For Hume's emphasis on economic justice rather than civic virtue and political liberty, see Istvan Hont and Michael Ignatieff, 'Needs and Justice in the Wealth of Nations: An Introductory Essay', in Hont and Ignatieff (eds), *Wealth and Virtue: The Shaping of Political Economy in the Scottish Enlightenment* (Cambridge, 1983), p. 7.

[10] Sir James Steuart, *An Inquiry into the Principles of Political Economy*, ed. A. S. Skinner (Edinburgh and London, 1966), p. 206. Steuart goes on to note (p. 207) that 'under this definition of liberty, a people may be found to enjoy freedom under the most despotic forms of government'.

conquest in India than English Whig emphases on constitutional checks and balances or even republican notions of participatory liberty.

A second overriding theoretical problem facing British empire builders in India was their appearance as strangers in a distant and little known land. Both European and Indian critics of Company rule commented on British ignorance of and lack of sympathy for local manners and customs, often appealing to the Montesquieuan notions about the contrasting spirit of different laws and constitutions. Yet this cultural deficit appeared less fatal if one accepted, with many leading political-economists, that 'the political conditions for economic success were everywhere similar'.[11] Even a figure like Sir James Steuart, who emphasised the need for a speculative person to 'become a citizen of the world', and to adapt the general principles of political economy to 'the spirit, manners, habits and customs of the people', still insisted that certain principles were 'universally true' at least in the abstract.[12] Adam Smith was firmly opposed to the Company rule in India, but his analytical style of reasoning in the *Wealth of Nations* was extended not just to the economic systems of Britain and Europe but also to China and India. The very universality of Smith's analytical approach appeared to undermine stark distinctions between the familiar and the alien which underpinned some critiques of early colonial rule in India.[13]

The rest of this essay looks more closely at two rival (north-) British theorists, Sir James Steuart and Adam Smith, both of whom directly addressed the emerging empire of British India as a problem in political economy. Steuart's and Smith's thinking about Indian affairs in the 1770s not only posed substantial challenges to Company rule in India, but also offered certain conceptual and theoretical resources for a beleaguered and unpopular Company government. Interestingly, both Steuart and Smith were at different moments approached to offer advice in an official capacity to the East India Company. This was a reflection not just of their reputations as experts in affairs of political economy, but also of the severe problems associated with the Company's evolution into a military and territorial power. In 1769–70, just four years after the Company had

---

[11] Rothschild, 'Global Commerce and the Question of Sovereignty', p. 11.

[12] Steuart, *Inquiry into the Principles of Political Economy*, pp. 16–17.

[13] For the suggestion that 'the Natural History of Man' as practised by Scottish conjectural historians helped to domesticate distant regions within British thought, and contributed to a renewed confidence in British capacity to rule distant peoples, see P. J. Marshall, '*A Free though Conquering People: Britain and Asia in the Eighteenth Century': Inaugural Lecture in the Rhodes Chair of Imperial History Delivered at King's College, London* (London, 1981), p. 10.

assumed the powers of *diwan* (or chief revenue collector of Bengal), the province was hit by a calamitous famine. Two years later, in 1772, the Company faced a financial crisis so severe that some thought it was on the verge of bankruptcy. This was the unpromising setting in which first Steuart, then Smith, put their formidable minds at work on the Indian Empire.

James Steuart and the Coin of Bengal

James Steuart, who had published his wide-ranging *Inquiry into the Principles of Political Economy* in 1767, wrote his *Principles of Money Applied to the State of Currency in Bengal* in 1772. Approached to compose this treatise by anxious directors of the East India Company, Steuart spent several months going over records from Bengal at the Company's head-quarters in Leadenhall Street, before addressing himself to the perceived crisis in the Bengal currency.[14] Now that the Company's financial health increasingly rested on its tax revenues and commercial investment in Bengal, successful management of the local system of currency based on the silver rupee was regarded as a policy priority. Yet Steuart noted that 'the complaints of a scarcity of coin in Bengal, once so famous for its wealth, are so general that the fact can hardly be called into question'.[15]

Connected to the issue of scarcity, many Company officials also thought that the coinage system in Mughal India was inherently corrupt, and they had made efforts at monetary reform, such as introducing new gold coins from the Company's mint in Calcutta. Many different varieties of coin circulated in the Company's new territories making monetary transactions complex and potentially expensive. Company officials also complained of the Mughal practice of allowing silver rupees to lose a certain portion of their nominal value each year after they were minted, as an inducement to 'shroffs' (money-changers) to bring damaged coins back to mint after a number of years. They thought that this system threw power into the hands of money-changers to impose arbitrary *batta* (exchange rates) on monetary transactions, which, it was argued, adversely affected the Company trade, private European trade, and disbursements of revenue from the interior.[16]

[14] S. R. Sen, *The Economics of Sir James Steuart* (London, 1957), p. 155.

[15] James Steuart, *Principles of Money Applied to the State of Bengal* (London, 1772), p. 56.

[16] Shubhra Chakrabarti, 'Intransigent Shroffs and the English East India Company's Currency Reforms, 1757–1800', *Indian Economic and Social History Review*, 34 (1997), pp. 69–94.

The first part of Steuart's treatise was taken up with a review of the Company's recent currency reforms. His method was first to establish the central categories of analysis (such as the distinction between money and coin) and also to abstract some main principles from his famous researches on monetary issues. Chief among these was the need to return coinage to its ancient simplicity, before modern rulers had contrived to impose 'arbitrary denominations to certain coins, beyond the proportion of their intrinsic value'.[17] A standard unit of account should be established as a fixed value in proportion to other denominations of coin, representing an invariable weight and fineness of silver. Steuart chose the current rupee as the standard unit of account in Bengal, which was not itself coined, but should be preserved as an invariable proportion (10:11) of the Bengal standard 'sicca' rupee. This last coin should be established by a general recoinage as the sole legal tender of Bengal, at a specified weight and fineness. Steuart was impressed neither by the old Mughal system of silver currency, which he thought was rife with abuses caused by arbitrary denominations and devious money-changers, nor by the Company's previous efforts at monetary reform, which he believed were unscientific and self-defeating. In particular, Company issues of gold coins had been deliberately overvalued to encourage money-changers to bring their gold bullion to the mint, but this (Steuart surmised) simply had the effect of driving silver coins out of the market.[18]

Steuart's treatise did not end with his proposed regulations for money and coin. Instead, he took a comprehensive view of the political economy of Bengal under Company rule, 'considering Bengal as a province by itself, not as making part of Hindostan'.[19] In explaining the apparent scarcity of coin, he diagnosed multiple sources by which the wealth of Bengal was being 'drained' out of Bengal by the Company and its servants. In his *Inquiry* of 1767, Steuart had explicitly rejected Hume's version of the quantity theory of money, which asserted that deficiencies in bullion or coin would be remedied by natural adjustments in prices.[20] Now he argued that the peculiar mechanism of the Company's investment in Bengal, paid for with local tax revenues, amounted to an unrequited drain of wealth, not compensated by accompanying imports of bullion or other goods. This was exacerbated by the Company's exports

---

[17] Steuart, *Principles of Money*, p. 4.
[18] Ibid., pp. 11–16.
[19] Ibid., p. 62.
[20] Steuart, *Inquiry into the Principles of Political Economy*, pp. 357–8.

of silver to China and its other trading stations, and by the remittance of private fortunes by Company servants.[21]

In this analysis, the Company's conquests had promoted a massive balance-of-payments crisis for Bengal; though Steuart also suggested, on rather slender evidence, that the drain of wealth may have been even more acute under the old system of tribute payments to the Mughal emperors in Delhi. 'It is vain to think of a remedy', Steuart argued, 'without sacrificing the interest of Great Britain, and of the Company itself to that of Bengal', by indemnifying the province for the 'gratuitous exportation of the many manufactures which we formerly bought with silver sent thither'. This should be done by supplying Bengal with raw materials for manufacture, by encouraging its trade with other nations and regions of India, and by sending bullion from Europe to pay for the trade in China tea.[22]

Thus, Steuart did not assume any easy identity of interests between Britain, the Company, and Bengal; rather the interests of the rulers needed to be circumscribed by the contradictory needs of the ruled. The most intriguing aspects of Steuart's proposed remedies were his broader prescriptions for the internal government of Bengal. Rather than considering the apparently 'absolute' character of Indian sovereignty as a source of corruption and misrule, Steuart argued that the Company should avail 'themselves of the principles of the feudal system of government' in making a comprehensive new land survey and leasing the rights to collect land rents to men of consequence considered as a type of 'superior lord'. Steuart followed conventional European wisdom in assuming that the Mughal emperors were sole owners of all lands, which were leased out to tenants-at-will. Yet he thought that such a system, if properly organised, could circumvent the elaborate chain of revenue farms which currently held up and reduced the flow of revenues, creating a more efficient circulation of the money in the economy as a whole. 'Let it be remembered', Steuart wrote, invoking a comparison at once surprising and illuminating, 'that William the Conqueror made a compleat survey and valuation of a country less known to him, than Bengal is to the East India Company'.[23]

---

[21] For a good analysis of Steuart's diagnosis of the monetary crisis in Bengal, see Walter Eltis, 'Steuart on Monetary Reform and Economic Development: His Advice for the Restoration of the Indian Economy', in Ramon Tortajada (ed.), *The Economics of James Steuart* (London, 1999), pp. 203–6.

[22] Steuart, *Principles of Money*, p. 64.

[23] Ibid., p. 73.

Perhaps this Indian version of the feudal law appealed to the sensibilities of an old Jacobite.

Meanwhile, Steuart ended his treatise with a proposal to extend the benefits of paper money to Bengal, inviting private investors to create a new bank regulated by the Company government, on the approximate model of the Bank of England. The starting capital of the bank would be provided by funds borrowed from Company servants. Subscribers to the bank would come together as directors, and establish branches of the bank in major cities. The bank would also be open to Indian investors, and Steuart imagined that Indian shroffs would naturally enter the new bank as directors.[24]

Steuart's prescriptions for Bengal echoed the broader emphases in his works on using determined government action to protect vulnerable agrarian economies, and especially in maintaining the quantity and velocity of the circulating specie.[25] A more efficient system of taxation could maintain the velocity of money in the economy, keeping it out of the hands of the wasteful money-changers, facilitating a buoyant demand for goods, and therefore employment and subsistence. As in his other works, Steuart was in favour of pre-emptive government action to prevent subsistence crises, suggesting that 'in the proximity of great cities, and in very populous districts, granaries might be established, and part of the rents might be received in grain for the supply of markets, at a price proportionate to the plenty of the year'.[26] A fascinating proposal sought to link the prompt payment of land rents to the Company, the encouragement of foreign trade, and the profits of the new general bank. The moment the Company's annual investment in a district was complete, and the rents paid (or adequate security given for payment), then the bazaars would be thrown open to 'even foreign merchants'. Thus it would be in the best interests of the inhabitants to pay their rents, and of the rent collectors and bankers to maintain the good credit of the inhabitants. 'What a new phenomenon in Bengal, a Shroff [money-changer], a director of a bank, from a blood-sucker is become the protector of the labouring man.'[27]

The very fact of Steuart's being commissioned to write this treatise on the coin tells us that Company directors saw the 'principles of political economy' as a valuable resource for solving the Company's financial

---

[24] Steuart, *Principles of Money*, pp. 77–9.
[25] For a wider view of Steuart's economic thought, see Hutchison, *Before Adam Smith*, pp. 342–3.
[26] Steuart, *Principles of Money*, p. 74.
[27] Steuart, *Principles of Money*, p. 81.

problems. From the directors' point of view, hiring an acknowledged expert like Steuart was also a further means of disciplining their servants overseas, providing intellectual heft to the critique of the Bengal council's monetary policies. Inevitably, however, Steuart's metropolitan theorising relied on Company officials overseas for his information on local affairs, and his treatise tended to parrot conventional views, common among Company servants, about the corrupt legacy of arbitrary Mughal government, wicked Indian money-changers, as well as the growing concern that the Company's own commercial policies were bleeding Bengal dry.[28] The production of Steuart's treatise suggests how the intellectual history of metropolitan 'theory' and the history of colonial politics were becoming closely entangled in this period.

Nonetheless, Steuart's highly technical discussion of the coinage problems seemed to offer a new, more scientific basis for proceeding to reform the currency, just as his broader proposals imagined the Company as a benevolent and energetic steward of the Bengal economy. Steuart's willingness to countenance absolute forms of sovereignty as no necessary hindrance to the freedom of the subject appeared to justify the Company's rule of conquest, tight control by government over landed property rights, and a vigorous taxation system as a means not just of profiting the government but also society as a whole through the medium of the Company's investment. Steuart's pragmatic approach to trade restrictions chimed well with the Company's basis in monopoly, and its preference for enforcing tight controls over the trade of its own officials and other foreign traders in Bengal. In commenting on controversial duties on internal trade in salt, betel-nut, and tobacco, Steuart noted that he was not in favour of 'open trade' simply for the sake of it, and indeed emphasised how excise taxes could boost the prices of commodities and hence of labour. He recommended that the Company impose excise duties on salt on the model of a similar tax in France.[29] Thus, Steuart's 'economics of control' appeared to offer intellectual backing to the Company's elaborate tax regime in Bengal as a source not of oppression and pauperisation, but of buoyancy and economic recovery.[30]

---

[28] For British encounters with local systems of administration in Bengal, see Robert Travers, *Ideology and Empire in Eighteenth-century India: The British in Bengal* (Cambridge, 2007), pp. 67–99.

[29] Steuart, *Principles of Money*, pp. 84–7.

[30] For the idea of Steuart as propounding an 'economics of control', see S. R. Sen. *Economics of Sir James Steuart*; for Steuart's advocacy of quality controls and price regulation to promote Bengal's industrial exports, see Eltis, 'Steuart on Monetary Reform', p. 209.

Adam Smith and the Declining State of Bengal

Four years later, Sir James Steuart's reputation as a political economist began its long eclipse, with the publication of the first edition of Adam Smith's *Wealth of Nations*. Smith did worse than refute Steuart's writings; he appeared to ignore them completely.[31] While Smith echoed Steuart's concern to delineate the systematic interconnections within commercial societies, the intellectual foundations of Smith's approach were quite different. Rejecting Steuart's emphasis on maintaining a favourable balance of trade to promote a fluid money supply, and also his more pragmatic approach to indirect taxation and commercial controls, Smith emphasised the fundamental importance of open exchange in promoting an efficient division of labour, increased productivity, and the accumulation of capital. Smith roundly condemned what he called the 'mercantile system' of restricted colonial trades, which unfairly diverted wealth away from producers and consumers and into the hands of grasping merchants, who used their political connections to distort the progress of commercial society.[32]

On the face of it, therefore, Smith appeared as a far more uncompromising critic of the monopolistic, mercantile sovereignty of the East India Company. Indeed, unlike Steuart, Smith had resisted the suggestion that he might act as an adviser to the East India Company in 1772. When the MP for Cromarty, William Pulteney, promoted his name as a possible member of a commission of 'supervisors' to travel to Bengal, Smith declared himself 'honoured', but also remarked (with perhaps a hint of irony) that Pulteney 'acted in your old way of doing your friends a good office behind their backs, pretty much as other people do them a bad one'.[33] Smith's friend David Hume discouraged him from the scheme, commenting that the proposed commission of nine supervisors was too many and that 'corruption will get in among them; and probably Absurdity and Folly'.[34]

[31] A. S. Skinner, 'Biographical Sketch', in Steuart, *Inquiry into the Principles of Political Economy*, p. lii.

[32] For a recent overview of Smith's economic thought, see Emma Rothschild and Amartya Sen, 'Adam Smith's Economics', in Knud Haakonssen (ed.), *The Cambridge Companion to Adam Smith* (Cambridge, 2006), pp. 319–65.

[33] Ernest Campbell Mossner and Ian Simpson Ross (eds), *The Correspondence of Adam Smith* (Oxford, 1987), p. 164.

[34] Ibid., p. 165.

By the time Smith published the first edition of the *Wealth of Nations* in 1776, the crisis in East India Company affairs had been temporarily remedied by Lord North's 'Regulating Act' of 1773. Yet the memory of the Bengal famine, and the air of scandal surrounding the Company, had by no means abated. Unlike Steuart, Smith wrote not as a paid adviser to the Company but as a confirmed critic. Moreover, again unlike Steuart, Smith's goal was to point out the deficiencies and destructive effects of the Company's mercantile sovereignty, rather than to propose detailed policies for the regeneration of Bengal. Smith devoted brief but careful attention to the East India Company as part of his broader attack on the 'mercantile system', but references to India and Bengal were scattered through the *Wealth of Nations* rather than forming the focus of any one section. In the context of his broader goals, the East India Company was almost too easy a target for Smith. He noted, for example, that the arguments against monopoly corporations like the East India Company were easier to articulate to a British audience, than those against the system of protected colonial trades in the Atlantic colonies. While the Navigation Acts appeared primarily to limit the trading rights of other nations and the colonies themselves, the monopoly rights of the Company were clearly directed against other British traders.[35] Smith was by no means the only metropolitan writer to critique the Company's exclusive trading rights, and he joined a long and venerable tradition of anti-Company polemicists.[36]

At the same time, while Smith was clear that the system of monopoly had severely restricted the potential benefits of the Asian trade to Britain and Europe, he also addressed the calamitous effects of Company rule in India. If the mercantile sovereignty of the Company was a 'nuisance' to the British economy, it was fundamentally 'destructive' to that of Bengal.[37] Smith's critique of Company rule rested in part on his wider theme of the role of extended markets in promoting the division of labour and hence productivity. A government of monopolists had the disastrous effect of curtailing demand for Bengal's goods, and therefore eating into wages. In the aftermath of the Bengal famine, Smith singled out those Indian territories under Company rule as his example of

---

[35] Adam Smith, *The Wealth of Nations, Books IV–V*, ed. A. S. Skinner (London, 1999), bk 4, ch. 7, pt 3, p. 215.
[36] For this longer history, see William Barber, *British Economic Thought and India, 1600–1858: A Study in the History of Development Economics* (Oxford, 1975).
[37] Smith, *Wealth of Nations, Books IV–V*, bk 4, ch. 7, pt 3, p. 226.

countries in a declining state where the funds for labour were decaying.[38]
The interests of the Company, its shareholders, and its servants in buying
cheap in India and selling dear in Britain were fundamentally at odds
with the interests of Bengal's producers and consumers. Smith made
telling observations on the incapacity of even right-minded directors to
police their servants across half the world, and of the circumscribed perspectives of Company servants who expected to spend no more than a
portion of their lives in India.[39]

Smith reiterated his determined opposition to the Company in an
extended series of additions to the third edition of the *Wealth of Nations*
in 1784. In 1783–4, the Company faced a new series of parliamentary
investigations as wars in India appeared to drive it close to bankruptcy
again. In this context, Smith emphasised what he regarded as the systemic
flaws inherent in joint-stock companies, in particular the separation of
management from ownership and liability, which encouraged profligacy
among directors and officials. Such pathologies were only redoubled in
the unnatural union of sovereign and merchant; 'no other sovereigns ever
were, or, from the nature of things, ever could be, so perfectly indifferent
to the happiness or misery of their subjects'. He thought that these systemic
flaws had rendered quite redundant the attempts by Lord North's government to regulate the Company's affairs.[40] As Sankar Muthu has asserted,
Smith's critique of Company rule rested not simply on the grounds of
economic inefficiencies, but on a deeply held notion of natural justice,
and his sense of the Company's curtailment of the rights of native peoples
to liberty of commerce broadly construed.[41]

Recent scholarship on Smith's relationship to the contemporary
empire has rightly regarded the *Wealth of Nations* as one of the most
powerful and coherent critiques of Company rule in India. Emma
Rothschild has suggested that Smith's ideal scenario would have been a
system of free commerce between Britain and India without the polluting
effects of conquest or sovereignty.[42] Similarly, Andrew Sartori has viewed
Smith's arguments at the very end of the *Wealth of Nations*, that the
Company's territories were 'the undoubted right of the crown, that is, of

[38] Adam Smith, *Wealth of Nations, Books I–III*, ed. A. S. Skinner (London, repr. 1999), bk 1,
ch. 8, pp. 175–6.
[39] Smith, *Wealth of Nations, Books, IV–V*, bk 4, ch. 7, pt 3, pp. 223–5.
[40] Adam Smith, *Additions and Corrections to the First and Second Editions of Dr Adam Smith's
Inquiry into the Nature and Causes of the Wealth of Nations* (London, 1784), pp. 72–4.
[41] Muthu, 'Adam Smith's Critique of International Trading Companies', p. 189.
[42] Rothschild, 'Global Commerce and the Question of Sovereignty', p. 21.

the state and people of Great Britain', and that they could be 'rendered another source of revenue more abundant perhaps than all those already mentioned', as a merely pragmatic accommodation to empire 'after the fact', which did not compromise Smith's 'principled stance against imperial expansion as such'.[43]

Nonetheless, Smith's advocacy of the crown's takeover of Indian territories, even if we regard it as a pragmatic response to less than ideal circumstances, was still highly significant. It placed him squarely beside other critics of the Company in arguing for root-and-branch reform of the Indian Empire through the extension of British sovereignty.[44] Smith supported Charles James Fox's efforts, through a parliamentary Bill of 1783, to effect a kind of parliamentary takeover of Indian territories, praising Fox's 'decisive judgement and resolution'.[45] Fox's Bill ultimately failed to pass in the House of Lords, after opposition from the king. In 1784, however, a watered-down version of Indian reform, establishing a ministerial Board of Control to supervise the Company, was passed by William Pitt the Younger's government. Supporters of the new settlement regarded this as a decisive resolution of the Indian problem in British politics, subjecting the Company to closer ministerial and parliamentary scrutiny, while maintaining the chartered rights of the Company and its shareholders in Asian commerce. Pitt's Act largely succeeded in neutralising the most virulent critics of the Company government, even if the campaign for ending the Company's commercial monopoly would gather strength in subsequent decades.[46] Thus, the imperial state's selective appropriation of Smith's and others' critique of the Company, accepting the need to differentiate commerce from sovereignty by interposing the

[43] Andrew Sartori, 'The British Empire and Its Liberal Mission', *Journal of Modern History*, 78 (2006), p. 630. Smith advocated the crown's rights to the Indian territories and revenues in *Wealth of Nations, IV–V*, bk 5, ch. 3, p. 549. Smith also wrote, however, that the crown should lighten the tax burden of 'those unfortunate countries'. E. A. Benians noted that Smith 'nowhere indicates with any clearness what place such possessions would hold in his project of an empire', but he 'seems not to have expected or desired the foundation of empires of some permanence' in Asia. See E. A. Benians, 'Adam Smith's Project of an Empire', *Cambridge Historical Review*, 1 (1925), pp. 269–70. Similarly, Jennifer Pitts noted that Smith made 'denunciations of existing imperial practice', but largely 'sidestepped the question of what Britain's relations with India ought to be': Pitts, *Turn to Empire*, p. 55.

[44] For a similar suggestion, that Smith's 'attitude was in many respects far more representative of the era than has been acknowledged', see Sudipta Sen, 'Liberal Government and Illiberal Trade', p. 139.

[45] Mossner and Ross, *Correspondence of Adam Smith*, pp. 271–2.

[46] H. V. Bowen, 'British India, 1765–1813: The Metropolitan Context', in P. J. Marshall (ed.), *Oxford History of the British Empire*, Vol. 2: *The Eighteenth Century* (Oxford, 1998), pp. 530–51.

legitimate authority of the British state, helped to make the Indian Empire respectable at last. Even though Smith had pronounced the Company unworthy even of a 'share' in imperial government, these reforms likely also helped to make Smith's theories safe, or at least safer, for official policy makers in British India.[47]

It is also important to note the ways that Smith's critique of the East India Company cut across the intellectual grain of other common charges against the Company. These often focused on notions of the dangers of 'eastern luxury' on habits of civic virtue, or on the corrupting effects of standing armies, which Smith's theories of the improving effects of modern commerce and the division of labour consciously rejected.[48] Smith had little interest in theories of the drain of wealth, which had animated James Steuart and other observers of Bengal. Steuart thought that the Company was enriching itself and Britain while draining Bengal of specie, but for Smith, the Company's restrictive practices and coercive methods were properly speaking preventing both Britain and India from profiting from a mutually beneficial overseas trade. Smith's analysis differentiated sharply between money and wealth, defining money as 'a great but expensive instrument of commerce', but forming 'no part' of the revenue of society.[49] He condemned the conventional obsession with ensuring inflows of bullion through a favourable balance of trade, arguing (in a similar vein to Hume) that the money supply was naturally self-adjusting. In the *Wealth of Nations*, therefore, the old problem of drain of currency and the Company's 'unrequited' exports from Bengal, often regarded as one of the crucial problems inherent in Company rule, was discounted.

A tantalising, yet ultimately unclear, reference in Smith's correspondence suggests that he may have advocated importing silver coin from Bengal to London in the late 1770s. For a brief period, Company finances in Bengal appeared quite healthy, and the old fears about a crisis of money supply in Bengal had died down. John Macpherson, later to become governor-general of India, wrote to Smith in November 1778 that in a meeting with Prime Minister Lord North he had 'pledged your authority about importing part of the dead treasure of Calcutta'.

---

[47] Smith, *Additions and Corrections*, p. 72.

[48] For fears about luxury and standing armies in relation to India, see Marshall, *Free though Conquering People*, pp. 7–8. For Smith's critique of older fears about the dangers of 'luxury' and standing armies, see Donald Winch, *Riches and Poverty: An Intellectual History of Political Economy in Britain, 1750–1834* (Cambridge, 1996), pp. 89, 117–19.

[49] Smith, *Wealth of Nations, Books I–III*, bk 2, ch. 2, p. 385.

Macpherson reported that North 'hesitated at a measure so novel. He thought the treasury of Bengal was a kind of Bank.'[50] Although the exact background to Macpherson's comments remains uncertain, this letter is at least suggestive that Smith was relatively unconcerned about India's supply of coin, and also that he believed that Bengal could indeed be made a profitable source of 'revenue' for the British state.

Arguably, indeed, Smith's confidence in the natural processes of adjustment between demand and supply in a system of open trade made it easier to imagine a coincidence of interests between British rulers and Indian subjects in a properly reformed empire than it was for James Steuart, who presented an unavoidable clash of interests between Britain and India which needed to be managed and mitigated. Smith argued that the fact of foreign trade as a means of extending markets was more important than who controlled the trade, noting that Egypt, China, and India had enjoyed long prosperity despite their overseas trade being controlled by foreigners.[51] Smith also implied that there was, if properly understood, a degree of mutual interest between the directors of the Company, considered as owners of Bengal and stewards of the Bengal revenues, and the people of Bengal as revenue producers, even if this shared interest had been obscured by mercantile prejudice and the short-term interests of Company servants and shareholders.[52]

It was certainly not the case that Smith abstracted issues of 'economic' justice from political or constitutional structures. Indeed, he was precisely interested in diagnosing the systemic flaws in trading companies as polities. In comparing the evident growth of population and resources in America with the declining state of Bengal, Smith contrasted 'the genius of the British constitution which protects and governs North America, and that of the mercantile company which oppresses and domineers in the East Indies'.[53] It is, however, very striking that he used the North American colonies as a foil for Company misrule, rather than previous Indian states like the Mughal Empire. Other prominent critics of the Company, notably Alexander Dow, Philip Francis, and Edmund

---

[50] Mossner and Ross, *Correspondence of Adam Smith*, pp. 236–7. The editors' note to this letter reads: 'perhaps he [Smith] had suggested that part of Calcutta's treasury holdings could be imported to Britain during the distresses of the American war without loss of advantage to Bengal'. Interestingly, North's response here picked up on Steuart's conception of the Company's Bengal treasury as the basis for a national banking system.
[51] Smith, *Wealth of Nations, Books I–III*, bk 3, ch. 1, p. 483.
[52] Smith, *Wealth of Nations, Books IV–V*, bk 4, ch. 7, pt 3, p. 225.
[53] Smith, *Wealth of Nations, Books I–III*, bk 1, ch. 8, p. 176.

Burke, argued that India had prospered under the benevolent rule of the Mughals, and that the Company had wilfully destroyed a viable ancient constitution.[54] But the language of 'ancient constitutions' was profoundly alien to Smith's brand of 'sceptical whiggism'.[55]

Smith's rather sparse and confusing references to Indian history suggest both that he shared the widespread view of India's ancient opulence, but that he may also have largely accepted conventional wisdom about the arbitrary nature of Asiatic despotism and its destructive effects on the development of commerce. On the one hand, Smith thought that 'in manufacturing art and industry, China and Indostan, though inferior, seem not to be much inferior to any part of Europe', and he commented on the large extent of the domestic market in India, as well as the role of the 'Mahometan' rulers in Bengal in funding public investments such as roads and canals.[56] On the other hand, in his lectures on jurisprudence from the 1760s, Smith had characterised the governments of Asia as 'military monarchies', where arbitrary practices undermined the security of subjects.[57] In the *Wealth of Nations*, Smith repeated a commonplace view that people in Asiatic countries were in the habit of hoarding money because of the pervasive insecurity created by tyrannical regimes.[58]

In this matter, at least, Smith's view of the arbitrary tendencies of Asiatic rulers may not have been far from the views of James Steuart about the corrupt forms of Mughal rule. Smith's Whiggism, and his advocacy of a mixed or balanced constitution, made him a very different figure within British politics to the sometime Jacobite Steuart. Yet Smith's thought also fitted into a broader movement within the Scottish Enlightenment that tended to shift the language of liberty away from republican-derived ideas of civic virtue, and away from notions of 'immemorial rights' within an ancient constitution, and towards a natural jurisprudential conception of liberty associated with the particular forms of social relations in a commercial society. David Lieberman has argued

---

[54] For a broader discussion of this tendency, see Travers, *Ideology and Empire in Eighteenth-century India*.

[55] For this, see Duncan Forbes, 'Sceptical Whiggism, Commerce and Liberty', in Andrew S. Skinner and Thomas Wilson (eds), *Essays on Adam Smith* (Oxford, 1975), pp. 179–202.

[56] Smith, *Wealth of Nations, Books I–III*, bk 1, ch. 11, p. 311; Smith, *Wealth of Nations, Books IV–V*, bk 4, ch. 9, p. 269, and bk 5, ch. 2, p. 429.

[57] Forbes, 'Sceptical Whiggism, Commerce and Liberty', p. 189. But see also Pitts, *Turn to Empire*, pp. 39–40, who argues that Smith was 'strikingly nonjudgmental' about China's and India's 'developmental differences', and tended to de-emphasise the notion of Asiatic despotism.

[58] Smith, *Wealth of Nations, Books I–III*, bk 2, ch. 1, p. 380.

that Smith 'joined an important body of contemporary political specula-
tion which emphasised the extent to which modern liberty in Britain owed
more to the integrity and independence of the law and the courts than to
structures of parliamentary representation'.[59] In Duncan Forbes's view,
the *Wealth of Nations* suggests that 'the freedom which is the end of
government'—a system of natural liberty defended by regular and
impartially administered laws—could exist outside the confines of a
'free government' as defined by institutions of aristocratic or popular
representation.[60]

If Smith was then a consistent and highly effective critic of the
government of a monopolistic joint-stock company, in a larger sense his
flexible conception of the relationship between 'political liberty' and 'natural liberty' was potentially useful in the consolidation of a new style of
colonial rule of conquest in India. His emphasis, shared with James
Steuart, on the role of an impartial administration of law in promoting
the well-being of commercial society was adaptable to a colonial setting
such as British India, where representative government was usually
regarded as unthinkable.

It is quite clear that Smith did not see the East India Company as an
agent of justice in India, and was horrified by the ill-effects of its rule. Yet,
fortified by the protection of the British state, a new generation of British
reformers after Pitt's India Act of 1784 would strive to represent the
Company's rule as a decisive break with a long history of Asiatic tyranny.
Central to their claims was the network of law courts set up under British
auspices, governed by written codes of administrative procedure, and
administering a complex and increasingly codified body of indigenous
laws. While the constitutional structure of British India was 'despotic', in
the sense of combining large executive, legislative, and judicial powers in
the hands of the governor-general and his council, the creation by the
1790s of a 'judicial branch' of administration separate from the 'revenue
branch' appeared to offer at least the semblance of an independent
judiciary and a regular government for Britain's Indian territories.[61]

---

[59] David Lieberman, 'Adam Smith on Justice, Rights, and Law', in Haakonssen (ed.), *Cambridge
Companion to Adam Smith*, p. 240.
[60] Forbes, 'Sceptical Whiggism, Commerce and Liberty', p. 192.
[61] For colonial conceptions of the 'rule of law' in India, see Radhika Singha, *A Despotism of
Law: Crime and Justice in Early Colonial India* (Delhi, 1998) and Nasser Hussain, *The
Jurisprudence of Emergency: Colonialism and the Rule of Law* (Ann Arbor, MI, 2003).

Steuart, Smith, and Imperial Political Economy

Clearly, neither Steuart nor Smith was a straightforward apologist for the British Empire in India. With quite different emphases, they situated themselves as reformers of an empire gone bad. As the Company's employment of James Steuart demonstrated, and Smith's fainter brush with Indian politics also suggested, contemporaries regarded the principles of political economy as a vital resource for tackling the new problems of Indian governance. These principles, stated and interpreted in varied and contentious ways, challenged domestic authorities to rescue the operations of the Company's empire from its ignominious beginnings. At the same time, the recitation of abstract theoretical principles, such as Steuart's discussion of the basic principles of money, or Smith's discussion of the sources of the wealth of nations, must often have appeared to offer a relatively secure point of reference in a field of imperial action that was highly confusing, deeply disputed, and still very little understood.

Even within Steuart's and Smith's treatises, the tension between political economy as imperial critique and political economy as a critical branch of the developing science of imperial legislation was already apparent. In the longer term, visions of economic development within authoritarian structures of government offered British rulers in India a form of compensation for the loss of older ideals of an empire of liberty. The close relationship between the Indian Empire and the intellectual history of British political economy in the eighteenth and nineteenth centuries reflected both the hope invested in political economy as a set of potentially universalisable principles of governance, and the continuing problems of justifying the messy realities of an empire of conquest within satisfying theoretical frameworks.[62]

In the short term, meanwhile, Steuart and Smith became significant players in crucial arguments over the shape of the new empire in India. Steuart's treatise on the Bengal currency had a mixed reception in official circles. His idea that the Bengal 'current rupee' should become the standard (if fictitious) unit of account was criticised by British officials in India, who pointed out that the current rupee was not a generally known

---

[62] S. Ambirajan, *Classical Political Economy and British Policy in India* (Cambridge, 1978); Sandra den Otter, 'The Political Economy of Empire: Freedom of Contract and "Commercial Civilization" in Colonial India', in Martin Daunton and Frank Trentman (eds), *Worlds of Political Economy: Knowledge and Power in the Nineteenth and Twentieth Centuries* (Basingstoke, 2004), pp. 69–94.

denomination in Bengal, but was confined mainly to European settle-ments.[63] Despite this, in 1774 the directors sent a copy of Steuart's trea-tise to Bengal as a point of reference for the Company's council as they framed reforms to establish 'an equitable rupee'.[64] Philip Francis, a member of the governing council in Bengal, subsequently corresponded with Steuart about plans for monetary reform, debating with him about the need for an 'ideal' standard of currency, and about the optimum silver content for new rupees. In a letter to Francis from 1777, Steuart expressed some frustration that his plans of reform had not yet been executed, and also that some of the information about the Indian currency included in Francis's letter was 'so different from what I learned at the time I wrote'.[65] The complications around Steuart's treatise illustrate the problems that the Company directors had in trying to manage the Indian Empire at a distance of six months' sailing time, especially when relatively few of them enjoyed local experience of conditions in Bengal.

The problems of communication between London and Calcutta, as well as the inherent difficulties of currency reform, vitiated Steuart's direct influence on policy making in Bengal, although the Company gov-ernment did fight a long and often difficult battle to restrain the power of shroffs by establishing a more uniform system of currency centred on the Company's sicca rupees.[66] In a broader sense, however, Steuart's 'eco-nomics of control' can be seen if not as a direct source for policy makers, then as symptomatic of a structure of thought which has perhaps been underemphasised in the history of early colonial state building in India. Ranajit Guha's evolutionist view of British economic thought in India, moving smoothly through the gears of contemporary theory, from mercantilist bullionism, to physiocracy, to Smithian free trade, tended to ignore a strand of British policy making which viewed (like Steuart) the absolute powers supposedly inherent in Indian sovereignty as a weapon of economic regeneration in the hands of enlightened British officials.[67] As in Steuart's treatise, the colonial state could appear as a masterful

---

[63] S. R. Sen, *Economics of Sir James Steuart*, pp. 173–4.
[64] Court of Directors' despatch of 30 March 1774, cited in ibid., p. 156.
[65] Sir James Steuart, *The Works, Political, Metaphysical, and Chronological of the Late Sir James Steuart*, 6 vols (London, 1805), vol. 5, pp. 136–7.
[66] Chakrabarti, 'Intransigent Shroffs', and Kumkum Chatterjee, 'Collaboration and Conflict: Bankers and Early Colonial Rule in India, 1757–1813', *Indian Economic and Social History Review*, 30 (1993), pp. 283–310.
[67] Guha, *Rule of Property*.

agent of economic improvement, deploying its powers of taxation, surveillance, and protection to ensure a fair distribution of resources.

A key figure here was Warren Hastings, governor of Bengal after 1772 and governor-general of British India from 1774 to 1785. Like Steuart, Hastings rejected the idea of an open trade in salt; rather than an excise scheme as Steuart suggested, Hastings established a system of state monopoly, whereby the Company sold salt on to Indian merchants and derived a substantial income from the trade. Hastings's system of farming out parcels of revenue rights for five-year terms between 1772 and 1777 bore certain similarities to Steuart's proposed farming system, aiming to settle the farms on responsible taxpayers and to infuse much needed cash into the system of collection.[68] Hastings's 1776 scheme to undertake a detailed land survey as a basis for a more permanent land settlement also echoed Steuart's treatise, though Hastings preferred to compare his plan to the land reforms of the Mughal Emperor Akbar, or to the evaluation of the British land tax in 1692, rather than Steuart's more quixotic invocation of the Domesday Book.[69] Finally, and perhaps most strikingly, Hastings suggested a plan for establishing a network of state granaries in Bengal to protect against the dangers of famine. Only one of these granaries was ever built, an imposing white building in the city of Patna, and Hastings admitted that the constraints on state expenditure made further progress towards an elaborate system of state protection unlikely.[70]

Hastings's brand of political economy excited ardent opposition, especially as the Company lurched into further expensive wars between 1778 and 1783, and seemed to be heading for bankruptcy again. Some of this opposition drew on notions of an 'ancient constitution', and the immemorial rights of Indian landowners that were allegedly being oppressed by Company tyrants and tax farmers. Hastings's opponents were also quick to co-opt Smith into their service; indeed, the loudest of these critics, Philip Francis, cited the *Wealth of Nations* as early as November 1776 to support his argument against Hastings's revenue

---

[68] Travers, *Ideology and Empire*, pp. 110–15.

[69] For Hastings's revenue survey, see Robert Travers, '"The Real Value of the Lands": The Nawabs, the British and the Land Tax in Eighteenth-century Bengal', *Modern Asian Studies*, 38 (2004), pp. 530–45.

[70] Hastings discussed his plans for grain reserves towards the end of his life in a letter to the newly appointed governor-general of British India, the Earl of Moira, dated 12 November 1812: see British Library (London), Additional MS 29234, fos. 18–19, where he described the plans (with heavy irony) as a 'monument to the profusion and wild imagination of its author'.

survey, urging Smith's authority (and also, confusingly enough, James Steuart's) for the proposition that leniency and fixity of tax assessments offered a better security for property than detailed, vexatious, and exactly proportionate assessments.[71] Again, part of the reason why Smith became a valued source for policy makers in India was that many of them, including Philip Francis, were also highly critical of the Company's monopolistic trading practices, and wished to open the commerce of Bengal to more thorough competition.[72]

Even though the Company's monopoly of European trade with Asia would persist into the nineteenth century, Company governors increasingly justified their internal government of Indian territories as a form of emancipation from the restrictive controls and arbitrary principles of Asiatic tyrants. Lord Cornwallis's 'permanent settlement' of 1793 decisively rejected experiments of revenue 'farming' and schemes for progressively increasing the land tax, by awarding full permanent property rights to Indian landholders, and by fixing the land tax demand in perpetuity. At the same time, Cornwallis re-established and rationalised a province-wide network of civil and criminal courts, and abolished the right of local landholders to collect dues on trade. The Company's regime, built on the land tax, salt, and opium monopolies, customs dues, and monopolistic controls over foreign commerce, could hardly be styled as an empire of free trade. Thus, Smith would continue to be invoked by the Company's critics as an intellectual heavyweight for ending commercial restrictions in Asian trade.[73] Yet the Company's abolition of local market controls in Bengal, and its broader effort to cut back on the allegedly vexatious, 'feudal' powers of local chiefs, turning warrior princes into improving landlords, also enabled Company ideologues to enunciate a discourse of commercial improvement under the benevolent stewardship of enlightened rulers, which claimed certain affiliations with Smithian arguments.[74]

At the same time, James Steuart's idea of creatively adapting the absolute powers of Asiatic despotism to draw out the untapped wealth of the country continued to resonate in some British Indian policy circles. For example, Steuart's emphasis on efficient taxation as a means of

[71] For Francis's invocations of Smith, see Guha, *Rule of Property*, pp. 117, 147.

[72] For the views of another Company servant, Thomas Law, who made use of Smith to argue for freeing up the India trade, see ibid., pp. 184–5.

[73] Ambirajan, *Classical Political Economy and British Policy in India*, pp. 45–6.

[74] See esp. Guha, *Rule of Property*, pp. 160–86, and Sudipta Sen, *Empire of Free Trade*.

increasing the flow of money in the economy was echoed in Francis Russell's tract defending the Company government in 1793, which viewed the Company's system of taxing and spending as a form of 'rapid circulation' of money maintaining the buoyancy of the local economy.[75] While intellectual historians tend to highlight the distinctions between formal theoretical models like Steuart's and Smith's, in day-to-day political language, principles of political economy became more mixed up and jumbled. Indeed, in the context of British India, the lines between Steuart's 'economics of control' and a Smithian conception of commercial liberty could easily blur. As Martha Maclaren has shown, a group of Scottish administrator-scholars who dominated the intellectual high ground of British Indian politics in the early nineteenth century invoked Enlightenment stage theories to draw an analogy between the absolutism of early modern European monarchies, and the regulated despotism of British India. Both appeared as transitional political forms, necessary for breaking down the arbitrary power of local chiefs, and cementing the centralised legal foundations of a true commercial society.[76]

Conclusion: Intellectuals, Ideologues, and the Historians

The grand meta-narratives that have structured histories of modern political and economic thought, specifically the narrative of the 'rise of liberalism' or 'classical political-economy', have tended always to work from the supposed centre outwards. The 'rise of free trade imperialism' is framed as a turn within metropolitan discourse that later diffused throughout the empire.[77] Intellectual historians wonder about the relationship between 'classical political-economy' and 'empire' or 'liberalism' and 'empire', in which the relational terms are neatly distinguished, and arguments turn on the nature of the fit or disjuncture between the two.

---

[75] Francis Russell, *A Short History of the East India Company* (London, 1793), p. 44, and the discussion in Barber, *British Economic Thought and India*, pp. 104–9.

[76] Martha Maclaren, 'From Anaylsis to Prescription: Scottish Concepts of Asian Despotism in Early Nineteenth-century British India', *International History Review*, 15 (1993), pp. 469–501. For a fuller exposition of Maclaren's analysis of a 'Scottish school' of political economy in early nineteenth-century India, see her longer work, *British India and British Scotland, 1780–1830: Career Building, Empire Building, and a Scottish School of Thought in Indian Governance* (Akron, OH, 2001), esp. ch. 11.

[77] Bernard Semmel, *The Rise of Free Trade Imperialism: Classical Political Economy, the Empire of Free Trade and Imperialism, 1750–1850* (Cambridge, 1970).

Recent imperial turns in the writing of European history, in which European states and societies are increasingly reconfigured not only as metropolitan agents of expansion, but also as provinces within their own colonial empires, pose new challenges for intellectual and political historians. Apart from the traditional question of the relationship between metropolitan or European 'theory' and the empire outside, new imperial histories will become increasingly concerned not only with feedback effects from colonial settings, or with webs of connection and comparison between different colonies, but also with breaking down the boundaries between histories of thought and practice, histories of intellectuals and of ideologies, and histories of texts and their diverse contexts.[78]

This essay started in noting the apparent tension between histories of imperial ideology—based largely on the forms of political language deployed by administrators in colonial settings, and intellectual histories of metropolitan political economy. In the former, political economy is often figured as a vital prop of the new imperialism in late eighteenth-century India; in the latter, it is recuperated as a source for anti-imperial critique. Both approaches are valid on their own terms; and their contrasting outcomes are relatively easily reconcilable within a familiar narrative of the ideological appropriation of philosophical arguments. Yet this form of reconciliation cannot properly account for the way that metropolitan theorists did not stand apart from empire, but were embedded within webs of knowledge generated in colonial contexts. Further, it may not fully account for the diversity of theoretical standpoints within colonial settings, and the complex histories of intellectual reception and adaptation in the colonies.

Situating James Steuart and Adam Smith in the context of transcontinental debates about the British Empire in India suggests how each writer spoke in contrasting and ambivalent ways to complex constituencies of political actors. A figure like James Steuart, who has sometimes been regarded as redundant within metropolitan intellectual history, especially after 1776, takes on a new importance in the light of the emerging political economy of Company rule. Similarly, Smith's *Wealth of Nations* can be seen not only as one of the most uncompromising attacks on the Company's empire in India, but also a source of usable strategies for reforming and legitimising British imperial rule. While Smith may have been deeply pessimistic about the global repercussions of European

---

[78] For an insightful review, urging historians to address the 'socio-historical constitution' of forms of knowledge, see Sartori, 'The British Empire and its Liberal Mission'.

commercial expansion, British imperial officials could read his account of the dynamics of commercial society within Europe as a source of improving knowledge and moral authority.

Recent intellectual histories have persuasively argued for putting the political back into political economy and resisting teleological readings of figures like Steuart and Smith as 'proto-economists'. But the political, for these purposes, has tended to mean conceptions of polity generated within Europe and about Europe, whereas political economists were read in relation not just to states but to empires and colonies. From the perspective of colonial state builders in India, mired within difficult problems of how to fit a rule of conquest within an imagined 'empire of liberty', and to manage the porous boundaries between commerce and government, writings on political economy helped to answer specific questions of money supply, taxation, or commercial policy, and to separate out these questions from conventional notions of political virtue and constitutional propriety. It was in the empire, perhaps, that the potential within writings on political economy for emancipating issues of economic justice from concerns about political liberty was most tenaciously pursued. And political economy quickly became a vital source of expertise in a government that styled itself as a rule of foreign experts.

Note. I would like to thank Duncan Kelly, Sankar Muthu, Emma Rothschild, and Chris Bayly for their advice on earlier drafts of this essay.

7

Colonial Emigration, Public Policy, and Tory Romanticism, 1783–1830

KAREN O'BRIEN

THIS ESSAY IS CONCERNED WITH a particular strand of British imperial activity—voluntary, white colonial emigration and settlement—following the loss of the first British Empire when emigration by British and Irish settlers first started to feature prominently in public and parliamentary debates. In particular, it examines the collective British imaginative engagement with the figure of the colonial settler, not so much as a standard-bearer of Britain's civilising mission, but as a casualty of industrialisation, war, and poverty, and as an economic migrant who nevertheless appeared to embody the potential for the recuperation of British society, in its expanded colonial form, at some stage in the future. My particular focus is upon the role of literature, and in particular that played by Romantic writers, in a new national imaginative investment in colonial settlement. This idea had been previously discredited by its association in the public mind with convicts, the dregs of Britain's Celtic peripheries, and rebellious Americans, but enjoyed a significant revival in this period. I am also concerned with a strain of Tory argument and policy making that promoted state involvement and the planning of the colonisation of white settler territories in Canada, the Cape, New South Wales, and New Zealand. This Tory strain of British imperialism itself issued, not from Enlightenment cosmopolitanism, utilitarianism, or incipient nineteenth-century imperialist liberalism, but from the Romantic critique of classical political economy, and in particular from the Romantic assault on Malthus's non-interventionist stance on poverty. Unlike liberal economists, its proponents advocated an active role for the state in managing poverty, population surplus, and the export of excess population to overseas colonies. By concentrating upon this Tory interest in the social potential of the settler colonies, as well as the imaginative dimension conferred by literary writers, this essay aims to shed more light on a

Proceedings of the British Academy **155**, 161–179. © The British Academy 2009.

(sometimes neglected) strand of imperialism that evolved in tandem with nineteenth-century liberal imperialism, but that differed profoundly from it. Proponents of liberal imperialism did, as Jennifer Pitts has suggested in her recent study of James Mill, J. S. Mill, and others, distinguish quite sharply between the settler and non-settler colonies, and had separate things to say about the former.[1] But, at least in the decades after the loss of most of North America, it was the Tories who really led the way in reformulating the political status and social purpose of the settler colonies.

The Romantic preoccupation with rural community and with the natural and ethical ties of men to their land can and has been seen as a backward, even nostalgic, turning away from industrial modernity. But it also played into what Anna Gambles has called, in her study of early nineteenth-century conservative economic discourse, the 'alternative imperial political economy' and 'constructive imperialism' of the Tories.[2] Wordsworth and Coleridge are part of this story, and an important connecting figure is their close associate, the Romantic poet and Poet Laureate Robert Southey.[3] He became a prominent advocate of assisted emigration, and a consultant to and commentator upon the Parliamentary

---

[1] Jennifer Pitts, *A Turn to Empire: The Rise of Imperial Liberalism in Britain and France* (Princeton, NJ, 2005), p. 113 (Bentham was an exception to this). Also Uday Singh Mehta, *Liberalism and Empire: A Study in Nineteenth-century British Liberal Thought* (Chicago, IL, 1999), pp. 70–1. See also Bernard Semmel on the imperialist 'agrarian' alternative to concepts of 'trading empire' in *The Rise of Free Trade Imperialism: Classical Political Economy, the Empire of Trade and Imperialism, 1750–1850* (Cambridge, 1970), pp. 48–75; Donald Winch, *Classical Political Economy and the Colonies* (London, 1965); John Cunningham Wood, *British Economists and the Empire* (London and Canberra, 1983), pp. 7–15.

[2] Anna Gambles, *Protection and Politics: Conservative Economic Discourse, 1815–1852* (Woodbridge, Suffolk, 1999). See also H. J. M. Johnston, *British Emigration Policy: 'Shovelling out Paupers'* (Oxford, 1972) and Peter Burroughs, *British Attitudes Towards Canada, 1822–1849* (Scarborough, Ontario, 1971).

[3] Coleridge once asserted that 'Colonization is not only a manifest expedient—but an imperative duty on Great Britain. God seems to hold out his finger to us over the sea. But it must be a national colonization, such as was that of the Scotch to America; a colonization of Hope, and not such as we alone encouraged and affected for the last fifty years, a colonization of Despair': *The Collected Works of Samuel Taylor Coleridge* (Princeton, NJ, 1971), Table Talk (4 May 1833), XXV, pp. 369–70. On Romantic writing and imperialism more generally, see Peter Kitson and Tim Fulford (eds), *Romanticism and Colonialism: Writing and Empire, 1780–1830* (Cambridge, 1998); Kitson, Fulford, and Debbie Lee, *Literature, Science and Exploration in the Romantic Era: Bodies of Knowledge* (Cambridge, 2004); and Alan Richardson and Sonia Hofkosh (eds), *Romanticism, Race and Imperial Culture, 1780–1834* (Bloomington, IN, 1996). On Romanticism and political economy, see Philip Connell, *Romanticism, Economics and the Question of Culture* (Oxford, 2001) and, most authoritatively, Donald Winch, *Riches and Poverty: An Intellectual History of Political Economy in Britain, 1750–1834* (Cambridge, 1996), ch. 11.

Select Committee reports of 1826–7 on emigration, authored by Tory Under-secretary of State for the Colonies (and Byron's cousin) Robert Wilmot-Horton. Wilmot-Horton made emigration an issue of pressing national concern, some time in advance of large-scale exoduses to the colonies, and he exerted a significant (if often unacknowledged) influence upon the man who really sold the idea of planned, state-sponsored emigration both to the government and to liberal political economists such as J. S. Mill: Edward Gibbon Wakefield. In all of these debates of the 1820s and 1830s, and in the coalescence of Whigs and Tories around Wakefield's vision of Britain's colonial future, an ancillary but important part was also played by Romantic ideals: notably that of the psychic wholeness and civic autonomy conferred by a close (preferably proper-tied) relationship between man and the land, as well as the richly imaginative mental condition of man adrift in wide, open spaces, seeking to reconstitute them as a version of the British home.

The first two decades of the nineteenth century brought a considerable expansion of opportunities for British colonial emigration.[4] A large proportion of colonial emigration was involuntary, including the tens of thousands of British and Irish convicts transported, from 1788 onwards, to New South Wales and Van Diemen's Land. Other colonies gave some hint of their future potential as new beginnings, refuges, and desperate last resorts for the 22.5 million or so people who ultimately left Britain and Ireland between 1815 and 1914. After the constitutional reorganisation, in 1791, of the remaining North American colonies, migrants began to trickle into Upper and Lower Canada, among them, after 1803, a number of Highlanders displaced by the clearances, as well as small numbers of settlers into the Cape Colony, acquired by Britain during the Napoleonic Wars. With new acquisitions in the Caribbean and, from 1818, the consolidation of East India Company supremacy in India, it was soon apparent how far Britain had recovered as an imperial power from the disaster of the American Revolution. State-assisted emigration, of the kind advocated by Southey, Wilmot-Horton, and Wakefield, only ever represented a small fraction of the total, but its advocates exerted disproportionate influence upon the reconceptualisation, in the first half of the nineteenth century, of Britain's relationship with its colonies, of

---

[4] See Charlotte Erickson, *Leaving England: Essays on British Emigration in the Nineteenth Century* (Ithaca, NY, and London, 1994); Helen I. Cowan, *British Emigration to British North America: The First Hundred Years* (Toronto, 1961); and Marjory Harper, 'British Migration', in Andrew Porter (ed.), *The Oxford History of the British Empire* (Oxford, 1999), pp. 75–87.

their nature, economic purpose, and the kinds of imperial future they might bring. Emigration to the colonies in the early nineteenth century was, in fact, statistically dwarfed by the numbers setting sail for the United States of America. This was a persistent cause of British cultural anxiety, and soon after American independence commentators sought to draw distinctions between Americans and other British settlers in the remaining colonies. The Scottish writer Anne Grant, for example, in her *Memoirs of an American Lady* (1808), differentiated between Americans and Canadians, not only in terms of their political situation and culture, but also in relation to the far more stable relationship to the land and agrarian values that, she claims, Canada's geography naturally promotes:

> The country, barren at the seaside, does not afford an inducement for those extensive settlements which have a tendency to become mere commercial from their situation [by which she means independent America]. It becomes more fertile as it recedes further from the sea. Thus holding out an inducement to pursue nature into her favourite retreats, where on the banks of mighty waters, calculated to promote all the purpose of social traffic among the inhabitants, the richest soil, the happiest climate, and the most complete detachment from the world, promise a safe asylum to those who carry the arts and the literature of Europe, hereafter to grace and enlighten scenes where agriculture has already made rapid advances.[5]

America's subsequent enemy status in 1812–14 further exacerbated anxieties, and ensured that the cultural vision for the colonial empire continued to be negatively defined by the American example. Keats, for example, wrote to his brother out in Albion, Illinois, urging him to resist Americanisation, and to be sure to infuse the new settlement with English genius and values.[6] Southey tried to define the difference between Americans and more recent British colonial settlers in terms of their very different approaches to settlement and colonisation, and of the superior instinct of the British settler to create civilised and domestic spaces:

> When Americans become restless, their bent is towards the wilderness; they move into the back settlements, and there become pioneers of civilisation. British and Irish adventurers, on the contrary, when removed to an uncultivated land, appear to pine after the haunts of men, and make when they can toward the centre of society instead of remaining beyond its frontiers. What to the

---

[5] [Anne Grant], *Memoirs of An American Lady: With Sketches of Manners and Scenery in America*, 2 vols (London, 1808), vol. 2, p. 340.
[6] *The Letters of John Keats*, ed. Hyder Edward Rollins, 2 vols (Cambridge, MA, 1958), vol. 1, pp. 397–8.

American back-settler seems the perfection of wild independence, they regard with dislike.[7]

English commentators rejected the Jeffersonian model of territorial expansion—the natural liberty of the pioneer settler pulling away from the social and political centre—and characterised too much frontier territory as detrimental to civilisation.[8] Not for them the colonial 'new men' of Crèvecoeur's famous formulation ('Everything [in America] has tended to regenerate them; new laws, a new mode of living, a new social system; here they are become men . . . Here all individuals of all nations are melted into a new race of men').[9] William Cobbett reasserted the similarities between Americans and English (except when it came to the American propensity for heavy drinking) in his account of his enforced, temporary emigration to the USA in 1817–18.[10] Later, Wakefield would argue with considerable bravura that this kind of American 'newness' was precisely what Britain should strive to avoid in her colonies:

> What are the ideas that we mean to express by the words New People? . . . We mean, it strikes me, a people like what the Canadians will be, and the United States' Americans are—a people though they continually increase in number, make no progress in the art of living; who, in respect of wealth, knowledge, skill, taste and whatever belongs to civilization, have degenerated from their ancestors . . . We mean, in two words, a people who become rotten before they are ripe.[11]

Throughout this period, America was an overwhelmingly prominent topos in British literature, and the figure of the Native American was central to the imaginative negotiation of ideas both of unlimited spaces and of common humanity.[12] More broadly, the vocabularies of savagery and barbarism, inherited from the Enlightenment and especially from Gibbon's epic accounts of mass migration in ancient Europe, were

[7] Robert Southey, *Sir Thomas More: or, Colloquies on the Progress and Prospects of Society*, 2 vols (London, 1829), vol. 2, p. 280.

[8] The best account of British cultural attitudes to America in this period is James Chandler, 'Concerning the Influence of America on the Mind', in *England in 1819: The Politics of Literary Culture and the Case of Romantic Historicism* (Cambridge, 1998), ch. 8.

[9] J. Hector St John de Crèvecoeur, *Letters from an American Farmer* (1782), ed. Albert E. Stone (Harmondworth, 1981), pp. 68 f, 70.

[10] William Cobbett, *A Year's Residence in the United States of America* (1818–19, repr. New York, 1969), p. 384.

[11] Edward Gibbon Wakefield, *A Letter from Sydney* (1829–30) in *The Collected Works of Edward Gibbon Wakefield*, ed. M. F. Lloyd Prichard (London and Glasgow, 1968), pp. 151–2.

[12] See Tim Fulford, *Romantic Indians: Native Americans, British Literature and Transatlantic Culture, 1756–1830* (Oxford, 2006).

valuable instruments through which literary writers could link questions of intellectual and economic impoverishment to those of man's relationship to the land.[13] There was a pressing practical need, at the political level, to redirect emigration away from the USA and towards the British colonies. This was accompanied (sometimes obligingly) by literary depictions of America as a place of rootlessness, failed aspirations, and danger. In one of his early *Lyrical Ballads*, Wordsworth told the story of Ruth, a lonely, motherless young woman swept off her feet by a young soldier from Georgia who is 'like a panther in the wilderness', and who tells seductive tales of magnolias, green savannahs, and fighting with the Indians.[14] He persuades her to marry him and to emigrate to America, but then simply takes off without her, just as they are preparing to sail. Wordsworth's implicit explanation is that, deep down, the Georgian is an impetuous creature of wild open spaces and Indian lore ('from Indian blood you [would] deem him sprung'), incapable of steadiness or of settling down.[15] The shock of this failed emigration leaves Ruth a broken vagrant, roaming the Somerset hills. She resembles many of Wordsworth's other solitary figures who are also internal migrants, displaced by emotional or economic misfortune; their displacement is obliquely linked to their deep imaginative sympathy with the natural environment and to their seeming unwillingness or inability to put down roots.

The link between this familiar side of Wordsworth as a poet who epitomised the human and his own condition as both a lonely communion with nature and a quest for settlement, and his subsequent advocacy of overseas colonisation may not at first seem clear. Certainly, there were those who descried a special connection between the spirit of Wordsworth and that of the pioneer colonist, for example Thomas De Quincey who commented: 'Wordsworth is peculiarly the poet for the solitary and meditative; and, throughout the countless myriads of future America and future Australia, no less than Polynesia and Southern Africa, there will be situations without end fitted by their loneliness to favour his influence for centuries to come.'[16] This was a connection that Wordsworth himself did

---

[13] J. G. A. Pocock, *Barbarism and Religion*, Vol. 4: *Barbarians, Savages and Empires* (Cambridge, 2005).

[14] 'Ruth' (1800) in *Lyrical Ballads and Other Poems, 1797–1800*, ed. James Butler and Karen Green (Ithaca, NY, 1992), l. 25.

[15] Ibid., l. 38.

[16] Quoted by Nigel Leask in 'Pantisocracy and the Politics of the "Preface" to *Lyrical Ballads*', in Alison Yarrington and Kelvin Everest (eds), *Reflections of Revolution: Images of Romanticism*,

something to encourage in the longest poem he published during his life-time, *The Excursion* of 1814. The poem tells the story of a five-day jour-ney around the Lake District undertaken by the poet himself and two characters, the Wanderer and the Solitary. Their conversations range across the whole of human life and contemporary society. Towards the end, the Wanderer reaches out to their implied listeners with a ringing endorsement of state-sponsored emigration:

> For, as the element of air affords
> An easy passage to the industrious bees . . .
> So the wide waters, open to the power,
> The will, the instincts, and the appointed needs
> Of Britain, do invite her to cast off
> Her swarms, and in succession send them forth;
> Bound to establish new communities
> On every shore whose aspect favours hope
> Or bold adventure; promising to skill
> And perseverance their deserved reward.[17]

This pronouncement comes in the context of the Wanderer's plea for Britain to assume responsibility for its poor through the provision of state-funded education. Industrial forms of labour, the exploitation of child workers, and rural displacement, he argues, are creating a mental underclass, 'A savage horde among the civilised/ A servile band among the lordly free'.[18] Both education and properly supported colonial emigration offer a remedy for these ills, with the colonies offering a global canvas upon which to reconstitute lost community and reanimate the human mind. All of this is offered as a vision of hope for the future in a poem that thematises both internal and external British migration. The Solitary and the Wanderer are both internal migrants from Scotland, but for the former alone migrancy is a pathological condition, starting from the moment when, driven by grief and political disillusion, he attempts to set-tle in America and to move west into Native American territory. He finds the natives merely 'Remorseless and submissive to no law', but, as the

---

(London and New York, 1993), p. 45. On Wordsworth and empire more generally, see Saree Makdisi, 'Home Imperial: Wordsworth's London and the Spots of Time', in *Romantic Imperialism: Universal Empire and the Culture of Modernity* (Cambridge, 1998), ch. 2. See also Karen O'Brien, 'Uneasy Settlement: Wordsworth and Emigration', in Michael Rossington and Clare Lamont (eds), *Romanticism's Debatable Lands* (Basingstoke, 2007), pp. 121–35.

[17] *The Poetical Works of William Wordsworth*, ed. Helen Darbishire and Ernest de Selincourt, 2nd edn, 5 vols (1952–9), vol. 5, *The Excursion*, ix, ll. 369–70, 375–82.

[18] *The Excursion*, ix, ll. 308–9.

poem makes clear, this is partly a reflection on him since he is, as he admits, like 'a damaged seed/ Whose fibres cannot, if they would take root'.[19] The Solitary approximates to the condition of savagery in his incapacity to settle or to form an economically and psychologically productive relationship to the land. It should be said that savagery, for Wordsworth, is not exclusively an ethnic ascription, but often a more generalised state of imaginative wildness. Wordsworth described his childhood self as 'a naked savage in a thunder storm', and used the term frequently to signal the way that the industrial poor are kept below the economic and mental threshold of civilisation. In a postscript to *Yarrow Revisited and Other Poems*, published in 1835, Wordsworth denounced the new Poor Law Amendment Act, comparing the English poor to the 'famished Northern Indian' and the 'savage Islander who . . . watches for food which the waves may cast up'.[20]

His notion of savagery is thus not limited to the notion of inferior ethnicity, although it often does certainly imply a loose anthropological hierarchy of savagery, rusticity, and Christian civility. It also meshes with imperialist ideas (current in Wordsworth's day) of human political competence in which colonisers are held to be superior to 'savages' because of their capacity to settle or develop waste lands. As a would-be settler, the young Solitary, like the native peoples he encounters, lacked this competence. Wordsworth offered a contrasting, successful example of colonial settlement in his most popular work, *A Guide through the District of the Lakes*, in which he admiringly describes the Dalesmen of the area. Originally Norse or Celtic settlers, Wordsworth tells how their ancestors migrated into the area, became freeholding peasant proprietors, like 'Robinson Crusoes', as he puts it, 'creeping into possession of their homesteads, their little crofts, their mountain enclosures', and transformed their settlement into an inheritance:

> Towards the head of these Dales was found a perfect Republic of Shepherds and Agriculturalists . . . The chapel was the only edifice that presided over the dwellings, the supreme head of this pure Commonwealth; the members of which existed in the midst of a powerful empire, like an ideal society, or an organized community, whose constitution had been imposed and regulated by the mountains which protected it . . . venerable was the transition, when a curious traveller, descending from the heart of the mountains, had come to some ancient manorial residence in the more open parts of the Vales, which, through

---

[19] *The Excursion*, iii, ll. 954, 889–90.
[20] *The Prose Works of William Wordsworth*, ed. W. J. B. Owen and Jane Worthington Smyser, 3 vols (Oxford, 1974), vol. 3, p. 243.

the rights attached to its proprietor, connected the almost visionary mountain republic he had been contemplating with the substantial frame of society as existing in the laws and constitution of a mighty empire.[21]

J. S. Mill cited this passage approvingly in his discussion of the merits of peasant land proprietorship in his *Principles of Political Economy* (1848).[22]

Apart from the remnants of this system of landownership in the dales, the only place at the time where small-hold landownership was widespread was the colonies, and Wordsworth's peasant proprietor certainly found an echo in Wilmot-Horton's conception of the ideal colonial settler. His colonisation schemes for New South Wales, Upper Canada, and the Cape rested upon the acquisition of smallholdings by industrious emigrants, and he drew a distinction between mere emigration (a movement of labour without capital) and colonisation (the mixing of labour and capital to bring 'waste land' into agricultural use). His hope was that, with a little capital grant from the British government (raised by means of advancing loans to parishes), the 'settler would be firmly fixed to the soil', as he put it in one of his parliamentary speeches:

> The distinction he drew between emigration where the individuals were fixed to the soil, and that desultory kind of emigration which consisted in merely conveying them to a certain place, and then leaving them to make their way as they could. He [Wilmot-Horton] would appeal to any man whether the advantages of the plan hitherto pursued [of giving emigrants land and support enough to become independent proprietors] were not almost too obvious to require argument. The settler would be firmly fixed to the soil, instead of taking his chance of obtaining subsistence.[23]

Wilmot-Horton began his sustained advocacy of parish- and state-assisted emigration in the 1820s, setting out his views in his pamphlet entitled *An Outline of a Plan of Emigration to Upper Canada* (1823).[24] Parts of his argument were directed at domestic concerns about overpopulation and unrest, particularly among the Irish Catholic population (and these have often been caricatured as a rage for 'shovelling out paupers'). But a substantial part of his ideas related to his vision for Britain's colonial future, and had a decidedly Tory Romantic tinge to

---

[21] *A Guide through the District of the Lakes* (1835 version), ed. Ernest de Selincourt (London, 1905), pp. 52, 58, 67.

[22] John Stuart Mill, *Principles of Political Economy*, 2 vols (London, 1848), vol. 1, pp. 300–1.

[23] Wilmot-Horton reported in *Hansard*, 16 (15 February 1827), p. 481.

[24] This was published in the *Report of the Parliamentary Select Committee on the Employment of the Poor in Ireland* (1823), pp. 173–8.

them. Malthus was privately sceptical, if publicly more circumspect about the plan.[25] Wilmot-Horton's distinction between mere migrants and colonisers might have appealed to Wordsworth, and they certainly did to Wordsworth's friend and neighbour Southey. Like the politician, he saw emigration as a chance to repair some of the damage done to Britain's social fabric by rampant industrialisation and the immiseration of the poor. Sometime before his correspondence with Wilmot-Horton and two years before the publication of *The Excursion*, Southey had already advocated state support for emigration as a means of siphoning off surplus population and of exporting British culture:

> It is time that Britain should become the hive of nations, and cast her swarms; and here are lands to receive them. What is required of government is to encourage emigration by founding settlements, and facilitating the means of transport ... imagine these wide regions in the yet uncultivated parts of the earth flourishing like our own, and possessed by people enjoying our institutions and speaking our language. Whether they should be held in colonial dependence, or become separate states, or when they may have ceased to depend upon the parent country ... is of little import upon this wide view of things.[26]

These remarks occurred in the context of a *Quarterly Review* essay on Malthus's *Essay on the Principles of Population*. Like Wordsworth and, later, Wilmot-Horton, he accepted Malthus's contention that the national population might outstrip material resources, along with a similar Anglican scepticism about the possibilities for human progress, but he did not share Malthus's belief that, like sand on the seashore, any surplus population scooped out for the colonies would simply replenish itself.[27] Southey's vision, like Wordworth's, was of a circle of colonists radiating out from an English centre, its expanding circumference giving an international dimension to the Anglican church and, above all, bringing a recuperation from a history of overpopulation and poverty in a new

---

[25] See R. N. Ghosh, 'Malthus on Emigration and Colonization: Letters to Wilmot-Horton', *Economica*, 30 (1963), pp. 45–62.

[26] Southey, 'On the State of the Poor, the Principle of Mr. Malthus's *Essay on Population, and the Manufacturing System*' (1812), in *Essays, Moral and Political*, 2 vols (London, 1832), vol. 1, pp. 154–5.

[27] See Malthus's discussion 'Of Emigration' in the *Essay on the Principles of Population* (1803 edn and after), which he characterised as 'a very weak palliative' for the problems of overpopulation: *Essay*, ed. Donald Winch (Cambridge, 1992), p. 81. The original 1798 edition characterised emigration as a last resort for the desperate, but conceded that 'a certain degree of emigration is known to be favourable to the population of the modern country': *An Essay on the Principle of Population* (London, 1798), pp. 109, 209.

spatial dimension. The colonies held out the prospect of an indefinite postponement of Malthusian history, and their open frontiers that of an alternative modernity to that offered by the political economists. To understand the genesis and force of this idea, it is worth looking still further back at Southey's earlier career when he first engaged himself and his fellow Romantic writers with ideas and fantasies of emigration. In the mid-1790s, he and Coleridge had seriously entertained a scheme of emigration to the Pennsylvania backcountry, to set up a utopian colony based upon communal property, farming, and agriculturally situated writing. Southey never did emigrate, although he made an internal migration from the south of England to Keswick, and he did encourage his brother to go out to Canada in the 1820s.[28] Around the same time as his emigration plans, he wrote a series of poems, the 'Botany Bay Eclogues' (published in his poems of 1797, along with one further poem published separately a year later). In these he gave voice to soldiers, sailors, prostitutes, and farmers, most of them outcasts stranded on the far side of the world, to whom New South Wales offers a harsh but potentially salutary asylum. This is the case with one of the characters, Frederic, transported for an unspecified, heinous crime, whose life in England had been one of indigence and dispossession ('I had no share in Nature's patrimony'), but who resolves, at the end of the poem, to come in from the wild to his hut, and finds solace, even redemption in self-reliant toil in the colony: 'I shall reach/ My little hut again! Again by toil/ Force from the stubborn earth my sustenance'.[29] Southey's idea for an eclogue of colonial new beginnings in turn owed something to *The Hurricane: A Theosophical and Western Eclogue* (1796) by his acquaintance William Gilbert, a poem that juxtaposes imperial violence with innocent and redemptive colonisation (in this case, by a little girl orphaned in a shipwreck, rescued, and resettled on Antigua), and Southey praised the poem in several of his letters.[30]

During this period, Southey was more generally preoccupied with questions of redemptive colonisation since he was writing the epic poem *Madoc* (1805) whose purpose was to celebrate an ideal of peaceful emigration and settlement using the legend of the first European discoverer

---

[28] On Tom Southey's plans for emigration, see Mark Storey, *Robert Southey: A Life* (Oxford, 1997), p. 299 and Southey, *New Letters of Robert Southey*, ed. Kenneth Curry, 3 vols (New York, 1965), vol. 2, pp. 243–5.

[29] *Poetical Works, 1793–1810*, ed. Lynda Pratt, Tim Fulford, and Daniel S. Roberts, 5 vols (London, 2004), 'Frederic' (1797), vol. 5, pp. 81–3. The lines cited are ll. 52 and 76–8.

[30] See Paul Cheshire, 'The Hermetic Geography of William Gilbert', *Romanticism*, 9 (2003), pp. 82–93. See Southey to William Wynn (26 January 1797), *New Letters*, vol. 1, p. 120.

of America, the twelfth-century Welsh prince Madoc. In telling how Madoc and his followers sail across the Atlantic from Wales to North America, Southey assures his readers that 'not of conquest greedy, not the sons/ Of Commerce, merchandizing blood, they seek/ The distant land'.[31] Instead, he depicts them as benign colonisers of pre-Columbian Florida, having been deprived of their native Welsh patrimony by treacherous relatives. They make positive use of their experience of dispossession when they espouse the cause of the Native American Hoamen tribe and liberate them from the clutches and idolatrous religious practices of the brutal Aztec ruling caste. At the end, the Hoamen and Welsh form a joint settlement, while the remnants of the Aztecs depart for Mexico, in Southey's words, to 'rear a mightier empire, and set up/ Again their foul idolatry'.[32]

Both before and after *Madoc*, Southey struggled to find an enabling myth of benign white colonial settlement, along with a credible, mythic founding father. Before he chose the subject of Madoc, he considered writing an epic on Brutus, the legendary Trojan founder of Britain, and a much favoured emblem, in numerous seventeenth- and eighteenth-century projected or half-finished epics, of enlightened colonisation.[33] Southey also had before him an example of a modern founding father of this type, Granville Sharp, who had established a colony in the Sierra Leone estuary in the late 1780s to provide a refuge for former slaves and other emigrants of African descent. In 1798, Southey published a poem in the *Morning Post* celebrating the humane and enlightened aspirations behind the Sierra Leone venture: 'They come to bid injustice cease,/ They come with science and with peace,/ To proffer happiness'.[34] In Southey's later works, Captain James Cook supplied the place of Sharp, Madoc, Brutus, and other real and legendary founding fathers as a figure for benevolent colonisation, and in *A Vision of Judgement* (Southey's, not

---

[31] *Poetical Works*, vol. 2, p. 459. See Lynda Pratt, 'Revising the National Epic: Coleridge, Southey and Madoc', *Romanticism*, 2 (1996), pp. 149–63, and Nigel Leask, 'Southey's *Madoc*: Reimagining the Conquest of America', in Lynda Pratt (ed.), *Robert Southey and the Contexts of English Romanticism* (Basingstoke, 2006), pp. 133–50.

[32] *Poetical Works*, vol. 2, p. 570.

[33] On Southey's Brutus plans, see Pratt, 'Revising the National Epic', p. 153. On the Brutus myth, see Karen O'Brien, 'Poetry and Political Thought: Liberty and Benevolence in the Case of the British Empire, *c.* 1680–1800', in David Armitage (ed.), *Political Thought in History, Literature and Theory, 1500–1800* (Cambridge, 2006), pp. 175–7.

[34] 'On the Settlement of Sierra Leona', ll. 19–21, *Poetical Works*, vol. 5, p. 169. On the Sierra Leone venture and on idealistic colonisation schemes in the Romantic period, see Deirdre Coleman, *Romantic Colonization and British Anti-slavery* (Cambridge, 2005), chs 2 and 3.

Byron's) he listed Cook as one of the worthies of the Georgian age who left 'a lasting name, to humanity dear as to science'.[35] Here, too, Southey stood in a long eighteenth-century tradition of writers (including his friend Anna Seward) who had mythologised Cook as a figure of atonement for the sins of earlier British imperialism and as the progenitor of a new kind of colonialism—humane, benevolent, and technocratic, rather than commercial and conquering. The idea of colonisation, which had started, with the 'Botany-Bay Eclogues', *Madoc*, and Southey's own migration to Keswick, as an exploration of psychological and moral recovery, became, in later works, a myth of British humanity institutionalised and writ large on the face of the globe.

Southey undoubtedly considered the hostility to the colonies of Malthus and other political economists as being merely of a piece with their non-interventionist and inhumane attitude towards poverty. Both he and Malthus became actively involved in the debate about the future of the settler colonies during the consultation process that issued in the publication of two Select Committee reports into the matter in 1826 and 1827. As well as summoning Malthus before the Committee, Wilmot-Horton, as chair, wrote to Southey for advice, and endeavoured to persuade the government to make generous grants of land and financial assistance to would-be emigrants. Southey warmly endorsed the Select Committee reports in the *Quarterly*, agreeing wholeheartedly that 'a regular as well as regulated system of emigration is required in the stage of society which we have attained', especially, he added at some length, for the surplus Irish population.[36] Over and above endorsing Tory policy in the 1820s, Southey continued to forge an alternative vision of the empire as a capacious, potentially enfranchising home for the poor (in Canada and Australia, but also in the newer Cape settlements)—a vision which, on occasions, he pursued into religious and racial sectarianism of the worst kind, but, which David Eastwood has argued, did offer a seriously considered reply to the political economists.[37]

---

[35] Southey, *Poetical Works* (London, 1837–8), vol. 10, p. 236. Compare Anna Seward, *Elegy on Captain Cook* (London, 1780).

[36] Johnston, *British Emigration Policy*, pp. 66–7; Southey, 'Of Emigration' (1828), in *Essays, Moral and Political*, vol. 2, p. 274.

[37] On Southey's *Annual Review* pieces on the Cape, see Geoffrey Carnall, *Robert Southey and His Age: The Development of a Conservative Mind* (Oxford, 1960), p. 79, and David Eastwood, 'Ruinous Prosperity: Robert Southey's Critique of the Commercial System', *Wordsworth Circle*, 25 (1993), pp. 72–6. See also Gambles, *Protection and Politics*, pp. 172–3.

Southey benefited greatly from the advice and input of his friend John
Rickman, the architect of the first population census of 1801 and a supporter of state-assisted emigration.[38] With the help of Rickman, he was
able to dispute Malthus's political prescriptions for poor law reform, and,
more generally, his infamous contention that there was no place at
'nature's mighty feast' for those unable to support themselves. Southey
was adamant that state intervention, national education, and assisted
emigration would ensure that there would always be a safety-valve, a
place overseas at nature's table ('if the land were full, and every acre husbanded like the garden-grounds of Flanders', he insisted, 'there is the sea
before us, and the way open to Canada, to South Africa, to Australia').[39]
Soon after the Select Committee reports Southey gave his ideas on empire
their most considered statement in his *Colloquies on the Progress and
Prospects of Society* (1829).[40] Here he renewed his call for a planned
national colonisation as a means of giving the poor an opportunity 'of
providing a sure subsistence, in all comfort and independence, for themselves and their posterity', but he also warned of the dangers of social
degeneration 'towards a lower standard of general manners' in the
colonies unless British institutions were properly transplanted and
nurtured. Fortunately, he did not air his view, expressed in some of his
letters, that forced emigration for the destitute might be a policy worth
considering.[41]

However much his views may have hardened, Southey clung on to
the idea that state-sponsored colonisation offered some redress for
poverty and social exclusion, even if that redress stopped far short of the
redistribution of property advocated in his earliest works. His vision of
the colonial future also retained the flavour of the Romantic agrarian
republicanism evident in his *Quarterly* essay on Malthus cited above,
where he stated that it does not matter whether the colonies separate from
the mother country so long as they remain enclaves of British yeomanry.
For Southey, the idea of portable, emigrant Britishness was not straightforwardly part of an aspiration for global dominance, and he recognised
and welcomed the fact that all colonial settlements, like those of
Wordsworth's Dalesmen, had an inbuilt republican logic of separation.

---

[38] On Southey and Rickman, see Winch, *Riches and Poverty*, pp. 311–14.
[39] Southey, 'On the State of the Poor', *Essays, Moral and Political*, vol. 1, p. 86.
[40] Southey, *Sir Thomas More*, vol. 2, pp. 276, 283.
[41] On forced emigration, see Carnall, *Robert Southey*, pp. 299, 326–7.

Throughout his life, Southey remained sanguine about Britain's loss of its American colonies, and anticipated a similar, though less violent, process of separation for Canada, Australia, and the Cape Colony. It mattered more to him that people of British origin, possessed of British energy and values, should have a large, freehold stake in the world. Indeed, he felt that migration and a degree of separation might be the very conditions for the renewal of the British culture of liberty, that had eroded in recent times by the industrial economy with its ever more thinly sliced divisions of labour. His emphasis was always upon the productive capacity of the settler, and he believed that modern empires, unlike the huge territorial empires of the ancient world, depended more for their success upon productivity than upon territorial extent. Like Thomas Carlyle after him, he thought that the existence of a colonial outlet for talented but under-employed individuals would help to restore the equilibrium of industry, landowners, and the lower class.[42]

The problems inherent in this kind of Romantic colonial thinking soon became apparent, not only in Carlyle's work, but in the popular fiction and promotional literature that bent the colonies so strongly to imaginative needs of the metropolis. One example is Mary Brunton's novel *Self-control* (1810–11), a best-selling work much admired by Jane Austen among others. Brunton's heroine, Laura Montreville, is the victim of an implacable aristocratic stalker, Villiers Hargrave, who kidnaps her and bundles her onto a ship bound for Quebec. She escapes by floating downriver in an Indian canoe, nearly drowns, but is rescued by a kind family of English settlers who take her to their 'plain, decent' farm, before eventually despatching her to home and happiness in Scotland.[43] Brunton's Romantic image of the British colonies as a space where wholesome rural domesticity remedies old world cruelty or corruption recurred many times during the nineteenth century. Another well known instance of this occurs in Elizabeth Gaskell's *Mary Barton* (1848) which tells the story of the bitter conflict between Manchester factory owners and their workers, up to the time of the rejection of the Chartist petition in 1839. The conflict is suspended and its resolution postponed at the end when the protagonist, Mary, and her husband, Jem, emigrate to Canada. The reader's last glimpse of them is in their idyllic cottage near Toronto where Jem is no longer a factory worker but an instrument maker to an

---

[42] On Carlyle's heroic conception of emigration, see the valuable discussion by John Morrow in *Thomas Carlyle* (London, 2006), pp. 112–16.

[43] Mary Brunton, *Self-control: A Novel*, ed. Sara Maitland (London, 1986), p. 426.

agricultural college. The idealised domesticity which Gaskell habitually associated with the English countryside, and which she derived from her deep love of Wordsworth, is here transposed onto a colonial landscape.[44] The colonial future she offers these characters, beyond the conflict and poverty wrought by industrialisation, is also, inescapably, a nostalgic enclave of pre-modern rusticity.

Edward Gibbon Wakefield, too, believed in the possibility of a colonial future, but he was much more wary of allowing his vision of the colonies to mutate into a nostalgic projection of the English agrarian past. As he said, 'you cannot recall the past, but you must deplore the present, and you may control the future'.[45] His first and most dazzling intervention in the debate about the future of the colonies came in the form of a piece of imaginative literature, the *Letter from Sydney*, published in 1829 at the end of a decade of colonial controversy. At the time he was in prison for abducting a rich heiress, and, in an imaginative effort of escape, he wrote the *Letter* in the persona of an independent gentleman farmer concerned about the faltering development of his home colony in New South Wales. Bad teeth, he writes, bad manners, scarce and uncooperative labourers, and, above all, more land than sense are the causes of Australia's hopelessly uncivilised newness. What is needed, the farmer argues, is a planned programme of emigration to bring over a properly sex-balanced workforce available to landowners and investors. Land itself should be sold at a price high enough to keep these workers in waged labour for a few years at least, and to finance further emigration.

Wakefield, a man of Whig affiliations, addressed himself first and foremost to the anti-colonial arguments of political economists, especially those who had argued that outflows of capital weakened the home economy, and that outflows of population were simply replenished by rising domestic birth rates (he won over John Stuart Mill, but Malthus remained sceptical).[46] Unlike his Tory and Romantic predecessors in the

---

[44] Jenny Uglow, *Elizabeth Gaskell: A Habit of Stories* (London, 1993), pp. 102, 176, 210. See also Diana C. Archibald, *Domesticity, Imperialism, and Emigration in the Victorian Novel* (Columbia, MO, 2002), pp. 30–2. Robert Grant gives a broad sense of the context of 'Arcadianist' and 'degenerationist' strands in attitudes to the British colonies in his period in his '"The Fit and Unfit": Suitable Settlers for Britain's Mid-nineteenth-century Colonial Possessions', *Victorian Literature and Culture*, 33 (2005), pp. 169–86.

[45] The best introduction to Wakefield is the *Dictionary of New Zealand Biography* entry by Miles Fairburn (www.dnzb.govt.nz). See also Friends of the Turnbull Library, *Edward Gibbon Wakefield and the Colonial Dream* (Wellington, 1997) and A. J. Harrop, *The Amazing Career of Edward Gibbon Wakefield* (London, 1928).

[46] See Ghosh, 'Malthus on Emigration', p. 60.

emigration debate, Wakefield gave the highest priority to the colonies' potential economic advantage to Britain, and, though he was concerned in all his promotional works with the development of cohesive and well governed colonial societies, he never accepted that eventual separation was either desirable or inevitable. Yet he also acknowledged a debt (largely ignored by his intellectual biographers, and denied by him in subsequent works) to Wilmot-Horton and to Tory colonial thinking about the possibility of reconstituting British society in the colonies. His vision for the colonies was, certainly, altogether more urban and more geared towards investment opportunities for the metropolis than to solutions to poverty at the colonial margins. He had no time for Wilmot-Horton's ideal of peasant proprietors, but he did have a residually Romantic preoccupation with the nature and meaning of settlement, the personal qualities needed for an emigrant to achieve rootedness, and the superior talent of the English (as opposed to Americans) for avoiding savage wildness and stamping their humanity on the wilderness. He also had as a goal the creation of a property-owning, largely self-governing society with enough leisure to support a colonial intellectual class (and he was broadly in favour of ending the transportation of convicts to Australia). Wakefield's ideas influenced the Whig-initiated Ripon Land Regulations mandating the end of free grants of land in New South Wales, and he was subsequently instrumental in the founding of South Australia, in the constitution of greater self-government for Canada, and in leading the push—in the teeth of considerable domestic support for Maori rights—for the Crown's annexation of New Zealand. Thereafter, he devoted his energies to promoting self-government for New Zealand, emigrating there himself in 1852. In all this, he remained committed to a vision of the British colony, not simply as a replication of the mother-land, but as a place of graduated opportunities for personal independ-ence for (strictly only) white settlers through dedication and hard work. Despite his public repudiation of the Tory and Romantic ideal of the colonies as agrarian communities, he did retain something of that Tory understanding of emigration as a project of national recuperation.

The American frontier, in Frederick Jackson Turner's famous thesis, holds the key to America's exceptional history and political culture.[47]

---

[47] Frederick Jackson Turner, *The Frontier in American History* (New York, 1920). Also on the British colonial frontier, see Robert Grant, '"Delusive Dreams of Fruitfulness and Plenty": Some Aspects of British Frontier Semiology, c. 1800–1850', in Mark Dorrian and Gillian Rose (eds), *Deterritorialisations: Revisioning Landscape and Politics* (London, 2003), pp. 101–9.

When that frontier ceased to exist on the North American continent, it could be extended into overseas regions through the workings of American imperialism. By contrast, the British frontier, in the formative Romantic imagination of the early nineteenth century, was, for the poorest, something that was experienced in the home country, and, in some measure, brought under control abroad. In a world where to move beyond one's parish boundary was to lose one's parochial settlement rights, all migrations from home involved a degree of expatriation, but, for the poor and the dispossessed, they might at least come to an end in a colonial settlement. In his celebrated report on Canada of 1839 (written with some input from Wakefield), Lord Durham claimed the territory as 'the rightful patrimony of the English people', implying that this was a settlement that was well on the way to becoming an enduring English community, and contrasting the English achievement with the failure of the French settlers ('There can hardly be conceived a nationality more destitute of all that can invigorate and elevate a people . . . they [the French Canadians] are a people with no history, and no literature').[48] This patrimony offered a future understood by those most actively involved with colonisation questions, not simply as a forward-projection of the past (like the stage-by-stage Enlightenment trajectory of economic improvement applied by James Mill to the future of British India), but as a compensation for history, a healing of the ruptures of the Napoleonic Wars, and of the regional and economic divisions brought about by accelerating industrialisation. Britain's settler colonies were not conceived to any significant degree, in this period, as part of Britain's civilising mission. But there were those, Wilmot-Horton foremost among them, who felt strongly that they had a wider value to the empire as a whole, and not just in terms of financial returns. Expatiating, as usual, on the 'colonial system' in the House of Commons in 1824, he said that 'he always felt that he was speaking of the wealth, the power, and commercial resources of the empire; and he was persuaded that, enlightened as the country now was by sound and rational principles of political science, the nation would be able to appreciate her colonial advantages, even though their precise pecuniary value could not be demonstrated on a balance sheet'.[49] In his later work *A View of the Art of Colonization* (1849), Wakefield quotes with emphatic approval a London banker who argues that the settler

---

[48] Lord Durham, *Report on the Affairs of British North America* (1839), ed. Sir C. P. Lucas (Oxford, 1919), p. 295.
[49] *Hansard*, 10 (12 March 1824), p. 958.

colonies serve the interests, not only of the metropolis, but of world order as a whole, of which Britain is the guardian:

> I am of opinion that the extent and glory of an empire are solid advantages for all its inhabitants, and especially those who inhabit its centre. I think that whatever the possession of our colonies may cost us in money, the possession is worth more in money than its money cost . . . For by overawing foreign nations and impressing mankind with a prestige of our might, it enables us to keep the peace of the world.[50]

For the domestic supporters of these colonies, their existence and slow flourishing showed Britain's capacity to offer social uplift to those white inhabitants living within its extended colonial polity, and, in showing that capacity, to demonstrate its fitness for imperial trusteeship elsewhere in the world.

---

[50] Wakefield, *Collected Works*, ed. Prichard, p. 811.

8

From Natural Science to Social Science: Race and the Language of Race Relations in Late Victorian and Edwardian Discourse

DOUGLAS LORIMER

OUR HISTORICAL AND CULTURAL STUDIES of racism look back to nineteenth-century science for the foundations of modern racist ideology. In this narrative, a leading role is given to Victorian anatomists and anthropologists whose science constructed classifications of humans by racial type, and depicted these types as having distinct and unequal characteristics determined by their biological inheritance. The elusive attempt to define 'racism' as an ideology often incorporates this narrative by making the belief in racial inequality dependent on a biological determinism derived from science. From the 1930s through to the 1950s developments in science, particularly human genetics and anthropology, led to a retreat from scientific racism and its biological determinism. After the Second World War, reaction to the Nazis' Final Solution, the new international consensus of the United Nations declarations on human rights and racial equality, the process of decolonisation prompted by colonial nationalist revolt, and advances in civil rights spearheaded by the mobilisation of the victims of racial oppression promised a new order free of the racism of the past. Nonetheless, forms of racial inequality and discrimination have persisted. To characterise this more recent form of racism since the 1960s, distinctions have been made between 'theoretical' racism relying on biological determinism, and 'institutional', or 'systemic', or 'pragmatic' racism which persists independent of an acceptance of scientific racism. The

Proceedings of the British Academy **155**, 181–212. © The British Academy 2009.

persistence of these forms of racism is one of the most problematic legacies of empire.[1]

While 'race' as a biological category is largely discredited, differences, even essentialised characteristics, assigned to culture as a product of language and history retain their currency. Regardless of how race and culture in their more recent post-1960s manifestations are characterised, the received narrative explains the origins of modern racist ideology from schemes of racial classification originating in the eighteenth-century Enlightenment. Although scientific racism was only fully articulated by the mid-nineteenth century (Gobineau in France and Knox in Britain being the usual benchmarks), this history forms the basis for the claim that science represented the dominant mode of thinking about race. It is time to reconsider this narrative, for it misrepresents the Victorian discourse on race, and consequently misconstrues the nineteenth-century legacy for racism and race relations in the twentieth and twenty-first centuries.

The flourishing field of cultural studies has deepened our understanding of the construction of racial identities within Victorian culture. We have no trouble finding representative Victorians articulating a robust racism to be subjected to our analysis.[2] Even though racism represented the dominant voice in the latter half of the nineteenth century, racial discourse was nonetheless contested territory. In attempting to reconstruct Victorian discourse, I have followed the fault lines where the disputes over

---

[1] E. Balibar, 'Is There a "Neo-Racism"?', in E. Balibar and I. Wallerstein, *Race, Nation, and Class: Ambiguous Identities* (London, 1991), pp. 17–28; Elazar Barkan, *The Retreat of Scientific Racism: Changing Concepts of Race in Britain and the United States between the World Wars* (Cambridge, 1992), *passim*; Antonio Darder and Rodolfo Torres (with Robert Miles), 'Does Race Matter? Transatlantic Perspectives on Racism after "Race Relations"', in *After Race: Racism after Multiculturalism* (New York, 2004), pp. 25–46; Barbara J. Fields, 'Whiteness, Race and Identity', *International Labor and Working-class History*, 60 (2001), pp. 48–56; Frank Füredi, *The Silent War: Imperialism and the Changing Perception of Race* (New Brunswick, NJ, 1998), pp. 7–8; Paul Gilroy, *Against Race: Imagining Political Culture beyond the Color Line* (Cambridge, MA, 2001), pp. 11–53; Michael Hardt and Antonio Negri, *Empire* (Cambridge, MA, 2000), pp. 190–5; Thomas Holt, *The Problem of Race in the 21st Century* (Cambridge, MA, 2000), pp. 3–24; Robert Miles, *Racism after 'Race Relations'* (London, 1993), pp. 1–23; Kenan Malik, *The Meaning of Race: Race, History and Culture in Western Society* (New York, 1996), pp. 9–37; Laura Tabili, 'Race Is a Relationship Not a Thing', *Journal of Social History*, 37 (2003), pp. 125–30.

[2] For example, Patrick Brantlinger, *Rule of Darkness: British Literature and Imperialism, 1830–1914* (Ithaca, NY, and London, 1988); H. L. Malchow, *Gothic Images of Race in Nineteenth-century Britain* (Stanford, CA, 1996); Robert J. C. Young, *Colonial Desire: Hybridity in Theory, Culture and Race* (London, 1995).

the meaning and significance of race occurred.[3] This strategy shifts the range of sources considered, for less attention is given to scientific theories of racial inequality, and to the cultural construction of identities of race, and more attention is paid to the language of race relations.

I

Robert Knox, the Edinburgh anatomist and author of *The Races of Man* (1850), is usually identified as the founder of modern scientific racism within Britain. Knox, who studied comparative anatomy in Paris, had a promising career as a professor of anatomy in Edinburgh ruined by his association with the murderers and grave robbers Burke and Hare. After professional disgrace, he struggled to make a living practising medicine in London and as a lecturer on 'transcendental anatomy'.[4] Knox wanted to prove that anatomical features signified inherited traits of intelligence, personality, and character within the British population. Having served in the British army in South Africa, he drew upon his experience of colonial racial encounters. From his comparative anatomy, Knox claimed that the races constituted separate species with separate origins. His polygenesis challenged existing ethnological thinking still dominated by the work of James Cowles Prichard and the theory of monogenesis or common origins. This view was compatible with biblical teaching and with the humanitarian outreach of the abolitionist and missionary movements. Aware of the mortality of Europeans in West Africa and of African resistance to European interventions in southern Africa, he warned that missionary and commercial visions of the conversion of Africans was contrary to the scientific laws of his comparative anatomy.[5]

Knox took delight in his role as an outsider at odds with prevailing ideas among scientists, and with the opinions of a larger public still attached to the anti-slavery cause.[6] A year after the publication of a

---

[3] D. A. Lorimer, 'From Victorian Values to White Virtues: Assimilation and Exclusion in British Racial Discourse, c. 1870–1914', in P. Buckner and D. Francis (eds), *Rediscovering the British World* (Calgary, 2005), pp. 109–34, and 'Race, Science and Culture: Historical Continuities and Discontinuities, 1850–1914', in Shearer West (ed.), *The Victorians and Race* (Aldershot, 1996), pp. 12–33.

[4] Clare L. Taylor, 'Knox, Robert (1791–1862), Anatomist and Ethnologist', *Oxford Dictionary of National Biography* (2004–6).

[5] George W. Stocking Jr, *Victorian Anthropology* (New York, 1987), pp. 62–9, and Philip Curtin, *The Image of Africa: British Ideas and Action, 1780–1850* (London, 1964), pp. 377–85.

[6] Robert Knox, *The Races of Man* (London, 1862), pp. v–vi, 23–8.

revised edition of *The Races of Man* in 1862, James Hunt, a young speech therapist, broke with the Ethnological Society to found the Anthropological Society of London. Hunt's promotion of his newly named science of anthropology aroused intense controversy. Defending Knox's treatment of races as fixed and separate species, Hunt and his followers rejected Darwin and evolution. Hunt also promoted the political applications of his new science by defending slavery in the Confederacy during the American Civil War, and by championing Governor Eyre's use of martial law to put down the Jamaica Insurrection of 1865. To the supporters of Charles Darwin and members of the influential X-Club, Hunt and his society were a scandal in the scientific community. After the death of Hunt in 1868, T. H. Huxley succeeded in reuniting the rival Anthropological and Ethnological Societies.[7]

The new Anthropological Institute, established in 1871, represented, according to George Stocking, a compromise which accommodated within an evolutionary paradigm both the older ethnological interest in the development of cultures and the new anthropological studies of humans and their races as part of nature. Scarred by the controversies of the 1860s, the members of the Anthropological Institute deliberately avoided political questions, even though the objects of their science were invariably persons of colour subject to western imperial interventions in Asia, the South Pacific, and Africa.[8]

In the last three decades of the nineteenth century, Knox was largely forgotten. His rehabilitation as the founder of modern British scientific racism began with the new scholarly interest in the history of racist thinking in the 1960s. For his influential work on *Images of Africa*, Philip Curtin saw Knox's *Races of Man* as a culmination of the paradoxical process of an increasingly negative view of Africans growing out of greater European knowledge of the continent. Scholars less concerned with the mid-Victorian encounter with Africa, and more concerned to place Knox in the history of racist thought ascribed greater influence to Knox's work and its popularisation through Hunt's anthropological science.[9] As Catherine Hall has shown for the metropolitan culture of

---

[7] J. W. Burrow, *Evolution and Society: A Study in Victorian Social Theory* (Cambridge, 1966), pp. 118–36, and D. A. Lorimer, *Colour, Class and the Victorians* (Leicester, 1978), pp. 131–61.

[8] Stocking, *Victorian Anthropology*, pp. 254–73.

[9] Curtin, *Image of Africa*, pp. 377–80; one of the first histories of racist thinking, Jacques Barzun, *Race: A Study in Superstition* (1937) (New York, 1965) refers to some British scientists but makes no mention of Knox. Christine Bolt, *Victorian Attitudes to Race* (London, 1971), pp. 1–28, Nancy Stepan, *The Idea of Race in Science: Great Britain, 1800–1960* (Hamden, CT,

Birmingham, Knox was only one source among many contributing to the growth of negative views of racial 'others' in the mid-Victorian period.[10] In his comprehensive work on Victorian anthropology, George Stocking notes that Knox 'is marginal to the mainstream of nineteenth-century British anthropological thought'.[11] After the controversies of the 1860s, beyond the occasional reference to past disputes, there were few citations to Knox in the proceedings of the Anthropological Institute or in *Nature*, the leading scientific journal aimed at a broader educated readership. Even the leading publicist of popular anthropological texts at the end of the nineteenth century, Professor A. H. Keane, who as a linguist retained a preference for distinct racial types with separate origins, identified Knox with the discredited school of American comparative anatomy.[12]

If there is any substance to the claim that racist ideology espousing biological determinist explanations owed its authority to Victorian scientists, then we have to look elsewhere than to the comparative anatomy of Robert Knox. There were two substantial outcomes from the controversies of the 1860s. First, the institutional development of anthropology among the learned societies was part of the professionalisation of the production of knowledge. Second, the evolutionary synthesis addressing the question of development over time, while shaped by the Darwinian revolution in biology, applied not only to humans as biological beings but to patterns of development in economics, politics, society, and culture.

Through the leadership of T. H. Huxley, Lionel Playfair, Norman Lockyer, and other prominent scientists, science was incorporated into the reformed universities, and initiatives were undertaken to promote government-sponsored research. This institutional development was part of the secularisation of knowledge freed from a biblical frame of reference, and part of the enhanced authority attached to knowledge claiming to be scientific.[13] The multiple applications of the evolutionary paradigm grew out of a lengthy history of evolutionary thought from the

---

1982), and George L. Mosse, 'Britain Lends a Hand', in *Toward the Final Solution: A History of European Racism* (New York, 1978), pp. 64–72, assign greater significance to Knox and Hunt.

[10] Catherine Hall, *Civilising Subjects: Metropole and Colony in the English Imagination, 1830–1867* (Cambridge, 2002), pp. 48–9, 276–84.

[11] Stocking, *Victorian Anthropology*, p. 65.

[12] D. A. Lorimer, 'Theoretical Racism in Late Victorian Anthropology, 1870–1900', *Victorian Studies*, 31 (1988), pp. 405–30, and '*Nature*, Racism and Late Victorian Science', *Canadian Journal of History*, 25 (1990), pp. 369–85; A. H. Keane, *Ethnology* (Cambridge, 1896), pp. 165–6.

[13] T. W. Heyck, *The Transformation of Intellectual Life in Victorian England* (London, 1982), pp. 81–119.

Enlightenment, and from the evident connections between social thought, principally Mathus's demography, and Darwin's theory of natural selection. The evolutionary synthesis and its multiple applications rested upon the confusion in Victorian thought between race and culture. Until the beginning of the twentieth century, there was no clear understanding of human biological inheritance, and, despite the logic of natural selection, many Victorians remained attached to Lamarckian claims of the inheritance of acquired characteristics.[14] For example, Herbert Spencer, who coined the phrase 'survival of the fittest', claimed adaptations from one generation passed on to the next by biological inheritance.[15] In the Victorian context of the ambiguities of race and culture, the precise meaning of 'biological determinism' remains unclear. Rather than the familiar racial types of comparative anatomy, the broader intellectual trend of 'scientific naturalism', in which humans were to be treated as part of nature, and human developments over time were presumed analogous to processes in nature, better captures the meaning and ambiguities of biological determinism in Victorian thought.[16]

To understand the biological determinist legacy of Victorian science for the early twentieth century, we need to shift the focus still further away from Robert Knox and the contentious debates of the 1860s, and look more closely at Francis Galton, his interest in human heredity, his role in the Anthropological Institute, and his patronage of eugenics. The shift in focus changes the historical context of the development of scientific racism to the period of 'high imperialism' from the 1880s to 1914. In addition to colonial expansion and conflicts overseas, these years were dominated by the paradoxical crisis at home of the so-called 'Great Depression' of 1873–96. The emergence of a more affluent urban mass culture, a greater awareness of poverty in the midst of plenty, a more militant and politically active labour movement, and the new politics of

---

[14] Stocking, *Victorian Anthropology*, pp. 233–7; Greta Jones, *Social Darwinism and English Thought: The Interaction between Biological and Social Theory* (Brighton, 1980), pp. 78–91; R. M. Young, 'Darwinism *Is* Social', in David Kohn (ed.), *The Darwinian Heritage* (Princeton, NJ, 1982), pp. 609–38.

[15] J. D. Y. Peel, 'Introduction', in Peel (ed.), *Herbert Spencer on Social Evolution* (Chicago, IL, and London, 1972), pp. xxi–xxiii.

[16] Evelleen Richards, 'The "Moral Anatomy" of Robert Knox: The Inter-play between Biological and Social Thought in Victorian Scientific Naturalism', *Journal of the History of Biology*, 22 (1989), pp. 373–436, and Frank. M. Turner, *Between Science and Religion: The Reaction to Scientific Naturalism in Late Victorian England* (New Haven, CT, 1974), pp. 17–30.

democracy informed the late Victorian and Edwardian discourse on race and culture.[17]

It was not until the 1880s that scientific racism established its academic credentials. Significant efforts to popularise this authoritative scientific view and to apply its lessons to colonial administration developed about a decade later from the 1890s onwards. Francis Galton (1822–1911), Darwin's cousin, an innovator in techniques of statistical analysis, and patron of the eugenics movement, pioneered studies of the relationship between heredity and environment. He coined the phrase 'nature versus nurture', and under his influence biological determinism gained new credibility. Galton first made a name for himself as an explorer and ethnologist. In *Tropical South Africa* (1853), an account of his travels in South West Africa in 1850–2, he claimed that innate differences accounted for African inferiority to Europeans. Although he served as honourary secretary of the Royal Geographical Society in the 1860s, he turned away from ethnology to pay greater attention to the statistical study of the British population. His views on inheritance first reached a broader public in his article 'Heredity Talent and Character', published in *Macmillan's Magazine* in 1865, and more fully in his book *Hereditary Genius* (1869). In these early works, Galton recognised he had to argue against the established presumption in favour of environmental explanations for human differences.[18]

By the 1880s, Galton had a more receptive audience. He used his position as president of the Anthropological Institute between 1885 and 1889 to promote the statistical study of populations including the anthropometry of the British population. Galton and other members of the Anthropological Institute from the biological sciences and medical schools thought that ethnography, including the evolutionary studies of

---

[17] For a recent comprehensive treatment of this period, see G. R. Searle, *A New England? Peace and War, 1886–1918*, The New Oxford History of England (Oxford, 2004); on imperial dimensions, see Andrew Porter (ed.), *The Oxford History of the British Empire*, Vol. 3: *The Nineteenth Century* (Oxford, 1999), esp. John Mackenzie, 'Empire and Metropolitan Cultures', pp. 270–93, and E. H. H. Green, 'The Political Economy of Empire, 1880–1914', pp. 346–68.

[18] Raymond E. Francher, 'Francis Galton's African Ethnology and Its Role in the Development of His Psychology', *British Journal of the History of Science*, 16 (1983), pp. 67–79; R. S. Cowan, 'Nature and Nurture: The Interplay of Biology and Politics in the Work of Francis Galton', in W. C. Coleman and C. Limoges (eds), *Studies in the History of Biology*, 7 vols (Baltimore, MD, 1977–84), vol. 1, pp. 133–208; D. W. Forrest, *Francis Galton: The Life and Work of a Victorian Genius* (New York, 1974); R. S. Cowan, 'Galton, Sir Francis (1821–1911), Biostatistician, Human Geneticist, and Eugenicist', *Oxford Dictionary of National Biography* (2004–6); Jones, *Social Darwinism*, pp. 99–108.

cultures and their material artefacts, had dominated the Institute's proceedings. They hoped to strengthen the role of physical anthropology and
make British practice closer to that of colleagues in France, Germany,
Russia, and the USA. Despite Galton's efforts, Institute members, many
with colonial connections and experience, still focused their attention
on exotic cultures and peoples, and their descriptive accounts seldom
provided the statistical information sought in the Institute's guide to
travellers.[19]

After four years as president, Galton ceased to play an active role in
the Institute. He remained an important patron of anthropological studies, assisting A. C. Haddon (1855–1940) in establishing anthropological
studies at Cambridge, and E. B. Tylor in his struggles at Oxford to establish a professorship in anthropology against the opposition of classicists
and theologians.[20] But he turned his attentions increasingly to eugenics,
another term he invented. By this time innovations in theories of biological inheritance, principally Auguste Weismann's theory of the continuity
of the germ plasm and Mendel's rediscovered work on genetics, had
weakened Lamarckian claims about the inheritance of acquired characteristics. With the intellectual defences of biological determinism reforti-
fied, and in a climate of self-doubt about Britain's world leadership and
national fibre in the aftermath of the South African War (1899–1902),
Galton found fertile ground for his new eugenic science. Up until 1914,
the Anthropological Institute continued to have an interest in anthropometry, and many of its members supported the eugenics movement. In
fact, Karl Pearson identified eugenics as a form of 'applied anthropology'.[21] Nonetheless, Galton's leadership in founding a separate study of
eugenics distinct from anthropology, and the foundation at the same time
of the new science of sociology, strengthened the identification of anthropology with its predominant focus, the study of non-European peoples
and the issues of race and culture.[22]

[19] Lorimer, 'Theoretical Racism', pp. 421–4.
[20] A. C. Haddon to F. Galton, 1 December 1891, University College, London, Galton Papers.
Haddon was professor of zoology, Royal College of Science, Dublin, and moved to Cambridge
in 1893, becoming a lecturer in physical anthropology in 1895: A. H. Quiggin, *Haddon, the Head
Hunter* (Cambridge, 1942), pp. 56–80, 93–5. E. B. Tylor to F. Galton, 29 May, 7 June, 18 June
1895, Galton Papers.
[21] G. R. Searle, *Eugenics and Politics in Great Britain, 1900–1914* (Leyden, 1976), p. 39.
[22] Philip Abrams, *The Origins of British Sociology, 1834–1914* (Chicago, IL, 1968), pp. 88–100,
149–50.

In keeping with the goal of making anthropology more scientific by improvements in statistical analysis and measurement, there was an effort to put the casual observations of travellers on a surer footing. As early as 1875, the Anthropological Institute had invited Herbert Spencer to present a paper on 'The Comparative Psychology of Man'. Proceeding in his customary deductive manner, Spencer compared the mind of the adult and the juvenile as analogous to the mind of the civilised and the savage.[23] Serious field studies began with the Cambridge Anthropological Expedition to the Torres Straits in 1898. Under the leadership of Haddon, anthropometric measurements of sense and motor functions and other psychological observations were undertaken by C. G. Seligman and W. H. R. Rivers, and his students, William McDougall and C. S. Myers. All these investigators later had distinguished careers in anthropology and psychology.

Rivers and McDougall contributed to the growing interest in 'instinct' as an explanation of human behaviour. Rivers, the nephew of James Hunt, claimed his anthropological interests originated with the bequest of his uncle's library. In his *History of Anthropology*, Haddon identified Hunt with the notorious negrophobia of the 1860s, but recognised him as one of the first anthropologists to take an interest in psychology.[24] As a psychologist at Oxford, McDougall, a member of the Eugenics Education Society, took an interest in intelligence testing, and encouraged Cyril Burt, his student, to develop means to test schoolchildren.[25] In contrast to Knox, Hunt, and mid-Victorian polygenists, the Torres Straits Expedition, as summarised by Professor R. W. Woodworth in 1910, came to a fairly sober conclusion: 'We are probably justified in inferring that the sensory and motor processes and the elementary brain activities, though differing in degree from one individual to another, are about the same from one race to another.'[26] Although he cited this observation with favour, Haddon, like Spencer before him, looked to childhood development to provide clues to adult traits. Like his fellow populariser, Professor A. H. Keane, he readily incorporated psychological profiles into his

---

[23] Herbert Spencer, 'The Comparative Psychology of Man', *Journal of the Anthropological Institute*, 5 (1875–6), pp. 301–15; also reprinted from *Popular Science Monthly* (1876) in M. Biddiss (ed.), *Images of Race* (Leicester, 1979), pp. 187–204.

[24] Haddon, *History of Anthropology* (London, 1910), pp. 53, 64–8, 79–80, 86; Quiggin, *Haddon*, pp. 95–108; on 'instinct' in psychology, see Jones, *Social Darwinism*, pp. 125–39.

[25] Searle, *Eugenics*, pp. 12–13, 52; Stephen Jay Gould, *The Mismeasure of Man* (Harmondsworth, 1984), pp. 234–9.

[26] R. W. Woodworth, *Science*, 31 (1910), p. 179, quoted in Haddon, *History of Anthropology*, p. 86.

classification of racial types.[27] Consequently, this new interest in psychological studies did not challenge existing generalisations, but gave a new authority to conventional stereotypes.

By the beginning of the twentieth century, students of anthropology felt sufficient confidence in their science to launch a sustained effort to gain recognition of the academic credibility and utility of their studies. Anticipating the conclusion of the South African War, the Anthropological Institute and the Folklore Society prepared a memorial to Joseph Chamberlain, the colonial secretary, urging him to establish a committee to investigate conditions of the 'native races' of the Transvaal and the Orange River Colony. The memorial was unsuccessful.[28] Quite independently, a group of humanitarian lobbyists, the South African Native Races Committee, investigated conditions in South Africa. In his review of its report in *Man*, the Institute's new magazine, E. S. Hartland drew a commonplace distinction between scientific and political questions. He found the first section of the report, which described the indigenous populations and their customs, of most interest, but noted that the succeeding section dealt with 'land tenure, the labour question in its various phases, the pass laws, education, taxation, the franchise, and the liquor laws'. Though the impact of civilisation on native cultures was a matter of scientific study, these topics were, he observed, 'of interest rather to the statesmen than to the anthropologist'.[29]

Unsuccessful in their bid to be part of a government commission on South Africa, the anthropologists were more successful in gaining public honours. In 1907, Edward VII graciously awarded the title 'Royal' to the Anthropological Institute. The report in *Man* reiterated the practical benefits of anthropology especially in colonial administration, and particularly at a time 'when the "Native Question" is assuming formidable

---

[27] Haddon, *History of Anthropology*, pp. 81–7, and his *The Study of Man* (London, 1898), pp. xxv–xxix; for examples of racial stereotyping, see Haddon's *The Study of Man*, pp. 16–29, and his *The Races of Man* (Halifax, 1912), pp. 24, 28, 34–5, 60–1, 70–6, 80–2, 101–2, and A. H. Keane, *Man, Past and Present* (Cambridge, 1899), and his extensively illustrated *The World's Peoples: A Popular Account of their Bodily and Mental Characters, Beliefs, Traditions, Political and Social Institutions* (London, 1908).

[28] The Memorial of the Anthropological Institute of Great Britain and Ireland and of the Folklore Society to Joseph Chamberlain, Secretary of State for Colonies, Royal Anthropological Institute (RAI) Archive, London, Council Minutes, 12 June 1900, A10(3).

[29] E. S. Hartland, 'Review of *The Natives of South Africa; Their Economic and Social Condition*', *Man*, 1 (1901), pp. 90–1, and South African Native Races Committee, *The Natives of South Africa: Their Economic and Social Condition* (London, 1901).

proportions in many of our colonies'.[30] Given this pressing need, in 1909 the Royal Anthropological Institute appealed to Prime Minister Asquith to establish a government-funded bureau of ethnology. This appeal followed the publication of an amusing yet informative article in *The Nineteenth Century* by one of the Institute's better known members, Sir Harry Johnston. The African traveller, administrator, and popular author began his essay on 'The Empire and Anthropology' with a striking contrast between 400 million people of the empire and the limited resources of the Institute. It was housed in one and a half rooms in Hanover Square, had a membership of about 500, and an annual budget of £500.[31] He observed that once anthropology was seen as 'a boring fad', but it was now becoming a required subject for the colonial service.[32] The memorial to Asquith stressed the utility of anthropology for administrators, missionaries, and traders in the colonies, and warned that their rivals, the Germans, spent substantial sums for the study of ethnology. It also mentioned the domestic applications of anthropometry in studying children and army recruits, and in investigating the question of the physical deterioration of the British population.[33] March 1909 was a poor time to ask the government for money. David Lloyd George was in the midst of his People's Budget with its costly dreadnoughts and old age pensions. The Institute revived the scheme in 1911 at the Imperial Conference, appealing to the dominion premiers to sponsor an imperial bureau of anthropology.[34] Unsuccessful in its appeals to the heads of governments, the Royal Anthropological Institute had greater success in organising the professional academic community. Along with the British Association, the Institute formed a committee of civil servants and academics to promote the teaching of anthropology at the universities.[35]

The advocates of anthropology, especially the promoters of its application to the problems of colonial administration, had envisioned

---

[30] 'Anthropological Institute: Augmentation of Title', *Man*, 7 (1907), p. 112.

[31] H. H. Johnston, 'The Empire and Anthropology', *Nineteenth Century*, 64 (1908), pp. 133–5; the essay was reprinted in Johnston's *Views and Reviews* (London, 1912).

[32] Johnston, 'Empire and Anthropology', p. 137.

[33] RAI Archive, Council Minutes, 5 May 1908, A10(3); *Journal of the Anthropological Institute*, 38 (1908), pp. 489–92; *Man*, 9 (1909), pp. 85–7; *The Times*, 10 March 1909, p. 10d; see also Adam Kuper, *Anthropologists and Anthropology: The British School, 1922–72* (Harmondsworth, 1975), pp. 125–7.

[34] Memorial on Imperial Bureau of Anthropology, printed copy, RAI Archive, no date, A56; *Journal of the Anthropological Institute*, 42 (1912), p. 5; *Man*, 11 (1911), p. 157.

[35] 'Proceedings of Societies—Anthropological Teaching in the Universities', *Man*, 14 (1914), pp. 57–72.

a network of universities to provide research and teaching facilities. Following the controversial birth pangs of anthropology in the 1860s, and especially in the period since 1880, scientific racism, made potent by the presumptions of a scientific naturalism that accommodated the ambiguities of race and culture, managed to establish its academic credentials. It did so within the context of the late nineteenth-century expansion of empire and intensification of global racial conflict. At the same time, the institutional basis of the production of knowledge had been transformed. This new institutional context of the modern university, staffed by professional academics ready to serve the interests of state and empire, made the scientific construction of race authoritative. The expansion of state education and improvements in print technology also gave the scientists access to a larger public. The production and sale of textbooks, reference works, and serialised magazines, often illustrated with photographs of the 'primitives' that the text classified by racial type, first appeared in the 1890s. While there is little sign that colonial officials premised policies on these typologies, scientific racism and its popularisation conveyed the more general message that the inequality of the human races was sanctioned by science. Beyond this general influence, the western science of man, or anthropology, as it stood in 1914, was itself a cultural artefact of colonialism.[36]

II

The anthropologists and biologists constructed this natural inequality of the human races by depicting each racial type within what the scientists described as its natural habitat. The task of modern colonialism or tropical development, according to advocates such as Benjamin Kidd, was to transform these natural habitats into modernised productive economies participating in the global market. In this task, Kidd recognised that the process of development necessitated the use of what he termed the 'natives' or 'coloured races'.[37] The recruitment, training, and discipline of the peoples of the tropics might well require the use of coercion, and

---

[36] D. A. Lorimer, 'Science and the Secularization of Images of Race', in B. Lightman (ed.), *Victorian Science in Context* (Chicago, IL, 1997), pp. 212–35, and Terence Ranger, 'From Humanism to the Science of Man: Colonialism in Africa and the Understanding of Alien Societies', *Transactions of the Royal Historical Society*, 26 (1976), pp. 115–41.
[37] Benjamin Kidd, *The Control of the Tropics* (London, 1898), pp. 1–5, 20–4.

certainly colonial advocates had no doubt that politically and socially coloured colonial labour would be subordinate to white administrators, employers, and traders. In other words, the task of colonial development involved the construction and management of new forms of race relations.[38] The anthropologists and biologists defined their field of observation as the 'natural' or 'primitive' as distinct from 'modern' human-made environments. From a contentious past and from their creed of 'objectivity', they also deliberately abstained from the world of politics. The construction of new forms of race relations under late nineteenth-century and early twentieth-century colonialism was an intensely political exercise. It should come as no surprise that the authors who had the most interesting and influential observations to make about the inequality of racial groups were those who understood and were ready to engage in the political arena. In the course of their deliberations, they invented a new language of race relations.

Unfortunately, our histories of racist thought tend to overlook the construction of racial inequality in the political practices, the law and its administration, and in the emerging social conventions of multiracial colonial societies. As Michael Adas has ably shown, the confidence, even arrogance, of nineteenth-century Europeans, who believed in the moral legitimacy of their colonial interventions and in their political capacity to effect this modernising transformation, did not come in the first instance from theories of racial superiority. Developments in western science and technology, most evident in the emergence of industrial economies and the growth of western-dominated world trade, provided the readiest measure of the comparative status of the world's peoples, and the best test of the presumed superiority of western civilisation. Although Adas sees racist ideology, which he defines in terms of biological determinism, as a secondary theme in the construction of western imperial ideology, its civilising mission and its secularised goal of modernisation, the power of the ideology of race grew out of the ambiguity of race and culture.[39] Although he puts more weight on technology as a Victorian measure of development, in cultural terms Adas's assessment is not dissimilar from

---

[38] There is an extensive literature on colonialism, slavery, and labour. Frederick Cooper, Thomas Holt, and Rebecca Scott, *Beyond Slavery: Explorations of Race, Labour and Citizenship in Postemancipation Societies* (Chapel Hill, NC, 2000), provides a useful introduction: on Africa, see Cooper, 'Conditions Analogous to Slavery: Imperialism and Free Labour Ideology in Africa', pp. 107–49.

[39] Michael Adas, *Machines as the Measure of Men: Science, Technology, and Ideologies of Western Dominance* (Ithaca, NY, and London, 1989), pp. 9–16, 194–8, 204–36, 338–42.

Peter Mandler's 'civilisational perspective'. Victorian liberal elite culture had confidence both in its sense of superiority and its belief in the progress of the 'barbarian' and the 'savage' towards a civilised ideal over time. Here the evolutionary paradigm provided a vastly longer period of historical time, and defined stages of development in economics, society, and politics as well as in biology and culture. The many applications of the evolutionary stages of development with their ambiguities about race and culture fuelled the colonisers' confidence that both the coloniser and the colonised would benefit from the conversion to conditions of modernity.[40]

Like an earlier generation of abolitionists, enthusiasts for colonial development greatly underestimated the immensity of their modernising project. They faced one evident political reality—the colonial subjects of colour who were to be the instruments of this transformation did not behave in accordance with the stereotypical attributes ascribed to them by the scientific experts. Therefore, social, political, and legal relationships had to be constructed out of a mixture of coercion and consent that defined the negotiated outcomes between the colonisers and their colonial subjects of colour. In the task of constructing colonial race relations, policy makers and political commentators had in mind the norms of the metropolitan culture. These norms were not even those of an 'invented tradition', but rather were the new practices of Victorian democracy. The discourse on race served the purpose of defining multiracial colonial societies as fundamentally different from the metropole, and thus the emerging conventions about the democratic rights of citizens as political participants and the rights of subjects under the law need not apply.

In the late Victorian and Edwardian period, the imperial metropole of London stimulated the creative ferment of new thinkers and new ideas about politics, society, and culture. The rich mix of Positivist, Progressive, New Liberal, Ethical, Fabian, Labour, and socialist, as well as other clubs and organisations, established a circle of friendship for discussion of the challenging issues of race, empire, and democracy. The leading and most influential participants, for example the members and associates of the Rainbow Circle (including J. Ramsay Macdonald, J. A. Hobson, Sydney Olivier, John M. Robertson, William Pember Reeves, Graham Wallas,

---

[40] Peter Mandler, '"Race" and "Nation" in Mid-Victorian Thought', in S. Collini, R. Whatmore, and B. Young (eds), *History, Religion and Culture: British Intellectual History* (Cambridge, 2000), pp. 224–44; Stocking, *Victorian Anthropology*, pp. 169–79, 285–314; Burrow, *Evolution and Society*, pp. 251–77; Lorimer, 'Victorian Values', pp. 115–17.

and L. T. Hobhouse), moved between the worlds of political advocacy, journalism, and the academy (mainly as lecturers in university extension programmes). For some, for example J. A. Hobson, their unorthodox opinions were an impediment to academic positions, but others benefited from the expansion of the universities and from the establishment of new chairs and departments in the social sciences. Here the lead was taken by the newly founded London School of Economics, but London, Oxford, Cambridge, and the new civic universities recruited established authors, many with experience as journalists, to staff these new academic ventures. Just as the natural sciences had led the way in the change from gentlemen amateurs to research professionals, so too the creation of new social science disciplines meant that the production of knowledge was increasingly, though never completely, in the hands of professional academics.[41]

In these formative years of the new social sciences, largely outside of the academy, the contentious matters of race and empire played a significant role in the social and political theories of leading authors. In large part, these considerations imposed themselves through external events, principally the South African War and the reconstruction of the new South Africa.[42] For this new kind of multiracial society, historical precedents or contemporary examples were few in number. As constructed by the late Victorians, the history of the West Indies since emancipation, including the use of indentured coolie labour from India, pointed to the need for some form of compulsion to produce a reliable, disciplined labour force. India was often cited as a successful model of benevolent bureaucratic rule by a small British elite over a much larger population alien in race and religion. The recent history of the southern states in America with its legalised segregation under Jim Crow and widely

---

[41] Heyck, *Transformation of Intellectual Life*, pp. 221–38; Harold Perkin, *The Rise of Professional Society: England since 1880* (London, 1989), pp. 116–70; Bernard Porter, *Critics of Empire: British Radical Attitudes to Colonialism in Africa, 1895–1914* (London, 1968), pp. 138–46, 156–68; Peter Clarke, *Liberals and Social Democrats* (Cambridge, 1978), pp. 9–27, 54–61; Jonathan Schneer, *London 1900: The Imperial Metropolis* (New Haven, CT, 1999), pp. 164–83; Michael Freeden, 'Hobson, John Atkinson (1858–1940), Social Theorist and Economist', *Oxford Dictionary of National Biography* (online edn, 2006); Michael Freeden, 'Rainbow Circle (act. 1894–1931)', *Oxford Dictionary of National Biography* (online edn, 2006).

[42] Ronald Hyam, 'The British Empire in the Edwardian Era', in J. Brown and W. R. Louis (eds), *Oxford History of the British Empire*, Vol. 4: *The Twentieth Century*, pp. 47–63; John Eddy and Derek Schreuder, *The Rise of Colonial Nationalism: Australia, New Zealand, Canada and South Africa First Assert their Nationalities, 1880–1914* (Sydney, 1988), pp. 19–62, 192–226; M. D. Blanch, 'British Society and the War', in Peter Warwick (ed.), *The South African War: The Anglo-Boer War, 1899–1902* (Harlow, 1980), pp. 210–37.

reported vigilante terrorism of the lynch mobs proved more troubling and contentious.[43] Some authors, for example L. T. Hobhouse and Graham Wallas, probed a broader theoretical concern about race, empire, and democracy. Both argued that biological differences of race, like differences of gender, should not impose limits on natural and civil rights, but recognised that an enfranchised white electorate, moved by imperial pride and race prejudice, would likely deny democratic liberties to persons of colour.[44]

Late Victorian and Edwardian commentators identified the problematic contradictions surrounding race, empire, and democracy as the 'Native Question', or the 'Race Question', or the 'Colour Question', or 'Colour Problem'.[45] In this discourse, the racial typologies of the physical anthropologists had at best a marginal role. Discussions of the 'Native Question' or the 'Colour Question' presumed persons of colour lived and laboured within a modernising colonial society in a status subordinate to white officials, employers, and settlers. Within these societies racial conflicts seemed endemic both from the assertions of persons of colour seeking to improve their position and from the colour prejudices of dominant whites. Trained in the classics, and drawn to make comparisons between

---

[43] John W. Cell, *The Highest Stage of White Supremacy: The Origins of Segregation in South Africa and the American South* (Cambridge, 1982), pp. 14–20, 160–70, 210–15, 230–5, 247–52; Saul Dubow, 'Race, Civilisation and Culture: The Elaboration of Segregationist Discourse in the Inter-war years', in S. Marks and S. Trapido (eds), *The Politics of Race, Class, and Nationalism in Twentieth-century South Africa* (London, 1987), pp. 71–80; D. A. Lorimer, 'Reconstructing Victorian Racial Discourse: Images of Race, the Language of Race Relations, and the Context of Black Resistance', in G. Gerzina (ed.), *Black Victorians/Black Victoriana* (New Brunswick, NJ, 2003), pp. 187–207.

[44] L. T. Hobhouse, *Democracy and Reaction* (1904), ed. P. F. Clarke (Brighton, 1972), pp. 13–57, 84–96, 156–69, 254–64; Graham Wallas, *Human Nature in Politics* (1908), 4th edn (London, 1948), pp. 6–10, 55–8, 269–96.

[45] The following titles reflect the currency of these terms: Aborigines Protection Society, *The Native Question in South Africa* (London, 1900); Alexander Davis, *The Native Problem in South Africa* (London, 1903); Sir Harry Johnston, 'The "Native" Problem and Sane Imperialism', *Nineteenth Century*, 66 (July–Dec. 1909), pp. 234–44; A. T. Wirgman, 'The South African Native Question', *United Empire*, 1 (1910), pp. 639–42; P. A. Silburn, 'The Native Question in South Africa', *Oxford and Cambridge Review*, 9 (1910), pp. 36–48; Anon., *A Question of Colour: A Study of South Africa* (London, 1906); Leonard Alston, *The White Man's Work in Asia and Africa: A Discussion of the Main Difficulties of the Colour Question* (London, 1907); Roderick Jones, 'South African Union and the Colour Question', *Nineteenth Century*, 66 (July–December 1909), pp. 245–56; William Archer, *Through Afro-America: An English Reading of the Race Problem* (London, 1910; repr. Westport, CT, 1970); H. H. Johnston, 'Racial Problems', *Views and Reviews: From the Outlook of an Anthropologist* (London, 1912), pp. 200–42; B. L. Putnam Weale [Bertram Lenox Simpson], *The Conflict of Colour: Being a Detailed Examination of Racial Problems throughout the World with Special Reference to the English-speaking Peoples* (London, 1910).

the British Empire and its Roman predecessor, colonial officials recognised that modern racial tensions and colour prejudices were unknown in the Roman world.[46] Pessimistic about the future of empire, they forecast that racial conflict would lead to the decline of the British Empire in the new twentieth century. Commentators looking more to the future than to the past were equally certain that the twentieth century would be unlike the nineteenth as the peoples of Asia and Africa asserted their rights in the modern world order. In 1900, in the imperial metropolis, the Pan-African Conference, representing the peoples of Africa and the African diaspora, and the peoples of colour more generally, issued its Address to the Nations of the World. It began with W. E. B. Du Bois's famous prediction that the problem of the twentieth century would be the problem of the colour line.[47]

The commentaries on this perceived crisis, as evidenced by developments in the self-governing dominions, India, South Africa, and the USA, gave rise to a new and modern language of race relations. This language had a rich vocabulary to describe conditions of racial inequality. Its richness and utility depended not on its biological determinism but on the ambiguous meanings of race and culture. In 1902, James Bryce, a noted constitutional expert, a Liberal MP, and a Pro-Boer, gave the Romanes Lectures on *The Relations of the Advanced and the Backward Races of Mankind*. Bryce based his lectures upon his extensive travels in the USA, and his recently published *Impressions of South Africa* (1897). Bryce used the commonplace language of 'higher and lower races', 'inferior and superior races', and 'dominant and subordinate races', but his title of 'advanced and backward races' was an innovation.[48] Like Benjamin Kidd before him, who had used the terms 'progressive and unprogressive races' and 'undeveloped races', this language cast racial groups within an evolutionary or developmental framework subject to

[46] The Earl of Cromer, *Ancient and Modern Imperialism* (London, 1910), pp. 73–107; Sir Charles P. Lucas, *Greater Rome and Greater Britain* (Oxford, 1912), pp. 91–111.

[47] 'Address to the Nations of the World by the Pan-African Conference in London, 1900', in J. Ayodele Langley (ed.), *Ideologies of Liberation in Black Africa, 1856–1970: Documents on Modern African Political Thought from Colonial Times to the Present* (London, 1979), pp. 738–9, and Schneer, *London 1900*, pp. 203–26. See also H. H. Johnston, 'The Rise of the Native', *Quarterly Review*, 212 (1910), pp. 121–51, and Weale, *Conflict of Colour*, pp. 85–121.

[48] James Bryce, *The Relations of the Advanced and the Backward Races of Mankind*, Romanes Lecture 1902 (facsimile University Microfilms International, Ann Arbor, MI, 1979), pp. 5–20, and *Impressions of South Africa* (London, 1897), pp. 584–7; John Stone, 'James Bryce and the Comparative Sociology of Race Relations', *Race*, 13 (1972), pp. 315–28; Christopher Harvie, 'Bryce, James, Viscount Bryce (1838–1922), Jurist, Historian, and Politician', *Oxford Dictionary of National Biography* (online edn, 2006).

change over time. According to Bryce, as the so-called 'backward' races advanced or adjusted to conditions of modernity, racial conflicts would not diminish but would intensify.[49]

Bryce looked for the roots of this racial conflict not in the racial typologies of the anthropologists, nor in the economic and political conflicts of class and labour, but in the psychology of the dominant whites. The phrase 'colour prejudice' had originated with the anti-slavery movement in the 1820s and 1830s, and the term was still in use at the end of the nineteenth century by humanitarian lobbyists, critics of empire, and administrators addressing the political repercussions of white racism.[50] As an alternative to 'colour prejudice', Bryce coined a variety of new terms—'race antagonism', 'race aversion', 'race repugnance', 'race-pride', 'race repulsion', 'race-rivalry'. Other commentators deployed variants such as 'race or colour antipathy' and 'race instinct'.[51] The point of this vocabulary was to normalise or naturalise racism by making it part of the psychological make-up of dominant whites, and therefore beyond their rational control. In the analysis of Bryce, New Liberals such as Gilbert Murray, and others, it also became part of their constructed political reality. Only utopian ideologues would champion ideals of race equality in the face of the psychological reality of white race instinct.[52] In the adaptations made by white settlers in the colonies, this psychology of prejudice, including the demographic, economic, and physical threat from Asia in the form of the 'yellow peril' or its adaptation in Africa as a 'black peril', including a sexual threat to white women, became the most powerful defence of exclusionary immigration laws, and of legalised forms of racial discrimination and segregation.[53]

---

[49] Bryce, *Relations*, pp. 30–1, 36–7, and Kidd, *Social Evolution* (New York, 1895), pp. 48–52, 59–60.

[50] *Anti-Slavery Reporter*, 4, 13 (1893), p. 156, and 27 (1907), pp. 61–4; Sydney Olivier, *White Capital and Coloured Labour* (originally published London, 1910; Westport, CT, 1970), pp. 156–7, 160–2; Bacillus, 'Colour Prejudice', *East & West*, 11 (1912), pp. 657–66; Lucas, *Greater Rome and Greater Britain*, pp. 98–100.

[51] Bryce, *Relations*, pp. 17, 19, 27, 29, 46. On colour or race antipathy or race instinct, see Cromer, *Ancient and Modern Imperialism*, pp. 136, 140; Lucas, *Greater Rome and Greater Britain*, pp. 106, 108; Wallas, *Human Nature*, pp. 55–8. Archer, *Through Afro-America*, pp. 7–9, 70–5, 113, 222–3, makes 'race instinct' the main explanation for racism he observed in the USA.

[52] Gilbert Murray, 'The Exploitation of Inferior Races in Ancient and Modern Times', in Francis W. Hirst, G. Murray, and J. L. Hammond (eds), *Liberalism and Empire* (London, 1900), pp. 118–57; Archer, *Through Afro-America*, pp. 7–9, 203; Newton H. Marshall, 'Empires and Races', *Contemporary Review*, 96 (1909), pp. 304–16.

[53] C. H. Pearson, *National Life and Character: A Forecast* (London, 1893), pp. 64–7; Richard Webb, 'The Imperial Problem of Asiatic Immigration', *Journal of the Royal Society of Arts*, 56

This discourse on race relations encompassed all the vastly different populations of the empire. On the imperial canvass there were really only two races—the whites and the others. Consequently, the term 'non-European' came into common use. 'Non-European' originated in the mid-nineteenth century as a linguistic distinction between European and other languages, but by the 1890s it was used to describe 'Europeans', all peoples with a European nationality, in contrast to all other peoples, most of whom would also be identified as 'coloured'.[54] Less commonly, a new term 'non-white' came into use in contrast to the long-established designation as 'white'.[55] The emerging pattern of institutionalised discrimination or segregation in the colonies, especially in South and Central Africa, came to be described as a 'colour bar'.[56] In 1911, Gustav Spiller, a German immigrant and member of the Ethical Society, convened the Universal Races Congress in London to address the global dimensions of the 'colour problem'. According to the press, which was largely favourably disposed to the Congress's purpose of promoting a better understanding between the races, its meetings addressed 'inter-racial problems' and 'inter-racial relations'. Around 1910 or so, the simplified term 'race relations', which probably had an American origin, also came into use in British discourse.[57]

(1908), pp. 585–97; Leonard Alston, *White Man's Work*, pp. 98–107; Robert A. Huttenback, *Racism and Empire: White Settlers and Colored Immigration in the British Self-governing Dominions, 1830–1910* (Ithaca, NY, 1976), pp. 59–138; Avner Offner, '"Pacific Rim" Societies: Asian Labour and White Nationalism', in Eddy and Schreuder (eds), *Rise of Colonial Nationalism*, pp. 227–47; Francis Bancroft, 'White Women in South Africa', *Englishwoman* (March 1911), pp. 262–9; 'White Women in Danger', *Daily Express*, 30 June 1911, p. 1g; 'Perils—Black and White', *Review of Reviews*, 44 (1911), p. 227.

[54] Kidd, *Social Evolution*, p. 60; 'The Self-governing Dominions and Coloured Immigration', C. P. L., Confidential, July 1908, TNA, C.O.886/1 Dominions No.1, pp. 52–3; Wallas, *Human Nature*, pp. 6–10, 288–9; Sir Charles Bruce, *The Broad Stone of Empire: Problems of Crown Colony Administration, with Records of Personal Experience*, 2 vols (London, 1910), vol. 1, p. 382.

[55] Wallas, *Human Nature*, pp. 8, 282–3, 288; Weale, *Conflict of Colour*, p. 101.

[56] *The Transactions of the Aborigines Protection Society, The Aborigines' Friend* (1907–9), 8 (May 1909), pp. 257–62; Bruce, *Broad Stone of Empire*, vol. 1, pp. 378, 380–1; 'Indians and the Empire', *The Times*, 12 September 1910, p. 9e–f; C. F. Andrews, 'Race within the Christian Church', *The East and the West*, 10 (1912), pp. 395–411.

[57] G. Spiller (ed.), *Papers on Inter-racial Problems Communicated to the First Universal Races Congress* (London, 1911; Miami, 1969); Lord Avebury, 'Inter-racial Problems', *Fortnightly Review*, 90 (July–December, 1911), pp. 581–9; *Review of Reviews*, 42 (1910), p. 335; Johnston, 'Racial Problems', pp. 237–42; Wallas, *Human Nature*, pp. 269, 288–90; R. P. Brooks, 'A Local Study of the Race Problem—Race Relations in the Eastern Piedmont Region of Georgia', *Political Science Quarterly*, 26 (June 1911), pp. 193–221. Olivier, *White Capital*, pp. 172–3, and Archer, *Through Afro-America*, p. x, both used the term 'race relations'.

III

Using the new language of race relations, colonial officials, journalists, and social scientists anticipated that increased contact between divergent peoples and cultures, a greater possibility for racial conflict, and the advance of democracy would make the new twentieth century quite unlike the nineteenth. For some colonial officials, experienced in the diplomacy of the exclusionary immigration policies of the self-governing dominions, or in the administration of colonies with a coloured majority composed of various ethnic groups, the increase in white exclusiveness threatened the viability of the empire itself. To some degree, they looked back to an anachronistic mid-Victorian liberalism confident in its social hierarchy based on class distinctions and ready to let individuals regardless of race or colour find their own level in the social order. This principle was clearly stated in the often-cited proclamation of Queen Victoria to the people of India in 1858 following the Mutiny and its repression: 'No native shall, by reason only of his religion, place of birth, descent, colour, or any of these things, be disabled from any place, office, or employment under the Government.'[58] Colonial officials and others sought to explain why the mid-Victorian ideal of a colour-blind empire no longer had credibility at the beginning of the twentieth century.

Sir Charles Bruce, formerly governor of British Guiana and Mauritius, published a number of essays on labour, race relations, and colonialism. In *The Broad Stone of Empire* (1910), Bruce attempted to draw a balanced picture of the contributions of Amerindian, African, and Indian labourers, but on the whole he held disparaging views of Africans and African culture. He defended the system of Asian indentured labour claiming that the migrants benefited from the system, and that after serving their indentures they had the right to residency and citizenship.[59] His rosy picture of past practices made him resist the new racism. In 'The Modern Conscience in Relation to the Treatment of Dependent Peoples and Communities', originally presented before the Universal Races Congress in 1911, he set out the basis of a stable colonial order under modern conditions. Bruce identified two possible strategies—a constructive policy or one of repression. The repressive policy he identified with South African laws prescribing both the separation

---

[58] Cited in Charles Bruce, *True Temper of the Times* (London, 1912), p. 66.
[59] Bruce, *Broad Stone of Empire*, vol. 1, ch. 10, 'Labour', pp. 306–69, and ch. 11, 'The Coloured Races', pp. 370–96.

and inequality of the races.[60] To serve the imperial policy of development, Bruce thought that the only option was a constructive policy. Extermination through conquest, and servitude through slavery or other forms of forced labour, belonged to past forms of colonialism, whereas 'amalgamation' was the only policy appropriate to modern conditions. 'Servitude' involved 'exclusion from civic rights', whereas 'amalgamation' viewed 'the native as a potential citizen'.[61]

For Bruce, 'amalgamation' was the only realistic option, because 'In the last analysis the struggle for the control of the tropics is a struggle for the control of the only agency by which they can be made of value,—the coloured population.' He asked the rhetorical question of whether such control could be exercised 'by force or by consent', and argued that a policy of consent involving the identity of the population with the colonial regime through participation in the political process as citizens was the only viable long-term policy.[62] Under the modern conditions of the early twentieth century, he observed two principles had to be recognised: 'first, that labour and freedom are indivisible, and secondly, that the social class that develops the material resources of a territory cannot be permanently excluded from a share in the administration of the developed area'.[63] Writing in 1910 and again in 1912, this affirmation was not simply a matter of liberal principle, but a part of the new political reality exemplified by Japan's defeat of Russia in 1904–5. As a consequence of this victory, Bruce claimed, 'the theory of a monopoly of capacity inherent in the trinity of race, creed, and colour peculiar to the West was destroyed'.[64] While not ready to accommodate Asian and African nationalist demands for political or cultural autonomy, Bruce affirmed that in the long term an oppressive racism would only engender conflict and disaffection.

While Bruce's commentary assessed the potentially harmful outcome of racism institutionalised in the law and practice of colonial and dominion governments, he did not attempt a sustained analysis of the sources of racial conflict. Sydney Olivier (1859–1943), a colonial office civil servant, Fabian socialist, and colonial administrator in the West Indies, for a time governor of Jamaica, attempted to provide such an analysis. Even though his Fabian socialism was evident in his book's title, *White Capital*

---

[60] Bruce, 'The Modern Conscience in Relation to the Treatment of Dependent Peoples and Communities', *True Temper of the Times*, pp. 55–76, and *Broad Stone of Empire*, vol. 1, pp. 393–4.
[61] Bruce, *True Temper of the Times*, p. 57; *Broad Stone of Empire*, vol. 1, p. 379.
[62] Bruce, *Broad Stone of Empire*, vol. 1, p. 393.
[63] Ibid., p. 373.
[64] Bruce, *True Temper of the Times*, p. 68.

and Coloured Labour, first produced for the Independent Labour Party in 1906, it was his West Indian experience that gave him an original perspective. He thought that too often the southern United States served as a model of modern race relations, and he feared that the American example of a rigid black–white divide institutionalised in legalised segregation might be inappropriately applied to South Africa.[65]

While his commentary was still infused with familiar racial stereotypes of African and Afro-Caribbean peoples, even a measure of respect for African 'primitive' difference after the fashion of Mary Kingsley, Olivier identified the issue of labour as the key to understanding race relations. Concerned with questions of colonial development, and especially the problem of recruitment of waged workers, Olivier turned conventional wisdom on its head. Recognising that patterns of labour in non-industrial societies conformed to traditional practices, he made the astute observation that forms of regular, disciplined, intensive labour originated only recently with the industrial revolution. The creation of a landless proletariat, dependent on wage income and peculiarly vulnerable to capital's extraction of surplus value, were, in Olivier's political economy, recent historical creations peculiar to western industrial societies. The 'lazy native' was not the source of the problem of colonial workers. Rather the problem was how to reproduce in a non-industrial colonial context conditions for the unusual regularity and intensity of industrial labour.[66]

In addition, Olivier's West Indian experience gave him a sense of comparative differences in race relations. While admitting that colour prejudice was evident in the British Caribbean, he claimed that, unlike the USA, neither formalised segregation nor violent racial antagonisms existed. Olivier accepted that inequalities in social status between racial groups rested upon differences in class and culture. Nonetheless, he rejected crude biological claims of racial superiority which he termed the 'race-barrier theory', or the 'race-differentiation formula'.[67] In *White*

---

[65] Olivier, *White Capital*, pp. 34–5, 43–60. See also George Bernard Shaw, 'Some Impressions', and Olivier's 'The Transplanted African', an address to the Church Congress, Southampton, 3 October 1913, in Margaret Olivier (ed.), Sydney Olivier, *Letters and Selected Writings* (London, 1948), pp. 13–18, 189–95; Francis Lee, *Fabianism and Colonialism: The Life and Political Thought of Lord Sydney Olivier* (London, 1988); Norman and Jeanne MacKenzie, *The First Fabians* (London, 1979), pp. 58–60, 268–74; G. F. McCleary, 'Olivier, Sydney Haldane, Baron Olivier (1859–1943), Civil Servant, Politician and Author', *Oxford Dictionary of National Biography* (2004).

[66] Olivier, *White Capital*, pp. 72–84, 126–31.

[67] Ibid., pp. 51, 57, 59; see also 'Transplanted African', pp. 194–5.

Capital and Coloured Labour, he attempted to shift the focus away from 'race' to the nature of social relationships within multiracial communities:

> If we carefully compare the essentials of the situation as between a modern industrial community and a tropical dependency, where white enterprise is exploiting native resources, we shall, I believe, be forced to recognise that inhuman social conditions arise in them much more out of the opposition in the categories of Capital and Labour than out of the opposition in the category of race or colour.[68]

Olivier's thesis was an innovative, yet early statement of the view that racial conflicts were analogous to the conflicts of social class. Reviewing efforts to compel black labour to conform to the expectations of white capital either by the creation of a monopoly of white landownership or by taxation, Olivier thought that Africans in their resistance showed less servility than the white industrial proletariat. In his opinion, colonial developers could not rely on compulsion alone, but would need to come to terms with Africans' understanding of relations of capital and labour, and expectations of productivity and reward.

Comparing industrial societies and multiracial colonial societies, Olivier observed that the conflicts in industrial societies took the form of 'the class-opposition of capital and labour: in communities of mixed colours it takes form in race-opposition and colour prejudice'. With South African developments in mind, Olivier warned that whites would exclude themselves from manual labour, employers would be entirely white, and the working class would be constituted by the coloured populations. In these circumstances, 'the division in industrial relations does really come to correspond with the racial division, the class prejudices and class illusions that arise between the capitalist and proletarian section of civilised societies energetically reinforce the race prejudices and race illusions that dominate all barbarous peoples'. These prejudices and illusions develop into what Olivier termed a community or 'corporate consciousness'. His most immediate example was 'the recently prevalent absurdity of the myth of the "Anglo-Saxon" Race'.[69]

Olivier's politics and views on race relations came under the critical scrutiny of some of his colonial office colleagues including Joseph Chamberlain, the colonial secretary. Another colonial office civil servant, Sir Charles Lucas (1853–1931), an assistant under-secretary with long experience in dealing with the exclusionary immigration policies of the

[68] Olivier, *White Capital*, p. 122.
[69] Ibid., pp. 161–2.

self-governing dominions, also offered a commentary on race, class, and democracy, but reached a rather different conclusion. Like Sir Charles Bruce, Lucas looked back favourably on mid-Victorian liberalism and its ideal of a colour-blind empire, but he reached a more pessimistic conclusion fearing that racial antipathies would ultimately lead to imperial fragmentation and decline. Like Olivier, Lucas identified issues of race and class as the source of the problem but, in his view, racism gained its destructive potential from the rising forces of democracy.[70]

In 1907, at the request of Lord Elgin, the colonial secretary, Lucas prepared a memorandum on 'The Native Races in the British Empire'. It was intended for internal discussion within the colonial office in preparation for parliamentary sessions on constitutional proposals for the reconstructed South Africa, and more generally for a possible review of 'native policy'. Lucas remained attached to what he called the traditional 'English' policy of the law being blind to race or colour. His review of the franchise and immigration regulations of the self-governing dominions noted a variety of strategies which contrary to his statement of traditional practice excluded or discriminated against aboriginal peoples or migrants of colour. These discriminatory practices applied regardless of the individual's status as a British subject. Lucas was of the opinion that British subjects of colour fared less well in the dominions of white settlement, and better under crown colony government. There the colonial office and its administrators offered protection against the self-interested and racially prejudiced initiatives of local white oligarchies.[71]

In his remarks on South Africa, Lucas first set out the long-term objective of assimilation of all persons of colour—Africans, Cape Coloureds, Indian residents of Natal—to a common status as citizens with equal protection under the law. The difficult political task was in the short term to both satisfy the white population that their interests would not be swamped by the black and brown majority, and build transitional institutions to facilitate the long-term goal of equal citizenship. With some hesitancy he suggested that reserve lands could be set aside, but as a temporary measure designed not to preserve African cultural autonomy

---

[70] Lucas, 'Class, Colour, and Race', *Greater Rome and Greater Britain*, pp. 91–111, and Robin A. Butlin, 'Lucas, Sir Charles Prestwood (1853–1931), Civil Servant and Historical Geographer', *Oxford Dictionary of National Biography* (2004).

[71] 'Native Races in the British Empire', Confidential, C. P. L., 31 December 1907, TNA, C.O.885/19 Miscellaneous No.217, pp. 1, 6–9, 26–27; Ronald Hyam, *Elgin and Churchill at the Colonial Office, 1905–1908: The Watershed of the Empire–Commonwealth* (London, 1968), pp. 367–78.

but to facilitate assimilation to British standards. He suggested various possibilities for governance of these reserved lands and looked with favour upon Lord Lugard's innovations in indirect rule in Northern Nigeria. He realised that it would not be appropriate or possible to accommodate all persons of colour on reserves, and feared that Africans, coloureds, and Indians not in protected status would be vulnerable to the economic demands and prejudices of the dominant whites. His gravest fear was that the protected reserved lands would become permanent and the basis for a racially segregated society. Under these conditions, he perceptively predicted, rather than a preparation for the rights and liberties of British citizens, this policy would create an excluded, unskilled labour force with no prospect of attaining equality of citizenship.[72]

Lucas's memorandum provided an informative review by an experienced civil servant. His commitment to traditions of equality before the law and assimilation to British ways reflected an old-fashioned idealism no longer shared by leading Liberal politicians. Accepting the commonplace belief in the inequality of races, they were ready to accept special provisions under the law, even segregation, as a means to protect non-whites. They also wished to avoid provoking African resistance, and therefore were drawn to proposals which claimed to reconcile what they thought were African traditions with the need to preserve social peace. Within four months of Lucas's memorandum, Asquith appointed a new colonial secretary. Elgin's proposed review never occurred, and attentions focused on the immediate priority of reconciling the two white communities of South Africa—the British and the Boers.[73]

Lucas resigned from the colonial office in 1911, and became principal of the Great Ormond Street Working Men's College, originally founded by J. M. Ludlow and Charles Kingsley as a Christian socialist outreach to the self-improving working class. As a fellow of All Souls College, Oxford, he also lectured on colonial history, and continued his authorship of a multi-volume series on the historical geography of the British Empire. Having an interest in classical scholarship since his undergraduate days, Lucas published his comparison of the British and Roman empires in *Greater Rome and Greater Britain* (1912) in which he explored more fully how divisions of race and class threatened the Empire.

---

[72] 'Native Races', C.O.885/19, pp. 23–30.
[73] R. Hyam, 'African Interests and the South Africa Act, 1908–10', *Historical Journal*, 13 (1970), pp. 85–105.

Noting that the conditions of slavery and of freedom in the Roman Empire were not attached to any particular race, Lucas recognised that new ambiguities, not to say exclusions, affecting the status of British citizens and subjects made the mid-Victorian ideal of a colour-blind empire largely illusionary. The recently concluded Imperial Conference of 1911 made it evident that each dominion defined its own citizenship, at times not including British subjects, and often excluding persons of colour.[74] Even though Lucas thought that colour prejudice was a product of modern history, specifically from the enslavement of Africans in the Americas, he drew a distinction between such prejudice and 'colour discrimination' which was based on 'practical experience'. In contrast to colour prejudice, discrimination rested upon the firmer and more rational basis of national identity and social class:

> But the white man, or at any rate the Englishman, also finds more rational ground for discrimination, in that the qualities, character and upbringing of most coloured men are not those which are in demand for a ruling race, and are not, except in rare individual cases, eliminated by education on the white man's lines.[75]

In Lucas's opinion, distinctions of race had been accentuated as the distance between peoples had lessened, and as the forces of democracy, especially in the self-governing dominions, had advanced.

Leading the way in pressing for these distinctions, in Lucas's opinion, were labour parties, trade unions, and associated working-class organisations, most evident in South Africa and Australia. These agencies of democracy attempted to advance the interests of the white working class out of fear of competition from cheaper coloured indigenous or immigrant labourers. In contrast, Lucas pointed to the preceding advance of liberal reform since 1832, which, in his view, attempted to diminish class interests and to advance a 'common citizenship and equality of chances'. With the advance of democracy organised through labour parties, the politics of class re-emerged. The working-class majority, identifying itself as part of a white race, and seeking to protect itself against the competition of non-European labour, created a new conjunction between class and race or colour:

> We have then, as against the great fundamental class distinction in the Roman Empire between freemen and slaves, which was not based on race, a great

---

[74] Lucas, *Greater Rome and Greater Britain*, pp. 92–7.
[75] Ibid., pp. 99–100.

fundamental distinction in the British Empire which is based on race, and which class interest has adopted and accentuated.[76]

Lucas worried that within white populations an identity of class pitted labour against capital. He hoped that the sense of common nationality and citizenship, even 'the natural instinct of race', would prove stronger than the identity of class. The colonial office civil servant 'hoped that the race instinct in the British Empire, more natural, less associated with material gains than the bond of class, will in the end prove the stronger force among the white citizens of the Empire'.[77] Despite Lucas's liberal attachment to an older view of the Empire encompassing peoples of all races as equal subjects under the law, his wrestling with the issues of democracy, class, and a more exclusionary racialism led him to put greater trust in the kinship of a common British ancestry.

Just as his friend John R. Seeley had described in his influential *Expansion of England* (1883), Lucas accepted that the British Empire housed two different empires: one of self-governing white citizens, and a second of dependent, colonial non-European subjects. The future of the Empire he entrusted to the first. For the second empire, he foresaw that the 'colour problem' would be an ongoing difficulty. He put his faith not in the development of self-government but in the exercise of sound government by colonial officials according to the British 'race instinct' of pragmatic common sense.[78] This contrast between two empires, and the identity of white British populations with democracy, in the hands of some dominion nationalists, would come to justify racial exclusion as an essential arm in the defence of white privilege.[79]

While Lucas struggled to reconcile his imperialism with the advance of democracy, other commentators, more sympathetic to democracy, recognised that British imperialism needed to reconcile itself not just to democracy for whites, but for all peoples in the Empire. With an interest in exploring whether human nature imposed limits on the exercise of democracy, Graham Wallas explored the contradictions between democracy at home and imperialism abroad. At Oxford, Wallas, the son of an Anglican clergyman, became close friends with another son of a vicarage, Sydney Olivier. It was through Olivier that Wallas was introduced to the

---

[76] Ibid., pp. 102–7.

[77] Ibid., pp. 107–8. Lucas was not a friend of democracy: see B. Porter, *The Absent-minded Imperialists: What the British Really Thought about Empire* (Oxford, 2004), pp. 203–6.

[78] Lucas, *Greater Rome and Greater Britain*, pp. 165–78.

[79] Webb, 'Imperial Problem of Asiatic Immigration', pp. 587–8, 595–7.

Fabian Society. After a period as a schoolmaster, lecturer for the Fabian Society, and teacher of university extension courses, Wallas gained a lectureship at the London School of Economics in 1895. An active promoter of education, he was also elected to the London school board as a Progressive. Growing dissatisfied with the direction of the Fabians under the leadership of the Webbs and George Bernard Shaw, he left the Society in 1904. Researching and writing on historical and politics topics, Wallas became one of the leading figures among the New Liberals exploring the meaning of democracy.[80]

Shifting away from the traditional interest in political philosophy to examine questions of political behaviour, in *Human Nature in Politics* (1908), Wallas noted the 'growing urgency of the problem of race'. The extension of democracy since 1870 had occurred at the same time as improvements in communications and the expansion of empire had brought diverse peoples under imperial jurisdiction. Using the new and generic short-hand classification of 'non-European', Wallas, as a critic of imperialism, was unwilling to 'draw any intelligible and consistent conclusion from the practice of democratic States in giving or refusing the vote to their non-European subjects'. In addition to 'non-European', Wallas also used the newer and less common designation of 'non-white'. Looking at British colonial experience, he addressed 'the political questions raised both by the migration of non-white races and by the acquisition of tropical dependencies'. He asked whether the principle of 'no taxation without representation' should apply to Asiatic populations.[81] Turning to British possessions in Africa, he used the term 'non-European' to describe the diversity of peoples and variations of rule within colonial jurisdictions. He observed that 'the non-European majority of Kaffirs, Negroes, Hindoos, Copts, or Arabs is regulated on entirely different lines in Natal, Basutoland, Egypt, or East Africa'. This diversity was simply a matter of 'historical accident', and created conditions for racial strife:

> . . . either from aggression of the Europeans upon the right reserved by the Home Government to the non-Europeans, or from a revolt of the non-Europeans themselves. Blacks and whites are equally irritated by the knowledge that there is one law in Nairobi and another in Durban.[82]

---

[80] Martin J. Weiner, 'Wallas, Graham (1858–1932), Political Psychologist and Educationist', *Oxford Dictionary of National Biography* (2004); Clarke, *Liberals and Social Democrats*, pp. 9–14, 28–44.
[81] Wallas, *Human Nature*, pp. 6–8.
[82] Ibid., p. 9.

For Wallas, past experience, especially the humanitarian tradition of the anti-slavery movement, provided little guidance for the unprecedented conditions of the new twentieth century.

Realising that empires were built on power and not sentiment, and recognising the emotive power of popular jingoism, Wallas had little patience with appeals to 'the white man's burden'. In the first half of the nineteenth century, he observed that European colonists in contact with 'non-European races' were in 'their impulses and knowledge alike revolted from the optimistic ethnology of Exeter Hall'. Recognising the beginnings of nationalism among the peoples of Asia and Africa, he also was certain that 'the non-white races within the Empire show no signs of enthusiastic contentment at the prospect of existing, like the English "poor" of the eighteenth century, as the mere material of other men's virtues'.[83] Foreseeing a global struggle with imperial rivals, Germany and Russia were Britain's most likely opponents, Wallas saw two contrary tendencies at work. On the one hand, an imperial war was the likely outcome 'if the white inhabitants of the Empire are encouraged to think of themselves as a "dominant race", that is to say as both a homogeneous nation and a natural aristocracy'. On the other hand, 'the non-white inhabitants of the Empire' will be employed in this imperial war, and 'we must discover and drill those races who like the Gurkhas and the Soudanese, may be expected to fight for us and to hate our enemies without asking for political rights'. This imperial conflict, he predicted, would result in the conquest of territories with 'white and yellow and brown and black men hating each other across a wavering line on the map of the world'. Even the victor in the imperial contest 'will be compelled to consider the problems of race'. In this view he saw no escape from 'humanitarianism' in considering the ethical and political status of diverse peoples, and what he termed 'the practical problem of race relationship'.[84]

In the effort to reconstruct the late Victorian and Edwardian discourse on race, a number of cautionary notes may be in order. During this period, as in our own time, race was an intensely political subject. Consequently, race was a contested territory occupied by divergent and contentious viewpoints. The terms of the debate and the relative strength and authority of the combatants were determined by their historical context, and our task as scholars is to recognise differences among the historical actors

[83] Ibid., pp. 288, 282–3.
[84] Ibid., pp. 283–4, 288.

and to chart the field of play. To some degree, too much of our scholarship reflects a kind of tunnel vision in which particular authors or particular literary forms are selected as representative, and assigned an often untested yet implicit influence. The assessment of the influence of authors or of particular forms of thought is an enormously difficult, some would say impossible, task. In his *Absent-minded Imperialists*, Bernard Porter offers a useful corrective to the untested presumption of the impact of the culture of empire upon the larger Victorian and Edwardian public.[85] Nonetheless, from the selection of sources discussed above, one can see in prototype many of the variants of race thinking commonly assumed to belong to our post-1945 discourse.

Insofar as our received narratives of the development of racist ideology in the nineteenth century assign a special, even central, role to scientific forms of biological determinism, they need to be reconsidered. Historical and cultural studies have amply documented the ubiquitous presence of racial stereotypes and their uninhibited expression in all cultural forms including non-fiction prose, novels, the theatre, museums and exhibitions, popular entertainments, and advertising.[86] Victorian scientists neither critiqued nor tested these stereotypical constructions. Rather they tried to give them an 'objective' reality by offering a 'scientific' explanation for their existence. In this sense, the scientists' acceptance of racial stereotypes came from the larger cultural context that informed their science. In our narrative of racism, it may make more sense to put culture and empire before biology.

Within the Victorian discourse on race, the scientists brought a new claim to be authoritative producers of real knowledge as distinct from the mere sentiment of the humanitarians associated with the anti-slavery and missionary movements. The mid-Victorian comparative anatomists, such as Knox and Hunt, made this assertion, but their science was too eccentric to do more than create controversy. In the end, it was simply overtaken by Darwin's evolutionary synthesis. While the comparative anatomists may fit the mode of biological determinism, race thinking gained its power from the ambiguities surrounding race and culture. While it may be tempting to tease out from the web of cultural meanings specific biological determinist ideas as definitively 'racist', to do so intro-

---

[85] Porter, *Absent-minded Imperialists, passim.*
[86] For example, John Mackenzie, *Propaganda and Empire: The Manipulation of British Public Opinion, 1880–1960* (Manchester, 1984) and Mackenzie (ed.), *Imperialism and Popular Culture* (Manchester, 1986).

duces our own analytical distortion. The ambiguous linkages between race and culture were the source of the power and utility of Victorian and Edwardian racial discourse.[87] In this sense the manifold applications of evolution, some adapted from Darwin but in social and cultural thought of much longer and diverse origin, proved a more fertile paradigm upon which to construct the inequality of the world's peoples. With the greater acceptance of scientific naturalism, as a weaker but more pervasive form of biological determinism applied to human beings and their evolution, and the normalisation of anthropology within the learned societies and universities after 1871, the science of race gained a greater measure of institutional authority.

With his interest in 'nature' over 'nurture', Francis Galton tried to shift the agenda of the Anthropological Institute to the anthropometry of the British population and to his new science of eugenics, but the ethnographers prevailed, and made social and cultural studies the mainstay of British anthropology. A greater understanding of biological inheritance and Galton's promotion of eugenics gave biological determinist explanations more credibility though more evidently in biology and psychology than within anthropology. At the same time, a larger market for various forms of reading material, an expansion of secondary and post-secondary education, and a revolution in publishing technology created conditions for the popularisation of anthropology and human geography texts and illustrated reference works that simply did not exist in the 1860s. This reconstruction of the narrative of biological determinism shifts the chronology from the mid-nineteenth to the late nineteenth and early twentieth centuries. By this time the external political and intellectual context was clearly informed by colonial expansion and conflict, and by the perplexing contradictions between democracy in the metropole and imperialism in periphery.

By their creed of scientific detachment and by their troubled history, the anthropologists abstained from participation in the politics of colonial race relations. Their reluctance to enter into what they defined as political questions did not deter them from seeking government funding or from claiming their science had practical lessons for colonial administration. The anthropologists and other scientists made virtually no

---

[87] Mahood Mamdani, *Citizen and Subject: Contemporary Africa and the Legacy of Late Colonialism* (Princeton, NJ, 1996), pp. 3–34, 62–71, 90–6; Homi Bhabha, *The Location of Culture* (London, 1994), pp. 66–92; Lorimer, 'Science and the Secularization of Images of Race', pp. 213–14.

commentary on how the inequality of races might be constituted in the governance, law, administration, and social and economic arrangements within multiracial colonial societies. Here informed commentaries came from colonial civil servants and administrators, humanitarian lobbyists, or journalists and university lecturers in the new social science disciplines. While they all took some measure of racial inequality as a given, they were aware that colonised persons of colour did not conform to their stereotyped descriptions, and that conflict within modernising multiracial colonies seemed to be growing in intensity. The colonial administrators faced the practical problem of devising ways to manage race relations to provide for social peace and order, and often the racial prejudices of white settlers frustrated that goal. Critics of empire, especially in the context of the South African War, explored how the 'colour question' exposed the contradictions between imperialism and democracy. Together they invented the modern language of race relations. Here the racial types of the scientists had little utility, for in describing the impe-rial and global order the bipolar designations of 'European' and 'non-European' or 'white' and 'non-white' better captured the politics of race. By the beginning of the twentieth century, the science of racial types was already showing signs of its obsolescence.

If we include this language of race relations in our historical narrative of racism, then further reconsiderations may be in order. From the 1960s and after, our histories introduced a distinction between a theoretical racism resting on a biological determinism derived from science and insti-tutional or systemic or pragmatic racism which existed independent of its discredited intellectual justification. The language of race relations which informs this non-theoretical racism has its own long and neglected his-tory. In the nineteenth century, this discourse of race relations had an ori-gin independent of the racial theories of the scientists. Its own largely autonomous development goes back at least to the abolitionist discourses on slavery and race and to enquiries into the status of aboriginal peoples such as that undertaken by a parliamentary commission in 1837. It is also this language of race relations which informs racial discourse in the 1920s and 1930s.[88] For our understanding of the lineages of empire, this language of race relations also represents the most enduring legacy of Victorian and Edwardian racism.

---

[88] For example, Laura Tabili, *'We Ask for British Justice': Workers and Racial Difference in Late Imperial Britain* (Ithaca, NY, and London, 1994); Barbara Bush, *Imperialism, Race and Resistance: Africa and Britain, 1919–45* (London, 1999); Füredi, *Silent War*.

9

Harold Laski on the Habits
of Imperialism

JEANNE MOREFIELD

SINCE HIS DEATH IN 1950, most accounts of Harold Laski's anti-imperialism have been biographical rather than scholarly in nature. Chroniclers of Laski's life and historians of twentieth-century British imperialism alike have located this London School of Economics professor's greatest contribution to the politics of anti-colonial struggle in his close, mentoring, relationship with Krishna Menon, H. O. Davies, Jawaharlal Nehru, Kwame Nkrumah and other post-colonial leaders.[1] At the same time, explorations of Laski's political theory have paid scant attention to his contributions towards a larger critique of imperialism. Rather, over the years both critics like Herbert Deane and sympathetic readers such as Peter Lamb have interpreted Laski's writings on imperialism as not very original, Leninist addenda to his critique of sovereignty that merely ape Lenin's evolutionary account of capitalism in its expansionist, 'moribund' phase.[2] Depending upon their positions, Laski's reading of empire either becomes a crude derivative of an already economically

---

[1] Krisha Menon's biographer T. J. S. George argues, for instance, that Laski's approach to socialism 'remained the most abiding influence on Menon's ideas': T. J. S. George, *Krishna Menon* (New York, 1965), p. 68. For Laski biographies that discuss his relationship to future leaders of the post-colonial world, see Granville Eastwood's *Harold Laski* (London, 1977), and Isaac Kramnick and Barry Sheerman, *Harold Laski: A Life on the Left* (New York, 1993). For more on Laski's influence in the context of anti-colonial politics more generally, see Lews Feuer, *Imperialism and the Anti-imperialist Mind* (New York, 1986), and A. P. Thornton, *Imperialism and the Twentieth Century* (Minneapolis, MN, 1977).

[2] Herbert Deane, *The Political Ideas of Harold Laski*, 2nd edn (Hamdon, CT, 1972), p. 88; Peter Lamb, *Harold Laski: Problems of Democracy, the Sovereign State, and International Society* (New York, 2004). See also Ram Chandra Gupta's account of Laski's Leninist interpretation of capital in its imperialist phase in *Harold Laski: A Critical Analysis of His Ideas* (Agra, 1964). For Lenin on 'moribund' capitalism, see V. I. Lenin, 'Imperialism, the Highest Stage of Capitalism', *The Lenin Anthology*, ed. Robert Tucker (New York, 1975).

Proceedings of the British Academy **155**, 213–237. © The British Academy 2009.

reductionist politics or a crude, economically reductionist moment in a more elegant theory.

This essay analyses two of Laski's few works on imperialism, a 1932 piece 'Nationalism and the Future of Civilisation' and a chapter written in 1933 entitled 'The Economic Foundations of Peace'. It does so, however, from within the context of Laski's overall theory of sovereignty. I argue that when viewed as an extension of broader trends in his political thought rather than as a truncated exception to these trends, Laski's approach to imperialism appears much more internally sophisticated than the accounts of either his critics or champions suggest. The first section is thus devoted to an analysis of Laski's theory of sovereignty, in particular his sustained critique of the ideological 'habits' that condition liberal society. The second half of the essay argues that these theoretical sensibilities led Laski to frame imperialism in both Leninist terms (as an outward expression of capitalism in its final stage of development) *and* as the almost dialectical relationship of the habits of sovereignty with the 'habits of imperialism'. Laski thus argued that not only did the habits of inequality within sovereign capitalist states both rationalise and compel imperial expansion abroad but that authoritarian and racist practices designed for implementation in the colonies also reverberated throughout the domestic sphere in ways that created a 'cleavage' between the state's expressed ideological support for political equality and its inegalitarian economic policies. This 'cleavage' then exacerbated the heretofore concealed authoritarian tendencies that Laski associated with liberal capitalist forms of sovereignty. The essay suggests that Laski's thinking on imperialism resembles less a truncated Leninism than it does a critical analysis of the way ideology can both obscure domination and discipline subjects. Additionally, I suggest that while Laski's analysis of empire also revealed some of the most maddening contradictions of his political theory, these contradictions are themselves understandable given Laski's political activism and his deep commitment to democracy. In the end, it is precisely this commitment that makes Laski's theory of empire so germane for our own era as influential liberals like Niall Ferguson and Michael Ignatieff ratchet up their cry for a return to imperial order.[3]

---

[3] See, in particular, Niall Ferguson's discussion of the need for a reinvigorated, American-led, 'liberal empire' in *Colossus: The Price of America's Empire* (New York, 2004), p. 2. Michael Ignatieff makes similar, less explicit claims in, *Empire Lite: Nation-building in Bosnia, Kosovo, and Afghanistan* (London, 2003).

The Habits of Sovereignty

Laski's interest in the theory of sovereignty remained a central feature of his work even as his political orientation shifted in the 1920s from plural-ism towards socialism.[4] Indeed, until the end of his life, Laski's scholar-ship remained infused with many of the same primary concerns about state power and authority that characterised his earliest writings. For Laski, sovereign states effectively erased economic, political, and social differences—that 'complex of interests which struggle among themselves for survival'—within political society by incorporating these differences within one smooth projection of a national 'unity'.[5] 'What the Absolute is to metaphysics', Laski argued in 1917, 'that is the State to political theory'.[6] Laski maintained, on the one hand, that this projection of coherence suppressed alternative forms of social and political associa-tion. The 'apotheosis' of the state, he argued, created the conditions under which citizens cease to inquire into 'what things a creative freedom must embody' by narrowing the 'diversity' of opinions and experiences that informed both a complex theory of individualism and democracy. [7] On the other hand (and one sees this even in his earliest writings), Laski argued that the state masked economic inequality by enabling powerful interests to draw upon its unifying mien and project their own agendas as universal. Thus, in his 1919 essay 'The Pluralist State', Laski argued that the political apparatus of the state is frequently 'dominated by those who at the time wield economic power'.[8] The regnant interests of capital drew upon the alchemy of sovereignty, Laski maintained, to transform their

---

[4] 'Pluralism' here refers to the tradition of English political pluralism represented by thinkers such as Laski, John Neville Figgis, and G. D. H. Cole, all of whom were most active in the early decades of the twentieth century. Unlike the pluralism of later American thinkers such as Robert Dahl these pluralists were committed to a thoroughgoing critique of the kind of unlimited state sovereignty originally developed by Bodin and Hobbes. While these thinkers shared with Dahl an interest in non-state forms of political organisation, they read the existence of these alterna-tive groups as challenging the legitimate authority of the unified sovereign state. Dahl, by contrast, focused on the way such groups competed with each other to achieve their interests through institutional channels. For more on the political thought of the English pluralists, see Paul Q. Hirst (ed.), *The Pluralist Theory of the State: Selected Writings of G. D. H. Cole, J. N. Figgis, and H. J. Laski* (London, 1989); David Nicholls, *The Pluralist State: The Political Ideas of J. N. Figgis and His Contemporaries* (London, 1975); Julia Stapleton (ed.), *Group Rights: Perspectives since 1900* (Bristol, 1995).

[5] Harold Laski, *Foundations of Sovereignty and Other Essays* (New York, 1921), p. 27.

[6] Harold Laski, *The Problem of Sovereignty* (New Haven, CT, 1924), p. 6.

[7] Harold Laski, 'The Apotheosis of the State', *New Republic*, 7 (1916), pp. 302–4.

[8] Harold Laski, 'The Pluralist State', *Philosophical Review*, 6 (1919), p. 566.

private interests into a 'factitious popular support against which it is difficult to make headway'.[9] The ideological and material power of sovereignty plus capitalism thus normalised economic inequality while simultaneously bestowing upon the liberal state the patina of political universalism.

Laski's intellectual response to the 'grim fact of inequality' within the state was to develop a historical methodology that relentlessly unravelled the strands of economic, political, and social thought that had gone into the making of the modern conception of statehood.[10] The purpose of such genealogical inquiry, he argued, was to trouble the appearance of universalism at the heart of this conception thus revealing the philosophical contradictions and forms of economic domination within. 'When the internal history of the state is examined', he maintained, 'its supposed unity of purpose and of effort sinks, with acquaintance, into nothingness.'[11] Laski thus treated sovereignty as both an expression of actual material power and as a dense and multi-layered ideology whose very incoherence had congealed over time into a powerful set of widely accepted habits.

Not surprisingly given Laski's conflicted admiration for, and abiding disagreement with, Edmund Burke, his use of the term 'habit' both resembled and rejected a Burkean understanding of the word. Political life was, for Burke, the end result of a complicated accumulation of experiences and habits that both bound individuals to communities and structured their understanding of political possibility. This analysis clearly appealed to Laski as his lengthy discussion of Burke in *Political Thought in England* (originally published in 1920) suggests. In it, Laski spent a considerable amount of time dwelling approvingly on Burke's fine grasp of the 'intricate' nature of man and his rejection of simplified, 'mathematical' theories of politics that reduced human society to the organisation of discrete individuals for whom the habits of the ages could be easily dismissed in return for natural rights.[12]

This agreement with Burke's belief in the embeddedness of political subjects in their communities and communal habits may seem strange to liberal readers of Laski who have traditionally focused on his expressed

---

[9] Harold Laski, *Authority in the Modern State* (New Haven, CT, 1919), p. 96.
[10] Harold Laski, *The Recovery of Citizenship* (London, 1928), p. 5.
[11] Laski, 'Pluralist State', p. 566.
[12] Laski, *Political Thought in England*, 10th edn (Oxford, 1961), p. 166.

support for what, at times, resembled a kind of radical individualism.[13] Indeed, throughout his career, Laski did often couch his critique of the state in terms of the 'ultimate isolation of the individual personality'.[14] Laski's interpretation of the individual's 'isolation', however, differed from traditional liberal assumptions about human autonomy in a number of ways. For Laski, individuals were isolated *insofar as* what bound them together was material necessity rather than 'Mind' writ large. He appreciated the Aristotelian observation that humans are, if not inherently social, driven to create societies. 'Man', he thus maintained in the first line of the first chapter of *Authority in the Modern State*, 'is a community building animal'.[15] But the fact that people built societies, Laski argued, could not be explained by any single metaphysical accounting of their nature. Rather, he insisted, '[h]unger, drink, sex, and the need of shelter and clothing seem the irreducible minimum of human wants. All else is capable of transmutation to forms as various as the history of society.'[16] Therefore, while Laski appreciated the 'isolated personality' of the individual, he also recognised the extent to which these personalities were 'transmutable', pushed and pulled in a variety of directions by the associations—in a Burkean sense, the 'little platoons'—in which people happened to find themselves.

The fact that human nature was permeable to the influence of associations helped explain, according to Laski, the power of political habit, and grasping the sway of political habit helped explain the longevity and widespread acceptance of certain forms of institutional organisation over time. In the case of modern sovereignty, the 'nature of obedience', argued Laski, becomes clear when we examine it as a form of 'habit bred into the tissue of countless ages of subservience to the state'.[17] Likewise, the historical tendency of political philosophers to adopt a 'mystic monism' in their analyses of the state could be explained, he maintained, as a form of intellectual 'habit', common to modernity, of transforming the state into a single personality. Additionally, for Laski, juridical theorists' passive acceptance of the circular logic by which law was assumed to be

---

[13] Works by authors who read Laski as both an individualist and eventual traitor to his own individualism include Henry Meyer Magid, 'Laski: Individualistic Pluralism', in *English Political Pluralism* (New York, 1940); W. Y. Elliot, 'The Pragmatic Politics of Mr. H. J. Laski', *American Political Science Review*, 18 (1924), pp. 251–75; Carroll Hawkins, 'Harold Laski: A Preliminary Analysis', *Political Science Quarterly*, 65 (1950), pp. 376–92.

[14] Harold Laski, *Liberty in the Modern State*, 2nd edn (New York, 1949), p. 43.

[15] Laski, *Authority in the Modern State*, p. 20.

[16] Harold Laski, *A Grammar of Politics* (London, 1925), pp. 22–3.

[17] Laski, *Authority and the Modern State*, p. 33.

legitimate because it emanated from the state, and the state was assumed to be legitimate because it 'compelled the law', could also be understood as a form of unexamined 'habit', a habit that systematically reinforced 'the reality of the State's personality'.[18]

But the similarities between Laski and Burke end here. For Burke, humans were dispositionally drawn towards the customary, that beyond their 'nature, and education, and their habits of life . . . the people have not to give'.[19] Wise statesmen and thinkers must therefore take their cue from habit, must understand both politics and political theory as, what Oakeshott would much later call, 'an abridgement of political habits' rather than 'a preface to political activity'.[20] Laski, by contrast, argued that Burke was simply wrong to put his 'trust in habit as the chief source of human action' although his critique in this regard appears, at times, to be profoundly conflicted.[21] On the one hand, Laski often insisted that human nature was unfixed and 'capable of transmutation'. On the other hand, he just as frequently argued for a more universal definition of human nature as fundamentally rational. In these more humanist moments, Laski describes political subjects as both capable and desirous of critical thought and the 'continual expansion' of their personalities.[22] His critique of Burke was similarly conflicted, characterised not only by an appreciation of Burke's approach to habit but also by a tone of moral indignation at his refusal to extend the possibility of reason (or 'consciousness of right') beyond the aristocracy.[23] Under conditions where Burke's 'gift of inert acceptance' reigned supreme, he argued, the natural human desire to imagine different forms of self-expression and political/social organisation withered on the vine. 'It is doubtless true', he would go on to insist in 1929, 'that innumerable men obey the state simply because the government which issues an order is entitled in law to speak in its name. But analysis would, I think, show that most of such obedience is the product of habit or inertia, and that it is never creative.'[24]

---

[18] Laski, *Problem of Sovereignty*, p. 4. For more on Laski's interest in law, see his later article 'Law and the State', *Economica*, 27 (1929), pp. 265–95.

[19] Edmund Burke, *Reflections on the Revolution in France* (Oxford, 1999), p. 40.

[20] Ironically, and as if to purge the taint of Laski's activism from the minds of his new students, Oakeshott made this observation in his Inaugural Address, 'Political Education', given shortly after inheriting Laski's position at the LSE in the early 1950s. See Michael Oakeshott, *Rationalism in Politics and Other Essays* (Indianapolis, IN, 1991).

[21] Laski, *Political Thought in England*, p. 172.

[22] Laski, *Liberty in the Modern State*, p. 34.

[23] Laski, *Political Thought in England*, p. 173.

[24] Harold Laski, 'Law and the State', p. 275.

When arguing from this perspective, Laski seemed determined to differentiate between the kind of just political change associated with critical thought and the instinctual lure of the habitual.

On another level, however, Laski's understanding of the relationship between habit and critique was more sophisticated than this somewhat jarring turn to enlightenment rationality would initially suggest. In the very same text in which Laski excoriated Burke for not taking the critical capacities of the masses seriously, he also argued, in a much more genealogical and historical vein, that Burke's analysis simply did not account for actual political changes that had occurred during his life time. If human beings really were only capable of living a political life structured by the bonds of habit, then how does one explain the Industrial and French Revolutions? More precisely, how does one explain the rate at which the ideologies of both would become normalised? 'No system of habits', Laski argued, 'can ever hope to endure long in a world where the cumulative power of memory enables change to be so swift.' Laski went on to explain that Burke mistook the power of habit in political life for the moral necessity of a *certain kind* of habit, fixed in time. Thus, he maintained, 'the habits which Burke so earnestly admired' were not 'at all part of our nervous endowment in any integral sense'. Rather:

> The short space of the French Revolution made the habit of thinking in terms of progress an essential part of our intellectual inheritance; and where the Burkean school proclaims how exceptional progress has been in history, we take that as proof of the ease with which essential habit may be acquired.[25]

In this context, Laski argued that habit itself was 'capable of transmutation'. The ideological and societal power wielded by habit thus never disappears (as the 'intellectual inheritance' of the French Revolution suggests) but political actors are able to both reflect upon, and ultimately transform, its content by embracing and universalising the 'gift of criticism'. In Laski's words habit 'can have virtue only to the point where it is conscious of itself'.[26] I argue that Laski's political theory as a whole can be read as an extended effort to make habit conscious of itself. His historical writings in particular were often focused on revealing the ideological and material processes whereby forms of governance and social organisation *become* habitualised such that they appear to be

---

[25] Laski, *Political Thought in England*, p. 173.
[26] Ibid.

the 'inescapable inevitabilities of the social order' rather than historical artefacts reflecting relations of power during a particular era.[27]

Nowhere is this deconstructive approach to the ideological habits associated with liberal sovereignty more apparent than in his 1936 book, *The Rise of European Liberalism*.[28] In it he argues that, during the sixteenth and seventeenth centuries, the political, social, and economic habits of the medieval order in Europe, 'habits dominated by religious precepts', gradually came into conflict with the emerging lived experiences of the ascending bourgeoisie.[29] As these new classes became more powerful they began to feel 'limited by a body of moral rules imposed under the sanction of religious authority', and 'after 1500 those rules, and the institutions, habits, and ideas to which they had given birth, were no longer deemed adequate'.[30] Thus, over time, new forms of social organisation, attitudes towards the state, conceptualisations of the economic order—in a word, the new habits of liberalism—replaced those of the old order thus naturalising and justifying the new order's status. When looked at from this historical perspective, argued Laski, we can see the historically contingent nature of political liberalism as an ideology. One could not maintain, Laski later argued, that alternatives to liberalism were impossible precisely because liberalism was itself merely an alternative to an earlier set of political habits. 'There is hardly a doctrine', Laski noted in 1939, 'that is commonplace in our time that did not, to some earlier age, seem monstrous error.'[31]

Laski insisted, however, that the political changes associated with liberalism did not emerge over night and that the slow rise of liberalism to predominance reveals just how difficult it is to counter the habits of a hegemonic world-view. Thus, he contended, 'bourgeois habits' were literally worked up out of the stuff of life itself. 'New material conditions', Laski argued, 'gave birth to new social relationships; and, in terms of

---

[27] Harold Laski, 'A Plea for Equality', *The Dangers of Obedience and Other Essays* (New York, 1930), p. 225.

[28] Perhaps not surprisingly, of all Laski's work this book most resembled the critical historical sensibilities of his socialist contemporary, Antonio Gramsci. In some ways, Laski's analysis of habit here mirrored Gramsci's approach to 'common sense' as the predominant 'traditional popular conception of the world—what is unimaginatively called "instinct"'. See Antonio Gramsci, *Prison Notebooks* (New York, 1989), p. 199.

[29] Harold Laski, *The Rise of European Liberalism* (London, 1936), p. 12.

[30] Ibid., p. 16.

[31] Harold Laski, *The Prospects of Democratic Government* (Williamsburg, VA, 1939), p. 12.

these, a new philosophy was evolved to afford a rational justification for the new world which had come into being.'[32]

For Laski, liberalism was thus a 'living principle' first and a political crusade second. Changes in economic production and social organisation preceded the rise of political liberalism, a rise that took 'something like three centuries' to accomplish precisely because liberals were themselves engaged in a pitched battle with medieval 'habits and ideas which were as stoutly armed as any in the history of mankind'.[33] Once established as a 'living principle', however, the battle for liberal hegemony was always conjoined, Laski argued, to the rise of modern sovereignty, a marriage particularly apparent in the ideological quandaries of the Reformation. In his introduction to the 1924 translation of the *Vindiciae contra tyrannos*, for instance, Laski argued that the political and religious discontents who prefigured seventeenth- and eighteenth-century liberals were driven 'on the one hand, to limit the power of government, and, on the other, to destroy the papal right of interference by showing the sovereign, and therefore, independent character of the state'.[34] The notion of sovereignty finally realised in the treaty of Westphalia spoke directly to this problem by wrapping the 'independent character of the state' in the legitimising mantle of a 'national unity' thus reconciling liberal discomfort with papal power to a new ideological order conditioned by the habits of liberalism and capitalist forms of production.

Laski's work on sovereignty also suggested that the 'bureaucratic process' (or what he sometimes referred to as the 'routine of habit') implicit in the institutions of the modern state worked to both instantiate and reinforce the legitimacy of the emerging liberal order.[35] There was nothing strictly instrumental about this process, however, and Laski's early works on sovereignty were particularly astute and cutting in their analysis of the self-generating nature of state power. For instance, in *Authority in the Modern State*, Laski found the argument of 'deliberate malevolence' by wily government actors working to consciously and systematically undercut the public good to be unconvincing. Rather, he argued, 'authority has certain habits' which take on a kind of institutional life of their own thereby nullifying the 'intentions of those who hold the reigns of power'.[36] Laski described the rise of liberal habits and

---

[32] Laski, *Rise of European Liberalism*, p. 14.
[33] Ibid., p. 22.
[34] Harold Laski, 'Introduction', *A Defence of Liberty against Tyrants* (London, 1924), p. 5.
[35] Laski, *Authority in the Modern State*, p. 50.
[36] Ibid.

the rise of those bureaucratic habits associated with modern sovereignty in historically reinforcing, dialectical terms. Liberals not only used the power of the state to establish their hegemonic world-view; the inertial logic of the state itself perpetuated this view.

Finally, while Laski's analysis of habit lingered, for the most part, at this macro level of societal and institutional change, his writings also delved into the more microscopic functioning of habit as a means to actively discipline citizens towards accepting particular norms of the social order. In an almost proto-Foucaultian manner, Laski argued that the success of certain forms of statehood, economic production, and social organisation could not be explained by virtue of their habitual status alone. As he argued with Burke, if habit and tradition on their own were enough to ensure the longevity of certain forms of political society, then change would simply never occur. Rather, Laski maintained, the dominant social order—'the vast discipline in which we are all involved'—must peremptorily drive its necessary habits into the overall sense of the public good in order to maintain its hegemonic status.[37] This was particularly true, he argued, of the liberal 'acquisitive society' because of its schizophrenic attitude towards equality. Liberalism, he argued, could not avoid the indwelling tension engendered by its formal commitment to political equality and the widespread economic inequality of capitalism. The ideological habits of the liberal society were thus directed towards inculcating within citizens a belief in the egalitarian nature of the state while, at the same time, actively discouraging alternative forms of social/political organisation that might reveal liberal society's ineluctable class distinctions or pose alternatives to its own stultifying logic. The 'unequal society', argued Laski in a 1930 essay entitled 'A Plea for Equality', therefore 'demands a standardised and uniform outlook as the condition of its preservation'. This was 'fatal to individuality', Laski insisted, 'because individuality implies the novel and unexpected; and these are dangerous to conventional habits'. An 'unequal society', had to ensure that alternatives to its order remained unconscious by imposing 'upon its members beliefs, ideas, habits, rules which prevent that affirmation of the self from which the increase of civilisation flows'.[38] Laski argued that the state imposed these habits through education but that they were also disseminated and encouraged culturally through religion, accepted forms of artistic expression, and social organisation.

---

[37] Laski, *Grammar of Politics*, p. 19.
[38] Laski, ' Plea For Equality', pp. 26–7.

Ultimately, the monism at work in the theory of sovereignty, Laski maintained, transfigured this ideological nexus between the habits of state and society into a portrait of the national unity, a smooth-surfaced, common-sense understanding of *who we are* as a polity and a people. At the same time, Laski's historical inquiries and analyses of alternative forms of contemporary social organisation suggest (again in an almost proto-Foucaultian sense) that the reach of habit is never absolute, that the existence of the 'Levellers and the agrarian communists of that day, in a lesser degree, also, the Baptists and the Fifth Monarchy men' made clear that the liberal ideological project was never complete.[39] While Laski's work in this regard is more suggestive than concise, his long-standing interest in alternative social movements (like the cooperative societies) coupled with his intellectual fascination with historical moments of 'disruption' gesture towards a politics that takes advantage of this slippage to make 'conscious' the habits of liberal sovereignty and transform them into the habits of democratic possibility.[40] It is no doubt because of these sensibilities that Laski never abandoned the possibility of a democratic transition to socialism.

However, in his perennially contradictory way, Laski often undermined this more subtle and critical approach to political change with what looked like a kind of ham-fisted instrumentalism, an approach that grew more intense as Laski's politics shifted from pluralism towards socialism in the 1920s. In 1919, Laski argued for a differently dispersed, 'spatial' orientation towards statehood, where trade unions and voluntary organisations shared in the responsibilities of political authority thus reviving the kind of 'spontaneous' citizenship implicit in Aristotle's definition of the capacity to 'rule and not less to be ruled in turn'.[41] And, while he also believed that an overall redistribution of wealth was necessary to wrest both economic and ideological power from capital, as a pluralist, he was wary of empowering the state to do this through either electoral or revolutionary means. The alternative of 'complete state-management' he argued, with its excessive, potentially uncontrollable bureaucracy, was hardly an inviting proposition for anyone interested in

---

[39] Laski, *Rise of European Liberalism*, p. 70.

[40] For more on Laski's early discussion of the cooperatist movement, see *Grammar of Politics*, ch. 9, and *The Recovery of Citizenship* (London, 1928). For an example of his interest in political crises as illustrative of sovereignty's limitations, see his discussion of the nineteenth-century Scottish church in the 'Political Theory of Disruption', *American Political Science Review*, 10 (1916), pp. 437–64.

[41] Laski, 'Pluralist State', p. 570.

individual expression and the development of 'spontaneous' human freedom. 'Indeed, it may without exaggeration be suggested that the evils such a regime would imply are hardly less great than those of the present system.'[42] By the early 1930s and throughout the 1940s, however, Laski's political solution to the problem of sovereignty shifted, somewhat ironically, towards the creation of a socialist state that would allow for 'organised planning' in order to transform 'industry and finance to instruments and not masters of the social purpose'.[43]

The paradox of using state power to counteract the universalising sweep of capitalist sovereignty was not lost on Laski's critics during his life time, particularly British idealists whose understanding of an expanded welfare state Laski had castigated as an ahistorical metaphysics grounded in a faulty assumption of 'common mind'.[44] After his death in 1950, in the midst of a more generalised Cold War intolerance for socialism, it was this disconnect that prompted Carroll Hawkins to complain not only of Laski's knack for reducing liberal democracy to 'the end product of capitalism' but, later, his 'chronic attachment to contradictory and confusing views, his penchant for rhetoric, his periodic apologetics for communist totalitarianism', and 'his affinity for dogma'.[45] In 1954, Deane argued that Laski's turn towards state socialism required an abandonment of 'all his former warnings of the dangers to initiative and freedom involved in bureaucracy and state control'.[46] For Deane, such inconsistency was the inevitable result of Laski's embrace of socialism, of a political theory that understood both state and society 'solely in terms of economic class'.[47]

In his 2004 book, *Harold Laski: Problems of Democracy, the Sovereign State, and International Society*, Lamb challenges these traditional criticisms of Laski by asking us to read Laski's turn towards state socialism not as an obdurate refusal to recognise his own inconsistency but as an expression of a more subtle theory of sovereignty that took into account both economic power and the more complex, discursive terrain of ideol-

---

[42] Laski, *Authority in the Modern State*, p. 4.

[43] Harold Laski, *The Decline of Liberalism: The L. T. Hobhouse Memorial Trust Lecture*, 10 (Oxford, 1940), p. 23.

[44] Ibid., p. 13. For a brief discussion of Laski's idealist critics, see Jose Harris, 'Political Thought and the Welfare State, 1870–1940: An Intellectual Framework for British Social Policy', *Past and Present*, 135 (1992), p. 134, n. 61.

[45] Hawkins, 'Harold Laski: A Preliminary Analysis', p. 380; Carroll Hawkins, review of 'The Political Ideas of Harold Laski', *Political Science Quarterly*, 70 (1955), p. 603.

[46] Deane, *Political Ideas of Harold Laski*, p. 125.

[47] Ibid., p. 88.

ogy. According to Lamb, Laski's later belief that socialists should take control of the state, does not reflect 'an acceptance of the principle of state sovereignty; it was, rather, a theory that the state could be employed in the service of an egalitarian goal'.[48] Lamb seems to be saying (although he is not always clear about this) that Laski was not an orthodox thinker when it came to the state. Unlike most anarchist theorists for whom the state is simply and always oppressive, Laski was less concerned with the state *qua* state and more interested in the ideological qualities of sovereignty that allowed the state to mutate into a seemingly authentic representation of the social whole. Once socialists had stripped the state of this dense mask of sovereign authority, then we could see it for what it really was: a mere 'instrument' through which we distribute the 'common stock' of humanity that could thus be used to further, in Lamb's words, 'an egalitarian goal'.

Lamb acknowledges that this was a somewhat unsatisfactory response on Laski's part insofar as it didn't sufficiently address either the staying power of capital or the possibility of totalitarian socialism. But he does insist that rejecting Laski's theory of sovereignty simply because he hadn't fully worked through who was to do the 'planning' in a socialist society is to throw the baby out with the bathwater. Laski's work on the transformative logic of sovereignty continues to be relevant, Lamb argues, precisely because sovereignty is still a 'central tool' that states use to justify their authority.[49] In particular, he insists, Laski's thinking about the state in relation to international politics is especially cogent in that it exposes how the semblance of inevitability projected by sovereignty blinds us to alternative forms of international organisation.[50] In sum, Lamb maintains that despite Laski's somewhat inconsistent political solutions, his was a mature and subtle theory of sovereignty that still has much to offer contemporary political theorists and scholars of international politics.

But for all his insistence that we take the complexities of Laski's thinking on sovereignty seriously, Lamb still relegates his approach to imperialism to a dusty Leninist corner. With Ram Chandra Gupta and Deane, Lamb reads Laski's thoughts on imperialism as a reflection of Lenin's theory of capitalism in its highest phase. While Laski's reading of empire was indeed partly Leninist in its economic analysis, Lamb fails

---

[48] Lamb, *Harold Laski*, p. 112.
[49] Ibid., p. 113.
[50] Ibid., p. 172.

to address the extent to which Laski was interested in not only the external push of sovereign power into the imperial world but also in the reinforcing relationship between this external push and the internal, ideological, habits of life in the state. In other words, Lamb leaves Laski's analysis of imperialism in the same place that Deane left his analysis of the state; as a theory imagined 'solely in terms of economic class'.[51] The picture of Laski on imperialism that Lamb thus captures is somewhat stunted and disappointing. Laski's 'concern with imperialism is now rather outmoded', he observes, noting the theory's fairly 'crude' inability to adequately address the more complex forms of 'structural power' that characterise international relations in the post-war era.[52]

By contrast, the following argues for the need to view Laski's writings on imperialism as a continuation of his theory of sovereignty that embraced a complex constellation of ideological, cultural, and economic habits—habits that he believed were both self-reinforcing and 'capable of transmutation' in directions ultimately troubling for the future of democracy. Indeed, I argue that Laski's analysis of the potential impact of imperial habits on domestic politics provides us with a particularly rich example of this kind of analysis at work. In the end, while Laski's critique of the relationship between imperialism and democracy was, in key ways, politically and philosophically contradictory, these contradictions arose not from any unquestioned adherence to Lenin's economic analysis but, rather, from his refusal to accept the consequences that such an analysis implied.

The 'Habits of Imperialism'

Unlike his friend and fellow Fabian Leonard Woolf, Laski never wrote an academic treatise committed specifically to the topic of imperialism. Rather, his writings on imperialism during the early 1930s were, for the most part, tucked within analyses of a variety of different political and philosophical issues, including the prevention of war, the 'problem of nationalism', and the necessity for economic, social, and political equality. These moments are thus easy to miss and equally easy to reduce to the economic forces that Laski believed were fundamental to imperial expansion in the first place. 'Nationalism and the Future of Civilisation' and

---

[51] Deane, *Political Ideas of Harold Laski*, p. 88.
[52] Lamb, *Harold Laski*, pp. 137, 142.

'The Economic Foundations of Peace' are the two most obvious examples of Laski's embedded and often misinterpreted analyses of empire.

Laski discussed the economic forces behind imperialism extensively in 'The Economic Foundations of Peace', which appeared in a volume edited by Leonard Woolf in 1933, *The Intelligent Man's Way to Prevent War*. In this essay Laski argued that the economic causes of imperialism could be located in a basic clash between the forces and means of production within states at the 'highest' phase of capitalist development. With Lenin and Hobson, Laski believed that industrial development in the nineteenth century compelled international financiers to look for profitable investments for their surplus capital in 'territories which lacked the authority to compete on equal terms with their exploiters'.[53] For Laski, the logic of sovereignty made this kind of economic exploitation possible insofar as capital could draw upon both the authority of the state to protect its interests and nationalist sentiment to justify its continued expansion. Once attached to national pride, competitive imperial expansion by industrialised states became inevitable. With Lenin, Laski believed that this competition led to military conflicts between imperial states and that the First World War could be understood in these terms.[54]

Critical readers of Laski's work on imperialism like Lamb have tended to become preoccupied with his Leninist inflected description of imperial history as the direct result of a particular crisis in capitalism. But Laski's work on empire was more nuanced than either Lamb's critique or Laski's own admittedly sometimes reductionist language would imply. First, while Laski did indeed believe that the historical underpinnings of

---

[53] Harold Laski, 'The Economic Foundations of Peace', in Leonard Woolf (ed.), *The Intelligent Man's Way to Prevent War* (New York, 1973), p. 504.

[54] During the Second World War, Laski's thinking on the relationship between imperialism and war changed substantially. In an essay published by the Labour Party in 1940 entitled 'Is This an Imperialist War?', Laski argued that while socialists were right to understand the First World War as largely precipitated by the interests of imperialist states, the new war was different insofar as British and French imperialism was contracting while German imperialism was expanding: 'The Difference between the war of 1914 and the present war is, for Socialists, fundamental . . . Socialists do not need either to deny or forget all that is evil or ugly in the first; they need constantly remember the essential characteristics of the second' (Harold Laski, *Is This an Imperialist War?* (London, 1940), p. 5). The irony of course is that Laski, whom Hawkins and Deane would soon berate as an economic reductionist, was able to discern the difference between different kinds of capitalist states. His position also earned him no favours with his fellow socialists. Belgian Trotskyite Ernest Ezra Mandel, one of the leaders of the Fourth International, referred to Laski as 'one of the most dangerous lackeys of British imperialism, because he likes to drape himself in a red toga from time to time (from *The Fourth International*, 8, 2 (1947), Marxist Internet Archive, www.marxists.org/archive/mandel/1946/11/shachtman.htm).

imperialism were economic his analysis of what *perpetuated* imperial expansion was—like his critique of sovereignty—essentially ideological, embedded in a historical genealogy of the political habits that conditioned the dominant liberal order. Second, Laski was always attentive to, in his words, the 'internal' as well as 'external' sides to the imperial problem. Thus, for Laski, the political effects of imperialism were multi-directional, implying a deep and reinforcing connection between the 'habits of imperialism' and the indwelling habits of the state, never reducible to the mere efflux of industrial capitalism.

I think it is not inappropriate to assume that Laski began his analysis of the relationship between the 'internal' and 'external' qualities of imperialism in his 1932 essay 'Nationalism and the Future of Civilization', and then developed it more fully the next year in 'The Economic Foundations of Peace'. In some ways, Laski's critique in this essay resembled a basic Leninist take on nationalism as the ideological justification for imperial expansion, the emotional gloss on the imperial project. Laski thus argued that sovereign states under capitalism were naturally sympathetic to the interests of their dominant classes and that when these interests stretched to include economic exploits in other parts of the world so too did the discursive sheath of 'national unity' expand to cover these exploits in the legitimating glow of 'national feeling'.[55] Laski referred to this nationalist sentiment as the 'emotional penumbra' by which capitalists linked their economic goals to the state.[56]

Again, however, in his typically contradictory way, while Laski sometimes approached nationalism in this instrumental sense as a deep well of 'profound and irrational impulses' that the state could cynically deploy when the need arose he also saw it as a complicated disciplinary apparatus subject to the habits of history. And it is when he is interrogating nationalism in this second sense that Laski's analysis departed most dramatically from Lenin's. Thus, for Laski, the power of the idea of 'nationality' or 'national unity' lay in the fact that it provided the ideological grounding for the 'organised authority' of the modern state

---

[55] Harold Laski, 'Nationalism and the Future of Civilization', *The Dangers of Being a Gentleman and Other Essays* (New York, 1940), p. 215.

[56] Ibid., p. 226. In his understanding of nationalism as 'an emotional force', Laski's analysis here also resembled those of many mainstream, inter-war League supporters and internationalists. Alfred Zimmern, for instance, argued in 1918 for a deeply gendered division of labour between states and nations: 'Nationality, like religion, is subjective; Statehood is objective. Nationality is psychological; statehood is political. Nationality is a condition of mind; Statehood is a condition in law' (Alfred Zimmern, *Nationality and Government* (New York, 1918), p. 50).

itself.[57] Under conditions of liberal sovereignty, the state was justified in its authority only insofar as it claimed to represent the universal desires of 'the people' and 'the people' were comprehensible only insofar as they understood themselves to be defined by certain unitary characteristics. In other words, because it was based on a 'basic contempt for alternative ways of life', Laski argued, the sovereign state depended upon an 'erosion of all competing loyalties' and the continual fostering of that single, cohesive version of 'the people' which, since the late eighteenth century, the foundational logic of nationality had supplied.[58] Laski maintained, therefore, that sovereign states required 'all the mysticism which nationality secretes within itself' in order to legitimate their authority, eradicate alternative forms of political organisation, and obscure the basic class inequalities that characterised life in capitalist society. At the heart of this obfuscating 'mysticism' lay that constellation of habits implicit in the hegemonic social order—habits that must be driven into the logic of the 'national unity' through disciplinary practices, namely state sponsored education. Thus, Laski argued that:

> . . . every state-system of education bends its energies to the intensification of nationalism. You can see that intensification in the history books we use. All the energy and enthusiasm are lavished on the men who have given the nation state its present form and power. Our children learn amply of Nelson and Wellington, of Clive and Rhodes. Is there an equal effort to make plain to them the greatness of Jeremy Bentham, the noble protest of Bright against the Crimean war, the effort of Charles Bradlaugh to achieve genuine religious freedom?[59]

Just as Laski had argued in 'A Plea for Equality' that the 'unequal society demands a standardised and uniform outlook', so did he now maintain that this unequal society habitualised its subjects to accept a version of history that reaffirmed a national order capable of tolerating only its own approbation.

At the same time, Laski also parted ways from Lenin in this essay by suggesting that not only was nationalism 'the servant of economic imperialism' but that the ideological and political habits of an unequal society themselves contributed significantly to imperial expansion. In this sense, Laski argued that the impetus for imperial adventure arose not only from the ability of capitalists to link their profiteering adventures to the power of the state, flush with a national glow. In addition, he maintained, the

---

[57] Laski, 'Nationalism and the Future of Civilization', p. 210.
[58] Ibid., pp. 210, 240.
[59] Ibid., p. 228.

social, civil, political, economic ideology at the heart of the 'acquisitive society' itself engendered the move towards imperialism. 'Where there is repression within', Laski argued, 'there will be at least the straining towards violence without; we become to others what we have been content to be to each other.'[60] Just as Laski would later argue that the history of liberalism must be understood as a slowly evolving set of social and political habits that preceded its political solidification in the state, so too did he argue in this essay that imperialism only becomes possible once the internally repressive hegemony of capitalist ideology has worked itself up into state practice. In this sense, the 'habits of imperialism'—which Laski first mentions in this work—clearly begin at home. His analysis suggested that once the habits of inequality were incorporated into the state's institutional and ideological practices, they pressed outward, compelling it towards empire, towards the 'suppression of the demand for freedom among the people subject to imperialist domination'.[61]

But Laski did not stop at this outward expression of imperial might. Not only did he argue that imperialism 'is born of inequality' he also maintained that the state's oppressive imperialist practices in the colonies inevitably turned inward, forcing a heightened intolerance for democracy back into the dominant nationalist ideology that legitimated sovereign authority. Laski thus argued, 'I do not believe you can suppress freedom abroad without danger to its reality at home.'[62] He did not, however, go on to develop this theme very extensively in the 'Nationalism' essay. Instead, in a manner similar to an argument he made in an earlier piece, *Karl Marx: An Essay*, Laski located this intolerance in the actual persons of imperial envoys returning from service in the Empire. Thus, in 1922 Laski argued:

> No group of men who exercise the powers of a despot can ever retain the habit of democratic responsibility. That is obvious, for instance, in the case of men like Sir Henry Maine and Fitzjames Stephen, who, having learned in India the habit of autocratic government, become impatient on their return to England of the slow process of persuasion which democracy implies.[63]

It is surely no coincidence that Laski wrote these words a mere two years after dwelling so intensely on Burke in *Political Thought in England*. In that earlier work, Laski quoted extensively from Burke's 1783 'Speech in

---

[60] Laski, 'Nationalism and the Future of Civilization', p. 232.
[61] Ibid., p. 237.
[62] Ibid.
[63] Harold Laski, *Karl Marx: An Essay* (London, 1922), p. 38.

Commons on India', focusing particularly on what he called a 'magnificent passage' describing the corrupting influence of empire. 'The English youth in India', Laski quoted Burke as saying:

> ... drink the intoxicating draught of authority and domination before their heads are able to bear it, and as they are full grown in fortune long before they are ripe in principle, neither nature nor reason have any opportunity to exert themselves for the excesses of their premature power. The consequences of their conduct, which in good minds ... might produce penitence or amendment are unable to pursue the rapidity of their flight. Their prey is lodged in England.[64]

Thus, Laski's analysis of the authoritarian-inducing habits of colonial administration was, in 1922, deeply Burkean in the sense that the good habits associated with home (which Burke characterised as restraint and Laski found in evolving forms of democratic governance) were endangered by those who had grown accustomed to domination in India. Ten years later, he made an almost identical argument when he noted: 'I cannot help seeing significance in the fact that two legal members of the Viceroy's Council in India, Sir Henry Maine and Fitzjames Stephen, were both, after their experience of autocracy abroad, passionate critics of democracy upon their return to England.'[65] In both the 1922 and 1932 essays, Laski treated the habit of autocracy like Burke did, as a form of contagion picked up while abroad. Upon their return, both Burke's heady youths and Laski's administrators found themselves resistant to the more healthy habits of English political life.

A year later, as he moved towards his more sophisticated analysis of habit in *The Rise of European Liberalism*, Laski expanded this critique in a more dialectical direction. Just as his work on habit in a domestic context was concerned with the supportive interaction of the 'routine of habits' required by modern liberal society and the perpetuation of the authority of the state, his thoughts on empire in 'The Economic Foundations of Peace' now focused on the mutually reinforcing relationship between 'the development of autocratic habits in imperial and domestic affairs'.[66] Thus, in 'The Economic Foundations of Peace', Laski argued that the autocratic and oppressive 'habits of imperialism' learned by the British state as a whole in the colonies doubled back on themselves driving a deep 'cleavage' into the 'the national unity' between a putative

---

[64] Laski's quotation of Burke's 'Speech in Commons on India', *Political Thought in England*, p. 154.
[65] Laski, 'Nationalism and the Future of Civilization', p. 238.
[66] Laski, 'Economic Foundations of Peace', p. 527.

support for democracy at home and an intolerance for democracy in the colonies. The state was thus forced to openly 'deny equality which is the affirmation of its own essence by the democratic system . . . and a society which denies equality within itself is bound by the logic of its nature to deny it also abroad'.[67]

Read in abstraction from the broader corpus of his work, Laski's description in this very confusing paragraph of the danger posed by imperialism to a polity that both affirms and denies equality as a critical expression of its own essence is rather opaque. It makes considerably more sense, however, when we approach it from within the context of his thinking on sovereignty and the contradictory project legitimated by the habits of state. Again, Laski argued that the sovereign state was structurally committed to an understanding of itself as the sole legitimate reflection of a single and coherent unity. For the liberal state in particular, this unity was nominally committed to political equality while at the same time accepting and sanctioning economic inequality.[68] The legitimating ideology of the unequal society must work unceasingly to discipline its citizens and project an image of a state where political equality was 'the affirmation of its own essence'. Thus, for Laski, democracy in an unequal society existed in a permanently tenuous ideological state because it was always in the process of negotiating this contradiction.

Laski's use of the word 'cleavage' seems to imply that the turning inward of the 'habits of imperialism' upon the liberal state's embattled ideological project rendered democracy even more vulnerable than it was under conditions of state capitalism. The 'habits of imperialism' demand, Laski insisted, an overall disciplinary logic that must necessarily 'weigh the claims of other peoples differently from one's own'. The more the state acted towards colonised peoples in ways that explicitly denied them both democracy and humanity, the more it became habitualised to these policies and the wider the divide or 'cleavage' grew between the liberal capitalist state's already tenuous commitment to democracy and equality at home and its contempt for its subjects in the empire. Incorporating or, in Laski's words, 'driving' the justificatory and disciplinary 'habits of imperialism' back into the 'national unity' compelled the state to embrace an explicitly autocratic agenda as opposed to those more subtle disciplin-

---

[67] Laski, 'Economic Foundations of Peace', p. 527.
[68] As Laski maintained 'political democracy implies only political equality . . . In most states of the modern world it has not been followed by equality either in the social or in the economic sphere' (Laski, 'Plea for Equality', p. 211).

ary habits aimed at generating the acquiescence or consent of the governed for the hegemonic order. Laski noted, for instance, the significance of the fact that:

> ... pseudo-scientific biology which began by insisting on the superiority of the white race, has continued by a general affirmation of the biological superiority of the white rich over the white poor. It uses this affirmation to attack their claims to social reforms.[69]

The 'habits of imperialism' thus not only created 'cleavages' in the state's projection of itself as egalitarian, they also enabled the creation of new habits that more explicitly justified inequality within the state based on theories of race developed for the colonies. Imperialist habits thus explicitly racialised the imperialising state within its domestic ambit and fundamentally altered the extent to which the state could be identified as both democratic and egalitarian.

At this point, Laski again parted ways from Lenin's assumptions about the relationship between democracy, capitalism, and empire. For Lenin, the overall claims of the capitalist state to be democratic were laughable; democracy under these conditions was merely democracy for the bourgeoisie. All bourgeois democracy was inherently reactionary, argued Lenin, making revolution and the transformation of society into a socialist democracy the only solution to bourgeois intransigence.[70] Lenin predicted that the international conflicts brought about by imperialism would inevitably involve millions of workers who would then become radicalised by the crisis, thus setting the stage for this revolution.[71] But Laski was never, according to Deane, 'prepared to accept a Leninist solution to the problem'.[72] As noted above, despite his extensive analysis of the disciplinary or consent-making qualities of liberal sovereignty, Laski's sense that habit was never totalising (as the existence of the Levellers, the cooperatist movement, and other alternative forms of social organisation suggested) meant that he always believed in the possibility of making habit 'conscious' of itself. Because of this, he never abandoned the promise of parliamentary democracy and the gradual

---

[69] Laski, 'Economic Foundations of Peace', pp. 527–8.
[70] See Lenin, 'Two Tactics of Social Democracy in the Democratic Revolution', in *Lenin Anthology*, pp. 120–52.
[71] 'Imperialism is the eve of the social revolution of the proletariat', noted Lenin in his preface to the French and German editions of 'Imperialism, the Highest Stage of Capitalism', *Lenin Anthology*, p. 210.
[72] Deane, *Political Ideas of Harold Laski*, p. 88.

rather than revolutionary transition to socialism and a more richly democratic society. Thus, Lenin's revolutionary 'solution' to the problems created for bourgeois democracy by empire was of less interest to Laski than his economic explanation for the external reach of imperialism in the first place.

Deane read this unwillingness to follow Lenin towards revolution as yet another example of Laski's general philosophical inconsistency. One could not both accept what Deane argued was an economically deterministic approach to the state as an agent of capital (in either a domestic or international/imperial sense) *and* put one's faith in a 'gradualism', in a democracy that was itself conditioned by the needs of capital.[73] But for Laski, the fact that, under conditions of capitalist sovereignty, political democracy worked primarily for the preservation of the hegemonic order did not undermine its potential. Democracy, under conditions of liberal capitalist sovereignty, was always, he suggested, in a state of ideological flux precisely because its legitimating claims to political equality were constantly in conflict with the 'acquisitive' society's commitment to economic inequality. Laski believed that individuals and social movements could effectively take advantage of this flux, expose the habits of liberal capitalism to rigorous critique, and then, in a sense, *re-habitualise* the social order through a deliberate engagement with democratic processes themselves. While he was never very clear on the strategic details behind such a politics, Laski argued that even liberal capitalist democracies created small spaces where working-class people could agitate for social reforms and when these social reforms were even partially enacted, they could lead to an overall change in the habits of society itself. Increased access to education, for instance—presumably even one with a nationalist bent—could potentially encourage citizens to challenge the 'privileged position' of capitalists in the state according to Laski.[74]

It was precisely this hope in the transformative potential of liberal democracy that both differentiated Laski from Lenin and sharpened his belief in the dangers of imperialism. Thus, even though the above obser-

---

[73] Deane, *Political Ideas of Harold Laski*, p. 88. This is an inconsistency that Kenneth Hoover missed in his book, *Economics as Ideology*. Rather than dwelling in the somewhat ironic fact that Laski's gradualism might very well be read as a conflict within his analysis of hegemony, Hoover argued that Laski's evolution as a thinker was always towards a greater reliance on 'reductionist' arguments that would 'edge him ever closer to a Leninist position on the imperative of revolution'. See Kenneth Hoover, *Economics as Ideology: Keynes, Laski, Hayek, and the Creation of Contemporary Politics* (New York, 2003), p. 99.

[74] Laski, 'Economic Foundations of Peace', p. 528.

vations on imperialism appeared in a book devoted to exploring the causes of war and its prevention, Laski clearly believed that the impact of imperial habits upon even nominally democratic states was potentially more dangerous to the polity than war itself. In the worst-case scenario, Laski argued, the 'conflicts between imperialism and democracy' led, as in Italy and Germany, to an overall fascist takeover of the state characterised by 'the deliberate sabotage of equality in the economic sphere to preserve the privileges of a small class'.[75] But even in England and the USA, he maintained, where the 'Liberal tradition is still more firmly rooted', imperialism contributed to an overall suspicion of democracy and an increasingly proto-fascist sense that democratic principles could be sacrificed in the name of a national interest now understood in more explicitly imperialist terms. In essence, for Laski, imperialism had the power to transform sovereign states into more dangerous forms of themselves by exposing the contradictions of liberalism and then justifying these contradictions through the very 'autocratic habits' learned through colonial rule. The sovereign state, under conditions of imperialism, took its authority from the very fact that it *was* the state rather than through any connection to democracy, no matter how feeble or disingenuous that connection might have been in the first place. In Laski's words, in 'an imperialist society being devoid of moral principle, it is only natural that it should assume that its rights are a function of its power to get its will obeyed'.[76]

In sum, imperialism transformed sovereignty into a more naked form of what Laski had earlier described as the indwelling essence of the modern state, its 'implicit acceptance of a certain grim Hegelianism', its assertion of itself as an authoritarian personality whose legitimacy emanated not from the will of its members but from its status as a 'harmonious whole'.[77] Imperialism unmasked sovereignty, revealing the class and racial biases within, but the result of this unmasking was not necessarily revolution, as Lenin predicted, but fascism. And, for Laski, fascism was too high a price to pay for ideological purity or even, one might rightly add, his own theoretical coherence.

---

[75] Ibid., p. 529.
[76] Ibid.
[77] Laski, 'Apotheosis of the State', p. 302; Laski 'The Personality of the State', *The Nation*, 101 (1915), p. 115.

Conclusion

There are important ways that Laski's writings on sovereignty and empire reflect niggling contradictions within his broader political theory. For instance, while we know from Laski's writings that he believed the fraught status of democratic governance within the context of the capitalist state created the potential for its own transformation, the details by which we transform the habits of liberal capitalism remain rather vague. Additionally, Laski never satisfactorily answered the basic question that any critical theory of both ideological domination and political change must face. By what precise mechanism does the disciplined, thoroughly habitualised, 'transmutable' subject become 'conscious' of his or her own dependence on habit? How is it, in other words, that we transform what Laski called Burke's 'gift of inert acceptance' into the 'gift of criticism'?[78]

In another light, however, we can read the tensions in Laski's political theory as simply the contradictions of political engagement, the price any theorist must pay for stepping outside the mind into the world. Laski the political activist, the teacher and mentor of future post-colonial leaders, the anti-imperial crusader, the Labour Party leader, thoroughly lived these contradictions between theory and practice and was more or less aware of them throughout his career.[79] What's more, Laski also read the history of political thought through the same lenses. Thus, he noted in 1930:

> . . . political philosophy is, by its very nature, pragmatic. Its practitioners do not sit down to write a treatise as dispassionate and universal as an exposition of geometry. In a very real sense, what they attempt is autobiography, the reaction upon themselves of a special environment individually interpreted.[80]

Perhaps this is the best advice for how to interpret Laski's own work on the 'habits of imperialism'. On the one hand, it is deeply 'autobiographical',

---

[78] Laski, *Political Thought in England*, p. 173.

[79] See, for instance, his defence of Indian nationalism that stands alongside, and in explicit tension with, his critique of nationalism more generally in 'Nationalism and the Future of Civilization'.

[80] Laski, 'Machiavelli and the Present Time', in *Dangers of Obedience*, p. 238. This quotation also offers an example of Laski's ironic use of language from the history of English political philosophy. In this instance, his reference to 'geometry' seems a playful jab at Hobbes who described his approach to political society as a 'geometric' project of reconstructing human nature from its constituent parts. Laski's works are riddled with these winking references, including sharp evocations of Burke's 'little platoons', and ironic inversions of Locke's fraught notion of the 'inconveniences' associated with state of nature. In each of these instances, Laski turns this very language in on itself, adding another layer of subtle critique to his analysis.

filled with the tensions of Laski's own political life. On the other, it gestures beyond itself towards a complicated and remarkably prescient critique of the relationship between empire and sovereignty and the consequences of this relationship for democracy.

Indeed, examples of Laski's far-sightedness exceed the limitations of this essay. More work clearly needs to be done, for instance, on the manner in which Laski's work foreshadowed that of contemporary post-colonial writers interested specifically in the impact of educational policies and racial discourses designed for the empire on the metropole.[81] This essay has, however, demonstrated that Laski's theory of empire amounted to more than a Leninist tic. Rather it expanded upon the most sophisticated aspects of his theory of sovereignty and, in so doing, offers us a rich theoretical window through which to critique the status of sovereignty in liberalism during an age of renewed liberal interest in empire in both Britain and the USA. Most importantly, Laski's analysis of empire demonstrates the urgent need to bring the 'habits of imperialism' to consciousness or risk losing the promise of liberal democracy altogether.

[81] See, for instance, Gauri Viswanathan's analysis of English literature as a subject of study developed for schools in India 'long before it was institutionalised in the home country' (Gauri Viswanathan, *Masks of Conquest* (New York, 1989), p. 3). See also Saree Makdisi's work on the impact of colonial practices on the Romantics and on English society during the Romantic period at large in *Romantic Imperialism: Universal Empire and the Culture of Modernity* (Cambridge, 1998).

Index

The letter n indicates a footnote